AF270446

Advance praise for *And Hell Followed With It*

"I've covered many a tornado over the years, but after reading these chapters, it's the first time I've ever been in one. Great writing."

—Wes Lyle, award-winning Missouri-Kansas photojournalist; member, Missouri Photojournalism Hall of Fame

"Bonar Menninger has written a gripping yarn about a fateful day more than 40 years ago when thousands of Kansas residents going about their daily business were caught unaware by a freakish weather event. The narrative focuses on ordinary people caught up in the literal maelstrom of one of the most monstrous tornadoes ever to hit the continental United States, depicting the extraordinary confusion—and, in some instances, heroism—engendered by that singular event. Combining vivid character portraits with an impressive command of the science behind tornadoes, Menninger has penned a page-turner worthy of the best narrative nonfiction books produced in recent years."

—Dan Margolies, former reporter, *Reuters*

"So many of us who have spent our careers in weather and severe storms are primarily focused on research, prediction, and concerns about the next scientific or public safety challenge. As a result, we are perhaps not as aware as we could be of the tragedy and suffering these storms cause. This book takes that awareness to a whole different level for us. It is a powerful story that should be read by everyone involved in severe storm prediction and public safety. It also provides insight into the aftermath of these events and human beings' remarkable determination to carry on."

—Phil Shideler, retired meteorologist-in-charge, National Weather Service office, Topeka, Kansas

"A beautifully written account of ordinary people under extraordinary duress. Menninger not only conjures the random chaos and violence of an EF-5 tornado, but also captures immensely human stories of endurance."

—Joan Dean, PhD, professor of English, University of Missouri–Kansas City

"The 1966 Topeka tornado was a seminal event for tornado preparedness. The real-life narratives about the many people who survived this devastating storm reinforce the idea that there are things a person can do to increase the likelihood of survival, even when nature throws her most extreme storm at us."

—Joseph T. Schaefer, PhD, CCM, retired director, Storm Prediction Center, National Weather Service, Norman, Oklahoma

# And Hell Followed With It

## LIFE AND DEATH IN A KANSAS TORNADO

### BONAR MENNINGER

EMERALD BOOK CO.

Published by Emerald Book Company
Austin, TX
www.emeraldbookcompany.com



Distributed by Emerald Book Company

For ordering information or special discounts for bulk purchases, please contact Emerald Book Company at PO Box 91869, Austin, TX  78709, 512.891.6100.

Design and composition by Greenleaf Book Group LLC and Bumpy Design
Cover design by Greenleaf Book Group LLC and Faceout Studio

Publisher's Cataloging-In-Publication Data
(Prepared by The Donohue Group, Inc.)
Menninger, Bonar.
   And hell followed with it : life and death in a Kansas tornado / Bonar Menninger.—1st ed.
     p. : ill., maps ;  cm.
   ISBN: 978-1-934572-49-8
   1. Tornadoes—Kansas—Topeka.  2. Natural disasters—Kansas—Topeka. 3. Topeka (Kan.)—History.  I. Title.
QC955.5.K2 M46 2010
551.553/0978163                                        2010929150

Part of the Tree Neutral™ program, which offsets the number of trees consumed in the production and printing of this book by taking proactive steps, such as planting trees in direct proportion to the number of trees used: www.treeneutral.com

Printed in the United States of America on acid-free paper

10 11 12 13 14 15   10 9 8 7 6 5 4 3 2 1

First Edition

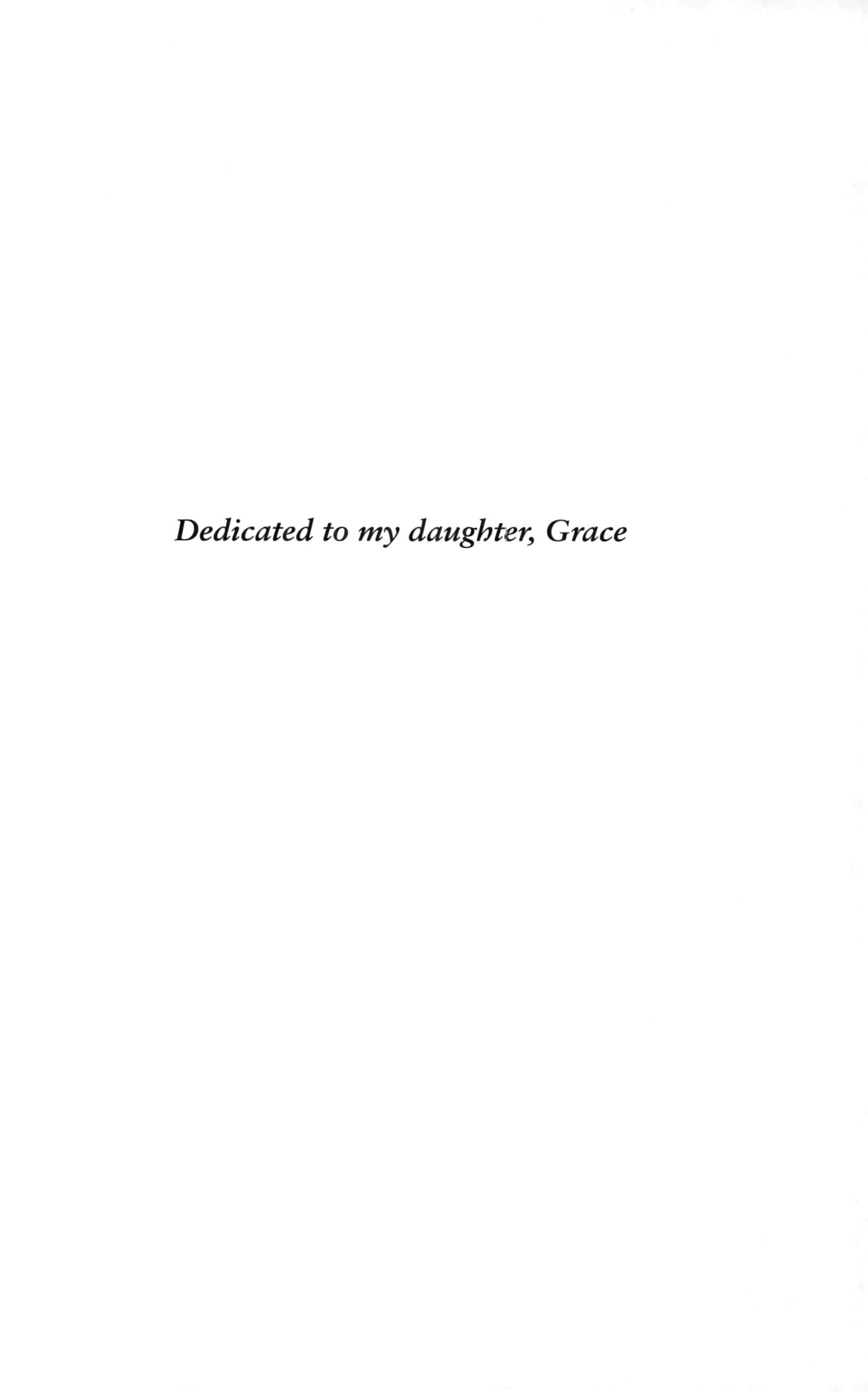

*Dedicated to my daughter, Grace*

# Contents

# Acknowledgments

This book could not have happened without the assistance, cooperation and support of a large number of people. First and foremost, I wish to express my gratitude to the many survivors of the Topeka tornado who took time to share their experiences with me. Their stories are the heart of this book. I appreciate not only their willingness to revisit often-traumatic memories but also their patience in working with me to ensure that I understood the facts correctly. I am particularly grateful to the next of kin of those killed in the storm and the relatives of tornado survivors now gone. Again, the memories were difficult for all, and I felt both honored and humbled that these people would share them with me.

Along with the individuals who had a direct connection to the tornado, numerous others provided expertise and insight in support of this project:

- Thank you to the following meteorologists for their time and patience in helping me get a handle on the complexities of severe weather: Phil Shideler, retired meteorologist-in-charge, Topeka National Weather Service office; Mike Akulow, retired warning coordination meteorologist, Topeka NWS office; Jennifer Stark, former warning coordination meteorologist, Topeka NWS office (now meteorologist-in-charge, Pueblo, Colorado, NWS); George Phillips, science operations officer, Topeka NWS office; Joseph Schaefer, retired director, NWS Storm Prediction Center, Norman, Oklahoma; and Bruce Jones, former meteorologist with KSNT-TV in Topeka. Thanks also to Mr. Shideler for his invaluable assistance in providing me with details about the early days of tornado preparedness efforts in Topeka and the role the late Richard Garrett played in that work.

- On a separate front, thanks also to Gary Wis-Ki-Ge-Amatyuk Jr., the great-great-great-grandson of Chief Abram Burnett, for his help regarding the history of the Potawatomis and Chief Burnett. (For more information on Chief Burnett, visit www.wiskigeamatyuk.com.) Thanks to historians Douglas Wallace and Don Chubb for assistance on the history of Topeka and the tornado's impact on the city. Likewise, thanks to Martha Imparato, the archivist at Washburn University, and Jim Kelly, documentarian with KTWU, Washburn's public television station, for their help in tracking down sources. Thanks also to Larry Broadbent, for sharing his historical knowledge of the Atchison, Topeka and Santa Fe Railway.

- Anita Miller Fry was a major help in locating numerous individuals and was an enthusiastic supporter of this project from the beginning. A big shout-out to KTWU, WIBW, cjonline.com and, most especially, the Topeka & Shawnee County Public Library, for having the foresight to collect written recollections of the tornado at the time of the storm's 40th anniversary in 2006. These documents were extremely helpful in tracking down tornado survivors.

- Thanks to the many reporters who preceded me on this story. Their hard work in chronicling the events of June 8, 1966 — both in the immediate aftermath of the storm and on subsequent anniversaries — made my job a lot easier. The same holds true for the documentary filmmakers, most notably Jim Kelly and Bill Kurtis.

- I am extremely grateful for the remarkable visual record of the tornado and its aftermath, created by an outstanding group of photographers working for the *Topeka Daily Capital* and the *Topeka State Journal* in 1966, including Rich Clarkson, Rod Hanna, Jack Kenward, George Olson, Perry Riddle, Delmar Schmidt, Barry Sweet and Hugh Tessendorf. Thanks to the current management of the *Topeka Capital-Journal* for generously allowing me use of the photos.

- Thanks also to Rick Schmidt, Lloyd Zimmer, B. T. Bradford, Martha Imparato and all others who provided additional photos.

- Thanks to Becky Eis of Ask Rebecca Secretarial Services for transcribing hundreds of hours of interviews, to Kim Mann for her initial design work, to Karen Alexander for her top-notch copyediting, to Topeka native Phil Thompson for his excellent maps, and to Steve Wilson Photography for key assistance with the pictures.

- Thanks to Dave Hathaway for providing me with a vast trove of documents, newspapers and other source material.

- Thanks to Bill Tiernan for his ideas, insight and support from day one.

- Thanks to Jan Hathaway for her faith.

- Thanks to Emerald Book Company and everyone at Greenleaf Book Group for all their hard work and for believing in this project.

Finally, I am grateful to the many colleagues and friends who took time from their busy schedules to read the first draft of the book. Not only did they catch numerous typos and make helpful suggestions, but they also reinforced my convictions about the relevance of this project. Special thanks to my mom, Catherine Menninger; my dad, Roy Menninger; and my stepmom, Bev Menninger. They were my biggest supporters from first to last and dutifully read every chapter when others likely would have lost interest. I tried to make them proud. Last but not least, thanks to my wife, Ann Cain, and my daughter, Grace, for putting up with countless evenings and weekends when all I did was work on my book. Ann was my first sounding board as chapters were produced, and her observations and instincts were never wrong.

Bonar Menninger
Kansas City

# Sources and Methods

The vast majority of individual experiences recounted in this book were recorded through face-to-face interviews with the persons involved or their next of kin. All historical conversations in the book, with the exception of surviving radio transcriptions, were recreated based on the recollections of participants. Most of the general information about the tornado's aftermath was culled from newspaper articles, primarily in the *Topeka State Journal,* the *Topeka Daily Capital,* the *Topeka Capital-Journal,* the *Kansas City Star* and the *Kansas City Times.* I am especially indebted to former *Capital-Journal* reporter Ralph Marsh for his excellent article titled "Tornado Watch No. 201," which appeared in the June 4th, 1967, edition of the *Topeka Capital-Journal's Midway* magazine.

# Warning

Certain scenes in this book depict persons seeking cover from an oncoming tornado beneath interstate overpasses. The National Weather Service has determined that taking shelter under highway bridges is extremely dangerous and should be avoided at all costs. Bridge openings accelerate the already fierce winds of a tornado and leave individuals vulnerable to a killing barrage of flying debris. If caught on the highway, persons should attempt to determine which way the tornado is moving and, if time and distance permit, drive out of its path. Failing that, they should get out of their vehicles and seek shelter in the lowest spot possible.

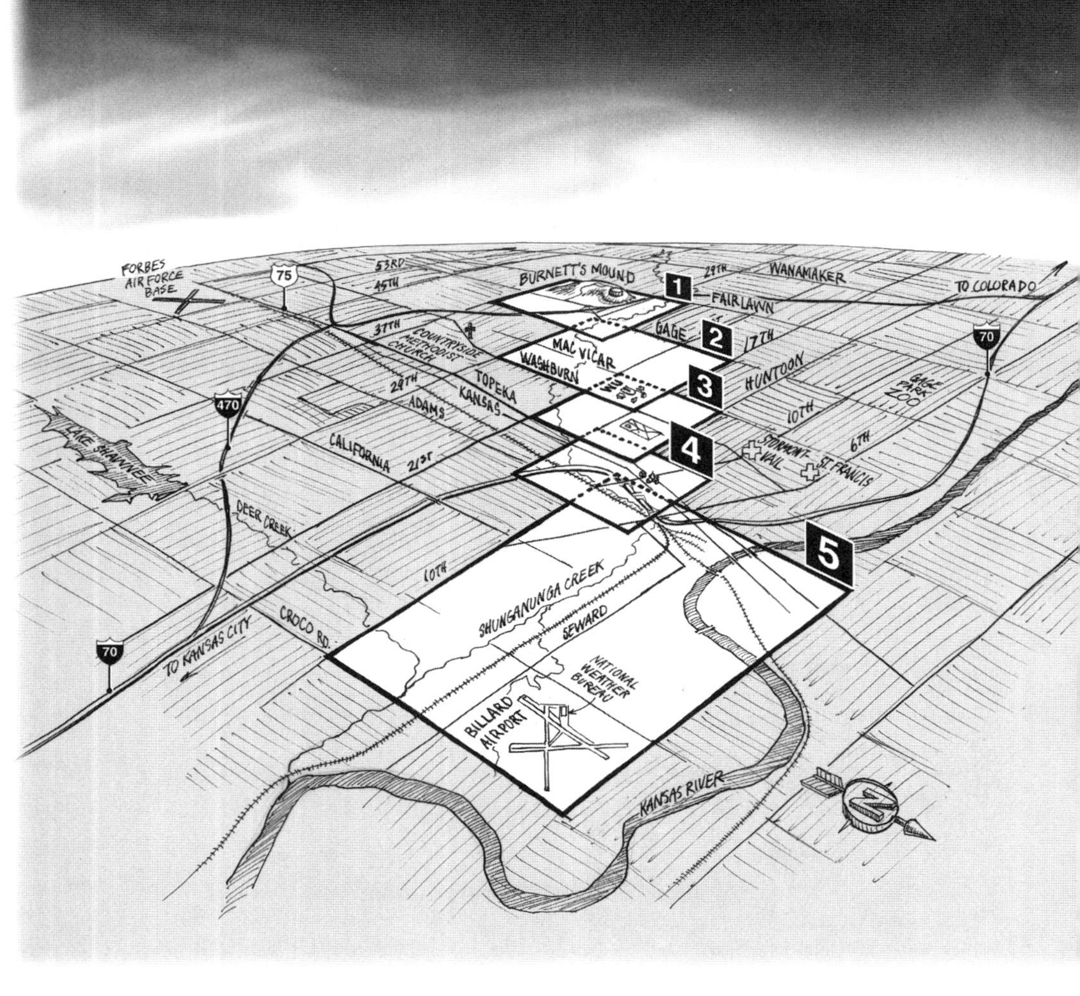


## Guide to Maps
## Topeka, Kansas — 1966

# CHAPTER ONE

# Hump Day

Glenn Nicely filled a paper cup from the push-button thermos perched on the tailgate of his pickup, took a long, steady pull, then spat a perfect jet into the gravel near his boots. The day was getting hot. It had rained hard the night before, and lingering clouds had drifted over most of the day. Now, at 4:30, the sun was burning through and the humidity was rising. The air was thick and close.

So summer was here. The days would grow steadily hotter. By the Fourth of July, the violent storms of spring and last night's driving, two-inch rain would be fading memories. By mid-August, the thermometer would regularly top 100 degrees and the wind would blow like a blast furnace until the earth wilted and pulled back into itself. Glenn had watched the seasons turn enough to know that summer on the plains could be just as savage as winter — that heat, humidity and frequent drought were just as merciless as the arctic winds that knifed down from Canada from December until March.

That was Kansas. You got used to it.

Fortunately, given the rising heat of the day, quitting time was near. Glenn crushed the paper cup, tossed it into the pickup bed and stared intently at the little building before him. With all the rain, it was a good thing he and Bud had managed to get the roof on last week. They had set in the big front window earlier and would finish putting up plywood by day's end. Siding would arrive tomorrow.

They could get that up in a couple of days and then go inside next week: setting the toilet and sink, building the counter, insulating, hanging Sheetrock and putting up trim.

Three months into it, maybe three to go. They were getting there.

Office workers and deliverymen hurrying to beat the yellow light at the busy intersection of 21st Street and Kansas Avenue in Topeka no doubt paid little attention to the two men working on the small structure nearby. But the fact was, a lot went into constructing a gas station.

You had your concrete work: pouring the slab and later, the eight-inch-thick cap for the tanks, and the island, too. You had your carpentry: framing and roofing and interior finish work. And the tanks: two 8,000-gallon steel beasts set in a hole 15 feet deep and 30 feet across. But before a crane could set them into place, you had to make sure they didn't leak. Air was pumped in and gauges set to measure any loss over a 24-hour period. A state inspector would come out to certify the results. After that, pipefitting: hooking up one-inch copper from the tank pumps to the dispenser pumps. And finally, welding: Roof panels for the canopy were arc-welded to a steel frame erected on two heavy posts bolted to footings five feet in the ground.

Glenn Nicely had gone through the apprentice program at Carpenters and Joiners Local 1445 after he'd been discharged from the Army in 1959. Now, seven years later, in June of 1966, there wasn't much he couldn't do. He'd been a cook in Germany. But Glenn was more like a Green Beret in the building and mechanical trades. Along with all the skills required to build a gas station, Glenn was qualified to do millwright work. He'd learned the trade — heavy machinery assembly, maintenance and repair — in apprentice school, and for previous employers, he'd worked on the giant steam turbines at the Kansas Power & Light power station by the river and on the big conveyors that moved tires through the Goodyear plant in North Topeka.

All of which was hard, physical work, and Glenn wasn't big, maybe five feet seven inches and 140 pounds. But what he lacked in size, he made up for in grit: He would attack a project with a quiet fury and go flat out until it was done. If he couldn't finesse the thing, he'd jam it, and if there was a problem, Glenn would quickly figure a way around. He worked smart and fast.

Glenn could be funny in a droll, hard-edged, job-site kind of way, co-worker Bob Clearwater recalled. One thing he didn't abide was ignorance. If Glenn thought something was wrong or impossible or foolish, like a schedule or a plan or a process or an idea, he wouldn't hesitate to speak up, fixing the boss with a flat, unwavering stare that suggested utter indifference to authority, if not outright contempt. He would argue his case steadily and fearlessly, and more often than not, much to his co-workers' silent amazement, the bosses would come around.

But now, as he picked up his tools at day's end, Glenn had no problem with anyone. Home was close. For three years, building service stations for the Uhl Company had meant working for one, two, even three weeks straight in far-off towns from eastern Missouri to western Kansas. At the end of the hitch, Glenn and his co-workers would drive back to Topeka and make the most of three days off before heading back out. But this particular job was right in town, not 15 miles from Glenn's trailer near Auburn, a farm town just southwest of the city. Miracle of miracles: He'd be home another night with his wife, Inge (pronounced "Inga"), and their six-year-old daughter, Angie.

It occurred to Glenn that he ought to drop by his father's barbershop after work to get a haircut. So he climbed into the cab of his brand-new, black Dodge pickup, lit a Pall Mall, nodded good-bye to Bud, and swung north on Kansas Avenue, heading downtown.

— • —

The languid pace of summer was slowly washing over the 127,600 souls of Kansas's capital city on Wednesday, June 8, 1966. School had been out for a couple of weeks, the big municipal pools had opened over the Memorial Day weekend, and for kids, a three-month carnival of baseball, swimming, bike rides, and endless TV had begun. Youngsters were especially excited about tonight's big event: The new

Charlie Brown special, "Charlie Brown's All-Stars," was set to debut at 7:30 p.m. on the local CBS affiliate, WIBW Channel 13. The show was one of the more obscure Charlie Brown specials of the 1960s and featured woebegone Charlie pitching the gang's baseball team to its 999th defeat. Older kids looked forward to the ever-popular *Lost in Space* at 6:30 p.m. or *Batman* on one of the Kansas City channels. Tonight's Batman episode was titled "The 13th Hat," and it sounded interesting in that weird, Batman kind of way, according to the listing in the paper: "When the Dynamic Duo meet the Mad Hatter, Batman gets stoned and Robin is mesmerized."

In the summer of '66, Topeka — or T-Town, as teenagers called it — wasn't a lot different from hundreds of other medium-sized cities across America. The community boasted four radio stations, two daily newspapers and one television station. There were three high schools, 166 churches of 42 denominations, 48 parks with a total of 1,100 acres, and 30 hotels and motels with 1,800 rooms. Topeka was heavily blue-collar and unionized, despite its large contingent of state workers. One of the biggest employers was the Atchison, Topeka and Santa Fe Railway shops, located northeast of downtown. The shops were among the largest railroad manufacturing and repair facilities in the country and employed 2,400. Topeka was a major transshipment point for wheat, corn, soybeans and other agricultural products, and some of the largest grain elevators in the world stretched for nearly a half mile along the Union Pacific tracks in North Topeka. Goodyear made tires at a sprawling plant north of the river, and DuPont produced 45 million pounds of cellophane annually at a foul-smelling factory just east of the city. Forbes Air Force Base, three miles south of town on Highway 75, was home to the 313th Troop Carrier Wing. Lumbering, jungle-camouflaged C-130 Hercules transports, some bound for Vietnam, were a common sight over the city.

On June 8 the *Topeka Daily Capital* reported that former actor Ronald Reagan had won the Republican primary for governor in California. Dr. Martin Luther King Jr. and Stokely Carmichael, the future Black Panther leader, had picked up the mantle for James H. Meredith and were marching south through Mississippi to the capital city of Jackson. Meredith, the first black to enroll in the University of Mississippi, had set off alone June 5 on a "March Against Fear." He intended to demonstrate that Negroes could walk safely through Mississippi and should not be afraid to register to vote. But the very next day, Meredith had been dropped by a shotgun blast in an ambush near Hernando. He recovered to finish the march in late June.

Closer to home, Local 22 of the Commercial Telegraphers Union had gone out on strike at midnight Tuesday after negotiations between the national union and Western Union collapsed. And in south-central Kansas, rain was slowing the annual winter wheat harvest. This was not good, as wheat was the backbone of the Kansas economy. In the 1870s and 1880s, German-Russian homesteaders had discovered that the hardy Turkish red wheat seed they'd carried over from the Ukraine did well in the rich soil and semiarid climate of the plains. The grain, which is used to make whole-wheat flour, is planted in early fall, peeks out of the ground by Thanksgiving and survives through winter under a protective blanket of snow. By early June, swaying fields two feet tall begin to ripen from green to gold. The wheat harvest starts in the southern tier of the state's 105 counties and moves north to finish by mid-July. In 1965, Kansas was by far the largest producer of winter wheat in the country, with 236.4 million bushels harvested, or about 23 percent of the U.S. total. Oklahoma, the next-largest producer, harvested 133 million bushels.

In weather news, the big story nationally was Hurricane Alma, which had raked Cuba and was setting its sights on Florida. The forecast for Topeka called for mostly cloudy skies with occasional showers or thunderstorms and a high around 80 degrees.

— • —

If Glenn Nicely happened to look as he drove past the car lots stretching along Kansas Avenue at the southern edge of downtown, he might have noticed a barrel-chested, sharply dressed man striding purposefully toward the Pla-Land bowling alley at 1024 Kansas Avenue. That would have been Lisle Grauer, the bowling alley's owner.

Grauer, who was 66 years old, was born in Summerfield, Kansas, a little town hard against the Nebraska line in the northeast part of the state. His father, Sam, had come from Germany in the 1880s and ran a bar called the Switzer House in Summerfield. It was a rough-and-tumble frontier joint, and Lisle (pronounced "Lyle") learned early on how to use his fists. A newspaper clipping from back in the day described how the strapping, teenaged Lisle had challenged the town bully to a fight and soundly whipped him.

Lisle never did back down. His son, Ron, years later remembered one night at the bowling alley. An obnoxious, loud-mouthed fellow had been making trouble during a pool game, so Lisle threw him out. Around midnight, after father and son had locked up and were heading for their car, there was that man again, standing across street and yelling: "Grauer, you son of a bitch! Get over here and I'll kick your ass!" Old Lisle shook his head and muttered, "I thought this might happen." He carefully removed his false teeth, put them in the pocket of his sport coat, took off the jacket and handed it to his son.

"This'll just take a minute," he said as he turned to cross the street. And sure enough, within a few moments, the malefactor lay battered and bleeding on the pavement. Then, much to his son's surprise, Lisle helped the man to his feet, put him into the car and drove to an all-night Chinese restaurant in downtown Topeka, where he bought Ron and the man a meal.

Baby-faced, jovial and always impeccably dressed, Lisle loved music and was a superb dancer. He'd taught himself to play piano, guitar, banjo and violin. In the '20s, Lisle joined a traveling jazz and ragtime band called the Blue Blazers. The combo played dancehalls across northeast Kansas and northwest Missouri, and it was at the Frog Hop in St. Joe that Lisle met Erma Anderson, his wife-to-be. As a young girl, Erma lived in a sod dugout on the plains of Kansas. Her mother was a pioneer who could ride two horses bareback at the same time like a circus daredevil, one foot astride each animal. Once, when Erma was very young, she awoke to an ear-splitting crash and felt something heavy tumble onto the bed. It was a cougar. Apparently the big cat had been sitting in the cabin's open window, perhaps eyeing a meal. But Erma's mother spied the danger in time and shot the panther dead.

After Lisle and Erma married, they'd come to Topeka to make their way. Lisle managed to borrow some money in the mid-1930s and he bought a roller rink near downtown. But catering to kids proved a hit-or-miss proposition. So a couple of years later, he gutted the building and put in a bowling alley, Topeka's finest at the time. The business did well enough, although in the days before air-conditioning, it could get pretty slow in the summer. Old Lisle used to joke that he made more money playing golf in the summer than he did with the bowling alley. And he probably wasn't kidding, for Lisle was a gambler and a good one. Golf mostly, but bowling, poker and pool all were fair game. He'd gamble on just about anything, Ron recalled. Decades later, Ron still had a baby grand piano his father had won in a poker game. And he had shotguns and pistols, too.

On this particular night, serious money in all likelihood would be changing hands at the bowling alley. Big-time bowlers from across the city would be converging at 7:00 p.m. for the first night of men's summer leagues.

Lisle hurried inside to get ready.

— • —

Glenn Nicely turned at the intersection of 6th and Kansas in the heart of downtown and glanced back toward his father's barbershop. The place was packed. Bankers, shopkeepers and state office workers were stopping in after work for a trim or a shave and shoulder massage. Glenn didn't stop. The haircut could wait. He kept driving west on 6th Street, past the carpenters' union hall and the Greyhound-Trailways bus terminal. Then he turned south and before long he was passing the stately, limestone buildings of Washburn University. The 160-acre campus, with its ivy-covered edifices, winding walkways, and ancient pines, pin oaks, and elms, looked more like a private school in the East than a small college on the prairie.

But Washburn had been a part of Topeka almost from the start.

In fact, the school was celebrating its centennial in 1966. Its predecessor, Lincoln College, was founded just after the Civil War by the Congregational Church. The name was changed a few years later, after a Massachusetts industrialist named Ichabod Washburn gave the school $25,000. In 1942, the citizens of Topeka voted to make Washburn a municipal university, one of just a few in the country supported primarily by local tax money. Enrollment by 1966 had reached 4,000. Washburn's law school was well known throughout the Midwest and well respected, at least among those in the legal profession. The school's mascot, "the Fighting Ichabod," was odd and quaint: a nattily dressed 19th-century chap in a top hat and bow tie, meant to resemble the school's benefactor and namesake.

Glenn was clear of the city as he turned onto Auburn Road, not five miles from home. The road shot straight south from the turn, rising and falling with the contours of the low hills that rolled easily toward the horizon. In the fields on either side of the highway, corn and soybeans muscled up from the rich, black soil and white-faced Herefords foraged on fresh prairie grass and brome. The occasional stand of hackberry, walnut and burr oak marked the creeks and draws.

Evidently, the rain wasn't finished. Glenn could see a storm building in the southwest. The temperature was falling. Fast, black clouds soon caught up to the sun and obscured it, and beneath the sudden, unnatural darkness, the rain began to fall. It came slowly at first, just a few, fat drops that hit the truck like splattering eggs. Then faster, tattooing the hood and roof with a steady roll. And finally, as Glenn turned into his driveway, the downpour became a battering torrent.

Glenn jumped out and sprinted past his parents' white, three-bedroom ranch (built on the site of his grandfather's homestead), leapt up the steps to his trailer and burst in, slamming the thin aluminum door behind him against the deluge.

"Coming down pretty good," Inge said.

"Yeah, it is," Glenn said, shaking the water off his hair.

"They said there might have been a tornado up by I-70. We're under a tornado watch, you know."

"Didn't hear that."

The television announcer's voice filled the family room off the galley kitchen as Inge reached into the refrigerator to start dinner. Twenty-six, with naturally curly, short brown hair and weighing maybe 110 pounds, Inge Nicely was a live wire and a long way from her homeland. She was born in Frankfurt, Germany, in 1940. Her father was a soldier and she'd lived in a small apartment building with her mother. Frankfurt was a major transportation hub and the target of heavy bombing during the war. All told, more than 5,500 residents were killed in the raids. Twice Inge and her mother were bombed out of their home. Inge remembered huddling on the banks of the Main River at night as flames danced across the water and fire engulfed the city.

Inge had learned English in school, and after the war she went to work in the purchasing department of Woolworth's Germany. At seventeen, in a tavern, Inge met a cocky, redheaded American soldier from Kansas. The friendship soon became something more, and a year later — much to her mother's horror — Inge and Glenn Nicely were married.

Now she was in faraway Kansas, raising a daughter, living in the country and working part-time in the bindery department at Hart Printing in Topeka. Strong and opinionated, she'd been through a lot in her young life. As a result, she was not at all intimidated by her new surroundings, Glenn's large, clannish family, or, for that matter, Glenn himself.

Glenn's co-worker Bob Clearwater remembered one telling incident. During a lunch break on the job site, the talk turned — as it often did — to women. Glenn was holding forth about how he was the boss at his home, how he wore the pants and how Inge did exactly what she was told, when she was told. As it happened, Inge had stopped by the job unannounced and, unbeknownst to Glenn, she was standing behind him in the doorway when he started in. Too late, co-workers caught Glenn's eye and motioned toward the door.

"You!" Inge barked, her German accent bristling with fury. "Outside! Right now!" Glenn got up and quietly walked out the door, where, according to Clearwater, a lively discussion ensued.

As fast as it came, the rain began to ease. To the west, the sun was breaking through. The Nicelys' six-year-old daughter, Angie, lay on the couch, thumbing through a picture book. A big Siamese named Tommy was curled up beside her. Inge dropped three hamburgers into the frying pan.

Growing up in the country, Glenn had always ridden, and in 1966, he kept five horses in the pasture below the trailer. One of them, a quarter horse–saddlebred mare named Pixie, was recovering from tendon surgery. The horse had either gotten tangled up in barbed wire or been attacked by coyotes; the doctor at Kansas State University wasn't sure which. But the surgery was successful, and now, two weeks later, Pixie was on the mend. With the rain slowing to a sprinkle, Glenn decided to go out and check on the animal. Mitzi, Inge's brown-and-white, bug-eyed, Chihuahua–toy terrier mix, bounded to the door, bouncing eagerly and shaking her stubby tail.

With a bottle of antiseptic, Glenn stepped outside and walked 50 yards to the low shed that provided shelter for the horses. The air was unsettled and the clouds still boiled, but it appeared the worst of the storm had passed. Glenn nickered to the horses and they slowly emerged, one by one, from the open shed. There was Red, the big bay mare. And Pedro, a mean Mexican brushtail that had once been wild and pretty much still was. Glenn stroked Pixie and then painted the purple antiseptic on her fetlock with an applicator. The wound looked good.

Inge was at the doorway when Glenn returned.

"Don't you come inside with those damn muddy boots!"

Glenn sat down on the step, unlaced his boots, pulled them off, and then set them on newspaper just inside the door. Inge looked up from her cooking. The weatherman was reporting that more heavy weather could be on the way. Just then, Inge remembered the new barbeque grill. It had a small glass window in the front to check the meat as it cooked.

"Could you go lay the grill down?" she asked Glenn. "I don't want the wind to knock it over and break that glass."

Glenn grumbled. She could have at least told him before he'd taken off his boots. He headed back outside barefoot, eased the grill over and pushed it up against the trailer.

It was just before 7:00 p.m.

Then Glenn gazed off toward the Bundy farm, three-quarters of a mile to the southwest across open ground. He squinted and looked again. It didn't make sense. Near the barn . . . a dump truck and a red, self-propelled combine — a massive piece of farm equipment weighing three tons or more — were tumbling end-over-end, 50 feet up in the air.

Glenn didn't hesitate.

"Tornado!" he shouted as he raced back up the steps and burst inside. "Tornado coming! Get your ass out of here. We'll go to Mom's. Let's GO!" He quickly lifted Angie into his arms and turned for the door. Inge was already moving from the kitchen to the living room, slamming windows down. Glenn raced down the steps, ran for his mother's house 100 feet to the north and slung open the back-porch sliding door.

"A tornado just hit the Bundy place! We gotta go!"

Mrs. Nicely, 61, stood in the kitchen in her housecoat and curlers. She looked straight at Glenn. Then she picked up the phone to call her husband. But the Nicelys were on a party line and the line was in use. She recognized the voice on the other end. It was a neighbor in the next house to the north, Clarice Wolf.

Mrs. Nicely interrupted: "This is Hazel Nicely. There's a tornado coming! You and Calvin need to take cover right now!" By now, Inge had finished closing up the trailer and had made the long dash to her in-laws' house.

"We gotta outrun it. Go! Go! Go! Get in the truck!" Glenn said, opening the side door to the garage and running through to the driveway with Inge and Mrs. Nicely close behind. They all jumped into the Dodge.

The keys . . . the keys! Where were the keys? Glenn fumbled for a moment. But time was running out.

"We'll go to the crawl space! RUN!" The truck doors flew open and bodies shot out. Everyone raced back to the garage. Glenn pulled the door down, grabbed Angie, stuffed her into the crawl space between the garage and the utility room and then pushed Inge in behind her.

But Mrs. Nicely would have none of it. She ran back out into the garage.

"No, I'm not going down there," she warned Glenn. "A tornado ain't hit here in 50 years and it ain't going to hit here now."

Glenn was yelling as he chased her across the garage.

"Get in the goddamn crawl space! Now!" he said.

At that point, the garage door panels started to rattle and buck. And then, oddly, the door began to lift on its own. So Glenn reached out to grab it.

And that was it.

The house exploded.

— • —

There was a man in Auburn on June 8 from the state of Maine whose name, unfortunately, is lost to history. He'd evidently spotted the tornado and, never having seen one before, decided with a friend to shadow it north along Auburn Road. The men had reached the Nicelys' lower driveway when debris flying across the road forced them to stop. Just after they'd come to a halt, the wind sucked the headlights out of their car. Then they looked up into the swirling gray cloud and saw Glenn's horses, all five of them, sailing 50 or 60 feet over the road. The men said the horses' legs were locked and their necks were lowered as if the animals were paralyzed or braced against the wind. Maybe that was the way they were standing when the wind picked them up; maybe they were frozen in fear. Maybe both. In any event, the horses were gently lowered back down in the pasture to the east, on the other side of the road. The herd regained its footing and, apparently unhurt, galloped away.

In front of the Nicely place were half a dozen white pines Glenn's grandfather had planted when he'd built the original family homestead in the late 19th century. Now the pines were mighty giants, 60- to 80-feet tall and three and a half to four feet in diameter at the butt. After the horses flew over, the men watched in astonishment as the massive trees violently corkscrewed in the wind and then shot out of the ground, one after another — "like carrots," the man from Maine said — and soared off to the northeast.

Not a bough or branch was ever found.

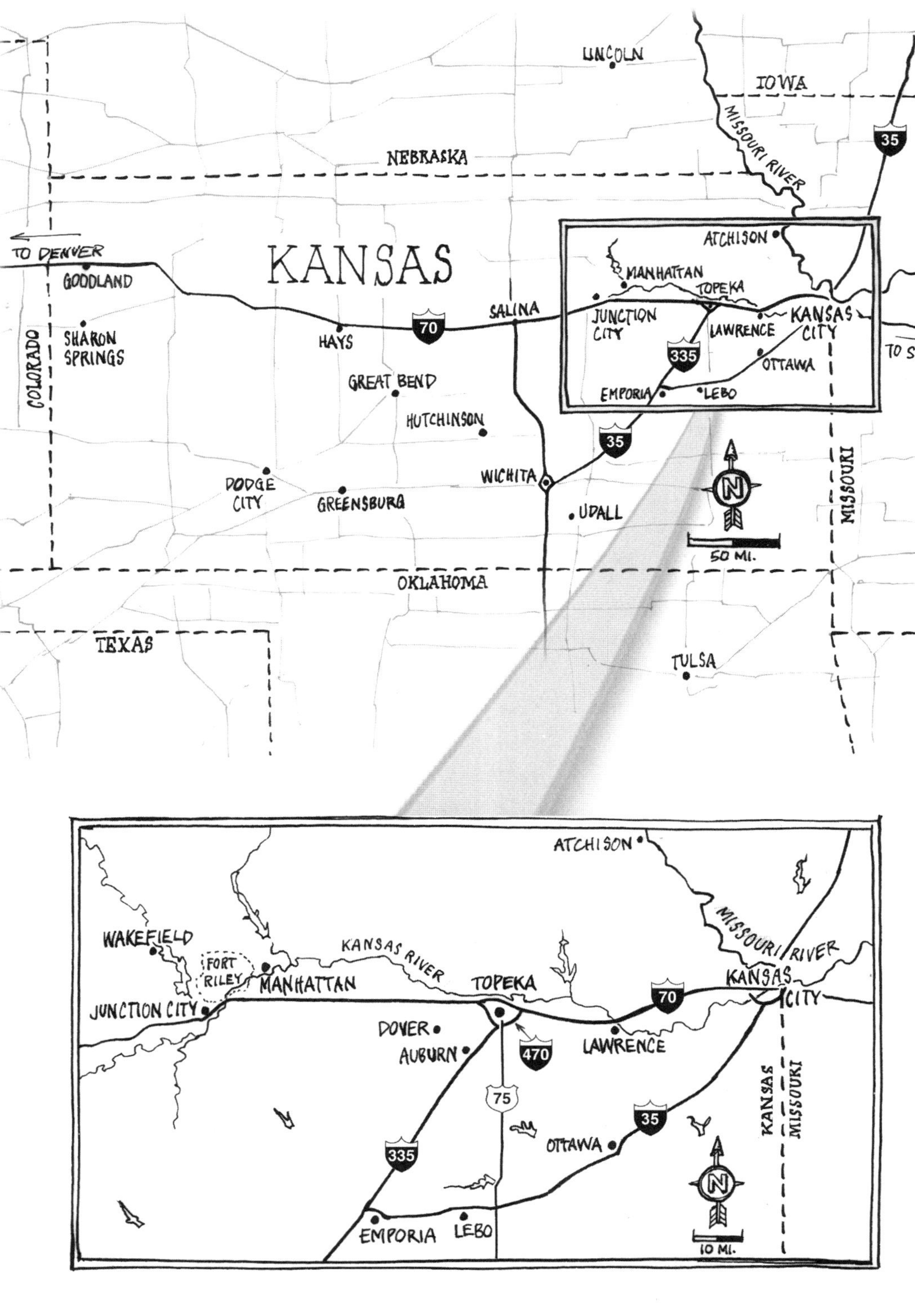

LINCOLN
IOWA
NEBRASKA
MISSOURI RIVER
35
TO DENVER
GOODLAND
KANSAS
ATCHISON
MANHATTAN
TOPEKA
SALINA
JUNCTION CITY
LAWRENCE
KANSAS CITY
COLORADO
SHARON SPRINGS
HAYS
70
335
TO ST.
GREAT BEND
EMPORIA
LEBO
OTTAWA
HUTCHINSON
35
MISSOURI
DODGE CITY
GREENSBURG
WICHITA
UDALL
N
50 MI.
OKLAHOMA
TEXAS
TULSA
WAKEFIELD
FORT RILEY
JUNCTION CITY
MANHATTAN
KANSAS RIVER
TOPEKA
ATCHISON
MISSOURI RIVER
KANSAS CITY
70
DOVER
AUBURN
470
LAWRENCE
75
335
OTTAWA
35
KANSAS
MISSOURI
N
EMPORIA
LEBO
10 MI.

# CHAPTER TWO

# Severe Weather Watch No. 201

The night of June 7 had been a wild one across Kansas. Severe thunderstorms pounded the state all evening. West of Hays, a five-inch deluge brought flash floods that swamped the creeks and draws. In Emporia, 200 miles to the east, 100-mile-an-hour, straight-line winds ripped across the airport just before midnight and hail piled up an inch deep. Golf ball–size hail was reported in Great Bend. And funnel clouds danced in the sky from Sharon Springs, near the Colorado line, all the way to Lebo, 300 miles to the east. But only a few touched down and no damage was reported.

The culprit behind the severe weather outbreak that struck during the overnight hours of June 7–8, 1966, was a powerful low-pressure system churning northeast out of the Oklahoma panhandle. Like a hungry bear, the low was devouring warm, moist air for hundreds of miles around, pulling the fuel toward its maw in a massive, counter-clockwise spiral. As the warm air slipped into the area of low pressure, it twisted upward into the cold, dry currents aloft. The vapor condensed and the storms exploded.

And it wasn't over yet. The jet stream was racing northeast at 50 miles an hour and dragging the low beneath it. On the stream's present course, the upper-level winds would carry the low's center — the most potent part of the storm — over Dodge City and eventually into northeast Kansas. At 2:40 a.m. on June 8, the Severe Local Storms

Forecast Center in Kansas City issued a brief statement indicating that severe thunderstorms likely would redevelop across Kansas by afternoon, once the sun reheated and recharged the atmosphere.

So it would be a stormy Wednesday. But what worried forecasters most was the tongue of hot, saturated air bottled up behind a warm front in southeast Kansas. The air was tropical, pushing up from the Gulf of Mexico. With a dew point of 72 degrees (the temperature at which vapor will condense to liquid), it nearly dripped with moisture. If the low continued moving east and the warm front kept creeping north, the ensuing collision could make the storms of the night before look tame by comparison.

In Topeka, the rain stopped around 3:00 a.m., although a few showers lingered as dawn slipped in under a heavy blanket of fog. At the city's U.S. Weather Bureau office, the day shift was beginning its morning routine. The office was located in a single-story building adjacent to the main terminal at Topeka's Billard Municipal Airport. The airport itself was a modest affair with three runways and a few commercial flights a day. It sat at the city's far northeastern corner, on bottomland close to the river, a few miles from downtown. Next to the airport were the working-class homes of the Oakland district.

Two weather technicians walked briskly toward a cinder-block building just west of the Weather Bureau office. They rolled up a tall, overhead door and entered a garagelike room, then attached a hose from a hydrogen tank to a large, gold-colored, latex balloon. The regulator was opened, the gas hissed and the balloon expanded to 10 feet in diameter. The men then tied the balloon off and attached a white metal container about the size of a large shoebox. The box held a battery, a small, cone-shaped antenna and an expendable instrument pack. The device was called a radiosonde. It would record and transmit a continuous stream of data on air pressure, temperature, humidity and wind speed as the balloon lifted into the sky.

These unmanned reconnaissance flights, known as upper air soundings, were a vital tool in providing forecasters with a real-time look at what was happening in the atmosphere. The soundings, or "runs," as the forecasters called them, were launched twice a day, every day, at 6:00 a.m. and 6:00 p.m., from nearly 100 Weather Bureau offices nationwide. Once the balloon was aloft, a receiver in the office would pull down the radiosonde's signals and spit the information out on a paper feed. Meteorologists would tear the paper off and then, wielding slide rules the way carpenters swing hammers, they'd construct a data set. The information was transmitted to the regional office in Kansas City and also plotted on a large table chart nearby.

It took the balloons just under two hours to rise to the edge of space, ascending at a rate of about 1,000 feet per minute. Above 100,000 feet, the balloons — now swollen in the thin air to 10 times their launch size — would burst, and the radiosondes would gently descend back to Earth on small, brightly colored red or yellow parachutes, the better to warn aircraft. The boxes were labeled with instructions to return them to the Weather Bureau office if found but few ever were.

Today's sounding would help meteorologists get a handle on the approaching weather. The two technicians flipped a switch on the data transmitter, synchronized the receiver and started a 60-second timer. The timer buzzed and, with a jerk, the balloon shot free and rose like a miniature moon against the metallic dawn.

Across Topeka on that gloomy Wednesday morning, thousands of people made ready for the new day. They showered and shaved, gulped coffee and scanned the headlines. They also walked, unwittingly, along the threshold of a great divide, moving through that fleeting moment between all that was and all that will be. Behind them was the past: familiar and comforting and probably not a lot different, they assumed, from what lay ahead. But fate can be a capricious thing. In truth, the lives of many were about to swerve sharply and inexorably down a different path. This day would mark the change. The transition for some would be difficult but manageable. For others, the scars — physical, emotional and financial — would linger for years. Still others would not survive the turn.

Human beings, of course, have always faced events that promised to alter them profoundly and, usually, not for the better: the looming prospect of combat. A long and difficult journey through a strange land. A debilitating illness, perhaps. But at least with those kinds of experiences, the human mind has a little time to adjust, to prepare, to make the necessary arrangements. What was different here was that so many did not know — could never have known — that the world they'd grown accustomed to was about to change forever, literally in the blink of an eye. For men and women, young and old, rich and poor, memories of all that preceded June 8 soon would be locked behind a barrier of new recollections: images, sounds and emotions shot through with unimaginable violence and terror.

Rick Douglass greeted the day with the confidence of a young man on his way up. Just 19 years old, Douglass already was one of Topeka's best-known citizens. You couldn't miss him in a crowd, with his helmet of wiry black hair, oddly serious features set against a wide, cherub face and a bowling pin body that tipped the scales at 270 pounds. It was his voice, though, that people knew. In the summer of '66, Douglass was one of Topeka's top disc jockeys. The voice was authoritative: a rich, deep tenor with just the right timbre for radio. And his elocution was precise. Douglass had worked hard to wring out any Kansas drawl or twang.

He was a heavy man, sure. But he always dressed exceedingly well. Jackets, pressed shirts, sharp ties and crisp trousers were the order of the day. Sometimes, with one of his pipes, he'd affect the thoughtful, pensive pose of an intellectual. But mostly, he was affable and down-to-earth. And always supremely self-confident. He seemed a lot older than 19. And in many ways, he was, for he'd been performing publicly since boyhood, and he had worked in radio since junior high. These days, Douglass was the afternoon drive-time voice of WREN 1250 AM, one of Topeka's top radio stations.

It had been a swift rise for the Topeka native. Douglass's father died before Rick was born, and the boy was raised by his mother, Lucille, and his maternal grandmother. The latter, Mrs. Byron Willcuts, was known locally as the Horseradish Queen due to the family business she'd taken over after her husband died. Byron Willcuts' Horseradish Sauce XXXX was sold at finer grocery establishments throughout the Midwest. Rick's mom was the company's bookkeeper but effectively ran the operation. The business did well.

As an only child, Rick enjoyed the undivided attention of his mother and grandmother. He was a precocious kid. In the early '50s, he put together a mini-vaudeville act. His mom would play some of the more well-known comedy monologues of the day on a record player, and the little guy would pantomime the acts, including Andy Griffith's famous "What It Was, Was Football," and Charlie Weaver's "A Letter from Mama." He had costumes for each character and would put on his show at school assemblies, church groups and the women's club downtown.

By junior high, Douglass's love of performance had sparked an interest in radio. In the ninth grade, he landed a part-time job at K-TOP, another local AM station. He started out ripping and sorting news stories as they rolled off the AP wire. But before long, he'd actually snagged his own show. Granted, it was on the virtually unused FM portion of the radio spectrum. Few people knew about FM and fewer still had receivers to pick it up. Nonetheless, every weekday evening, from 5:30 until 7:00 p.m., the Topeka High School sophomore hosted "Dinner Date with Rick," a mix of news, sports and dinner music.

Douglass learned quickly. So when a Sunday morning slot opened on the AM side, he stepped right into it. K-TOP was run by an old-time radio guy named Bailey Axton. His son, Charlie, had recently returned from the service, and he'd learned a thing or two out in the world. He urged his dad to lose the hymns and elevator music and adopt the new Top 40, rock-and-roll format. It was a can't-miss deal. The old man mulled it over and figured what the hell — why not?

K-TOP soon was the most popular station in Topeka and Rick "Fat Daddy" Douglass was the hippest DJ in town. He had his own beatnik shtick, kind of a Wolfman Jack–type act. He played Elvis and the Beach Boys and Little Richard and Chuck Berry. His popularity soared, and Axton quickly moved him to the 7:00–10:00 p.m.

slot, Monday through Friday. The evening hours didn't help Rick's grades, but he couldn't have cared less. Old Axton worried sometimes, though, that the station might get in trouble for employing a kid under the age of 18 full-time. Consequently, he'd ask Rick to make jokes on the air about his wife and kids, which, of course, he didn't have, and Douglass often wore a fedora in public to shield his baby face.

Douglass graduated in May of 1964 and turned 18 that August. Throughout '64, the music of the Beatles and the other bands of the British Invasion poured into Kansas. Overnight, it seemed as if the air itself had changed. To kids, anyway, the world was electric and alive in a way it had never been before. And Rick was right in the middle of it. He spun the records. He was popular with the girls. He was making some money. Not bad for a first job out of school. And maybe it could have gone on that way forever, except that in March of '65, old Axton decided he'd had enough. He sold K-TOP to a company from western Kansas. The new owners wanted to switch to an adult-oriented format and they didn't think "Fat Daddy" fit the bill. So just like that, it was over.

But Douglass didn't miss a step. After a brief stint at a Kansas City station, Douglass landed a job with WREN in Topeka. The station was owned by the venerable Alf Landon, a former governor and the 1936 Republican presidential candidate. For many older residents, WREN was the voice of Topeka: the go-to source for news, weather, sports and entertainment. Paul Harvey's commentary was on every weekday. The station played a lot of Sinatra, Bing Crosby, Dean Martin and Tony Bennett. Five thousand watts of nighttime power pushed the signal 450 miles west, all the way into eastern Colorado. Rick's mom was a big WREN fan and was thrilled her son was going to work for such a prestigious local institution. The station's management, for their part, hyped Douglass's return to the Topeka airwaves just about every way they could. For a week solid, advertisements in the local newspaper proclaimed: "Fat Daddy is making the big move to WREN!"

Douglass started as the station's morning man in the summer of '65, then moved to the afternoon slot a couple of months later. He soon settled into the job and picked up the additional duties of music director. In that role, he reinvigorated the station's moribund playlists with new, if safe, artists like Herb Alpert and the Tijuana Brass and Wayne Newton. WREN's ratings climbed.

Because WREN prided itself on spot news coverage, Douglass often found himself in the field, reporting on car wrecks, fires, shootings and robberies. If severe weather threatened, WREN disc jockeys, engineers and news directors alike deployed to various vantage points around the city to watch and report on the dangerous skies. More often than not, Douglass would be behind the wheel of the WREN-mobile, a cherry red 1962 Chevy II wagon with WREN-Mobile splashed in big white letters on the side. Bristling with two-way radio antennas and sporting a tall, red emergency light on the roof, the little family car looked like a circus wagon trundling down the street. But it was a reassuring sight for many to see the WREN-mobile motoring into the teeth of an oncoming storm.

When it came to severe weather, WREN did something else that earned the respect and appreciation of listeners. An engineer had come up with a novel idea for providing a reliable warning if nasty weather threatened. He'd taken the puck off of an old turntable and mounted it on a motor, then put a little notch in the puck and added a tone generator. The puck had a two-minute rotation, so with every complete turn, the tone generator was hit and a shrill *beep-beep-beep-beep* produced. Every time a tornado or severe thunderstorm watch was issued, the device would be activated and the beeps would go out every two minutes over the top of whatever was being broadcast, be it a baseball game, music, news or commentary. The beeps were remarkably effective at raising the public's awareness about the risk of severe weather.

On June 8, Douglass planned to head into the station early to sort through the newly arrived records and update the playlists before starting his 3:00–7:00 p.m. stint at the microphone.

There was another young man in Topeka on that Wednesday who likewise was preparing for an evening broadcast. Like Rick Douglass, Bill Kurtis started in radio at a young age, working as a part-time announcer at an AM station while attending junior college in southeast Kansas. Like Douglass, Kurtis had a deep, stentorian voice that seemed genetically engineered for broadcasting. But rather than sticking with radio, Kurtis had followed the television path. He'd been pulled toward the profession by the dramatic reporting network newsmen had done across the South during the civil rights movement in the '50s and early '60s. Kurtis was convinced that the networks' stories had played a decisive role in forcing America to confront the racism at its core. He wanted to be a part of a big story like that. His convictions about television's power were confirmed during the historic four days of round-the-clock coverage that had followed the assassination of President John F. Kennedy. CBS News anchorman Walter Cronkite was one of his heroes.

Fortunately for Kurtis, he had not only the voice for television but also the looks. He was all-American, frat-boy handsome, with a broad forehead, a cut jaw, large, dark eyes and a ready-for-TV smile. He had the build of a quarterback, which he was in high school. Born Bill Kuretich, in Pensacola, Florida, he was the son of Kansans: His mother, Wilma Horton, was from Independence in southeast Kansas. His father, William, was a Marine Corps brigadier general who'd fought on Okinawa. He was of Croatian decent. The family had moved around quite a bit before Bill's father retired in 1954 to Independence, where young Bill attended junior high and high school.

Kurtis earned a degree in journalism from the University of Kansas in 1963, and three years later — after a hitch in the Marine Corps reserve and a stint as a weatherman — he'd been promoted to part-time news anchor for WIBW Channel 13, Topeka's only TV station. He was 25 years old.

Yet even with the success he'd enjoyed and the passion he had for broadcasting, Kurtis was under no illusions about his long-term career prospects. The big television markets — New York, Chicago and L.A. — were the real launchpads for network jobs, and they might as well have been on the moon to a kid from southeast Kansas. Being the cautious and practical fellow that he was, Kurtis consequently hedged his bets when he began his broadcast career by enrolling in the Washburn University School of Law. Now, three years later, with graduation upon him, the decision that would shape the rest of his working life was front and center: Would it be TV or the law?

He chewed on the dilemma for months. There was his family to think about. Kurtis had married his high school sweetheart, Helen Scott, in 1963, and the couple's first child, Mary Kristin, was six months old in June of '66. Building a good life required money and you could make a lot of it as an attorney. Nor was Kurtis bereft of talent when it came to the law. At Washburn, he'd gotten involved in moot court, a competition that simulated trials and appellate work, and he'd been named outstanding advocate after one event at Washington University in St. Louis.

So while his heart was still in broadcasting, his mind insisted that he follow a more prudent path. Kurtis sent out his résumé and interviewed with a law firm in Wichita, and they soon offered him a job, assuming he passed the bar. Thus, by early June, Kurtis was spending most of his free time prepping for the bar exam. He was still working at WIBW, but his broadcast days were numbered. On June 8, Kurtis agreed to do the six o'clock news for a fellow broadcaster who wanted to get out of town for vacation a day early.

— • —

At the Weather Bureau office, forecaster P. N. Eland studied the data streaming in from the dawn balloon launch. It was late morning. Eland was in charge for the day; chief meteorologist Richard Garrett had gone to a two-day conference at the Weather Bureau regional office in Kansas City. Eland pored over the readings. It didn't look good. Although the wind at the surface was out of the south at five knots, the breezes stiffened and changed direction with altitude, swinging first out of the east at 20 knots around 2,000 feet and then, at 6,000 feet, shifting to the west-southwest at a steady 35 knots. Even higher, at 25,000 feet, the jet stream was racing west to east at 55 knots. These countervailing winds aloft, or shear, could set the stage for atmospheric rotation — a primary ingredient in a severe thunderstorm formation — as the day wore on.

Forecasters at the Severe Local Storms Forecast Center in Kansas City were aware of the reports from the Topeka station and from other offices across Kansas. They also were watching the powerful low-pressure system as it churned ever closer to the warm front crawling north over the eastern part of the state. No getting around it: The air masses in all likelihood would collide by evening and spark another round of severe weather.

At 11:00 a.m. on June 8, weather Teletype machines in law enforcement offices and newsrooms in Kansas and western Missouri snapped to life, and Severe Weather Watch No. 201 clattered across the wire at the rate of 80 words per minute:

> THE U.S. WEATHER BUREAU HAS ISSUED A TORNADO WATCH FOR PORTIONS OF SOUTH-CENTRAL AND EASTERN KANSAS AND WEST-CENTRAL MISSOURI. THE THREAT OF ONE OR TWO TORNADOES WILL EXIST FROM 2 PM UNTIL 8 PM THIS WEDNESDAY AFTERNOON AND EVENING. SEVERE THUNDERSTORMS WITH LARGE HAIL AND LOCALLY DAMAGING WINDS ALSO ARE FORECAST.
>
> THE GREATEST THREAT OF TORNADOES AND SEVERE THUNDERSTORMS IS IN AN AREA ALONG AND 60 MILES EITHER SIDE OF A LINE FROM 20 MILES SOUTHWEST OF HUTCHINSON, KANSAS, TO 60 MILES EAST OF KANSAS CITY, MISSOURI.
>
> PERSONS IN OR CLOSE TO THE TORNADO WATCH AREA ARE ADVISED BY THE WEATHER BUREAU TO BE ON THE WATCH FOR LOCAL WEATHER DEVELOPMENTS AND FOR LATER WEATHER STATEMENTS AND WARNINGS.

It was odd; it didn't seem like tornado weather. Typically, tornadoes are ushered in by a particular kind of day. The wind blows out of the south — hard, steady or in fluttering, desultory bursts — the temperature climbs to 80 degrees or more under a milky sky, and the air itself seems to sweat with humidity. Then the atmosphere becomes very still. But today, it had drizzled sporadically all morning, the sky remained overcast and by noon, the temperature was still in the mid-60s. The weather seemed more like September than early June. Nonetheless, Topekans heard the *beep-beep-beep-beep* on WREN and made a mental note. Most did, at least.

But Carol Martin was a kid. If she knew about the tornado watch, she didn't give it a thought. The 16-year-old had other things on her mind. She had just gotten her driver's license and was enjoying tooling around town in her own car: a baby-blue 1960 Dodge Dart with a white vinyl top and a push-button automatic transmission. She also looked forward to a trip out to Hutchinson, Kansas, on Thursday with Job's Daughters, a singing group affiliated with the Masons. The group was going to the central Kansas city to participate in a singing competition. One more practice was slated for tonight at the Masonic Temple downtown before the girls hit the road in the morning.

It would be good to get away.

Carol was tall and slender, with fine, straight, shoulder-length brown hair and bangs that touched her eyebrows. She had a narrow face and a big, open smile. She seldom removed her tortoise-shell, cat-eyed glasses, and they changed her appearance, as glasses will do. Carol was the only child of Cleve and Hazel Martin. Cleve was a barber at the sprawling Winter Veterans Administration Hospital near 21ˢᵗ Street and Gage Boulevard. The family lived within walking distance of the VA, at the edge of a blue-collar neighborhood adjacent to the grounds of the Kansas Neurological Institute.

Her father's people had homesteaded near Topeka before the Civil War and her great-grandfather had fought for the South. When Carol was a one-year-old, the Martins moved in from the country because her mom needed to be committed to the Topeka State Hospital. Hazel was a paranoid schizophrenic; she was not a happy person, and she was hospitalized on and off all through Carol's growing-up years. But Carol's dad was patient and kind, and he and Carol worked as a team. They took care of Hazel and the little family managed as best they could.

Carol, though, could always close her door and close her eyes and escape into her music. She enjoyed the stirring religious hymns she sang with Job's Daughters. But she loved rock and pop more. She probably listened to *Rubber Soul* every day that year. It was the Beatles' sixth album, released in December of '65, just in time for Christmas. So incredibly vivid: It was filled with light and shadow and a fleeting darkness that raced across the landscape like summer clouds and shined with a melancholy beauty that Carol was convinced could only have come from God.

And it wasn't just the Beatles. All the music that summer was amazing. The Rolling Stones' menacing incantation on the bleakness of life, "Paint It Black," became the new No. 1 single on the Billboard Hot 100 that Wednesday. The rest of the top 20 had something for everyone:

2.  "Did You Ever Have to Make Up Your Mind?" — Lovin' Spoonful
3.  "I Am a Rock" — Simon and Garfunkel
4.  "When a Man Loves a Woman" — Percy Sledge
5.  "A Groovy Kind of Love" — The Mindbenders
6.  "Strangers in the Night" — Frank Sinatra
7.  "Monday, Monday" — The Mamas and the Papas
8.  "It's a Man's Man's Man's World" — James Brown
9.  "Green Grass" — Gary Lewis & the Playboys
10.  "Barefootin'" — Robert Parker
11.  "Sweet Talkin' Guy" — The Chiffons
12.  "Cool Jerk" — The Capitols
13.  "Oh How Happy" — Shades of Blue
14.  "Opus 17 (Don't You Worry 'Bout Me)" — The Four Seasons
15.  "Rainy Day Women #12 and 35" — Bob Dylan
16.  "The More I See You" — Chris Montez

17. "You Don't Have to Say You Love Me" — Dusty Springfield
18. "Love Is Like an Itching in My Heart" — The Supremes
19. "Red Rubber Ball" — Cyrkle
20. "(I'm a) Road Runner" — Junior Walker and the All Stars

For Beatles fans, the new single, "Paperback Writer," debuted at No. 28.

— • —

Throughout Topeka that Wednesday, all kinds of people were looking ahead as summer gathered momentum. Jim Ward didn't like what he saw. The 28-year-old assistant U.S. district attorney was waist-deep in a major case and the trial date was closing in. With his slow drawl and steady gaze, the Topekan seemed more like a farmer or rancher than a lawyer. But his laid-back style belied a sharp and ambitious mind, and the way he'd won the U.S. attorney's office job said a lot about the young man. Back in 1959, Ward had earned an undergraduate degree from the University of Denver and returned to Topeka to attend law school at Washburn. After graduation, Ward went to work for one of the city's big firms, Rooney & Rooney, doing divorces, plaintiff work, financial claims and the like.

Rooney & Rooney was a major player in the Kansas Democratic Party. So when the state chairman asked the senior Mr. Rooney if he knew of any bright young prospects who might want to run for the U.S. House, Ward's name came up. Finding Democrats willing to take on incumbent Republicans in Kansas was never easy, given the state's hard conservative bent. But Ward gamely accepted the challenge. He ran an earnest and energetic campaign, and, to no one's surprise, he was soundly defeated. Still, the effort didn't go unnoticed. In 1964, U.S. Attorney and Kennedy appointee Newell George asked Ward to come to work in the federal prosecutor's office. The young lawyer jumped at the chance.

Now, two years into it, Ward was scrambling to assemble a complex and difficult criminal prosecution. The case involved a couple of con men who had allegedly bilked ranchers by promising them expensive, purebred cattle but instead delivering run-of-the-mill crossbreeds. A large number of Kansas cattlemen were caught in the scam and the dollar loss was huge. Ward was on his own pulling the case together. He'd been traveling the state for weeks, interviewing victims and gathering evidence. It was a heavy load for a young, relatively inexperienced attorney, and the clock was ticking. There was much to sort out before trial. So Ward was glad to be off the road on June 8, and he looked forward to forgetting about the case and perhaps shooting some home movies of his seven-year-old son, Greg, at the boy's little league game that night.

—  •  —

Like most of the kids around town, teachers also were downshifting with the end of the school year. Peg Griebat Marmet had kicked it into neutral. A few weeks earlier, the 26-year-old had submitted her resignation as girls' physical education instructor and gymnastics coach at Topeka West High School. Back in '61, winning the job had been a major coup for the plucky California native. Fresh out of Kansas State University and armed with a degree in physical education, Peg had gambled when she told board of education administrators she wasn't interested in teaching at the junior-high level. Instead, she wanted to work at Topeka West, the big new city high school scheduled to open that fall. First-year teachers typically started at a junior high school and worked their way up. But the woman slated for the Topeka West job had abruptly left town and a confident Peg stepped into the breach. Thus, at 22, she became one of the 35 original teachers at "West" when the doors opened in the fall of '61.

Despite her youth, Peg did have some teaching experience. She'd come to Kansas in 1954, her sophomore year in high school. Her parents ran a grocery store near Lodi, California, but were forced to close it when the state expanded the nearby highway. Rather than try again in the Central Valley, the family returned to her mother's hometown of Morrill, in extreme northeast Kansas. The Griebats purchased a 42-acre resort called Sun Springs, replete with campsites, picnic areas, a swimming pool, a skating rink and artesian mineral wells. The place did well and provided Peg and her three brothers with an opportunity to teach swimming, become lifeguards and generally help out running the business.

On the job at Topeka West, Peg's age — just four years older than the seniors when she started — along with her pretty smile and upbeat personality, made her popular with kids and faculty alike. Her coaching prowess didn't hurt either. She built a girls' gymnastics program from scratch and proceeded to coach the team to four straight undefeated seasons.

But all that was over now. Peg and her husband, Paul, a supervisory meat cutter at Falley's supermarket, wanted to start a family. Peg was worried that the Topeka school system would frown on a pregnant physical education teacher. So she decided it was time to move on.

Fortunately, when word got out that she was leaving, the PE department chair at Washburn University made her an offer to teach physical education in the fall, pregnant or not. Peg accepted and was looking forward to a summer off before stepping up to the big leagues, so to speak, in September. As for today, she and her husband planned to do some shopping before she headed out for the evening to a friend's wedding shower on the city's southwest side.

—  •  —

The intermittent sprinkles stopped as the afternoon wore on and the low clouds gradually started to lift. A little after 2:00 p.m., Dave Hathaway stepped outside. He felt the humidity rising and decided it was too hot for Baron. The big German shepherd looked up from the cool concrete slab in the shade of his backyard kennel and wagged his tail. He could stay home.

Hathaway went inside, put on his pressed blue shirt and badge, strapped on his Smith & Wesson .357 Magnum, grabbed his hat and walked out the door to the black-and-white K9 wagon parked in the driveway of his west-side home. Hathaway was 29. He was divorced. He looked like John Glenn. He had the same cocky grin, the same crew cut, the same aura of badass invincibility. He was five feet 10 inches and wiry, and this was his fifth year as a patrolman with the Topeka Police Department. As he drove in for roll call for the 3:00–10:00 p.m. shift, he felt the knot of anticipation that always surfaced about now. He hoped it would be a quiet night.

But you never really knew. Just the day before, Hathaway and a partner had disarmed a deranged woman. She was ranting and waving a cocked, loaded pistol. When she looked away for a moment, Hathaway grabbed the gun. Problem solved. Nobody hurt. If he was assigned to North Topeka tonight, there was a good chance he'd get called to a bar fight. Once, he'd rolled up on a disturbance at a tavern in North Topeka. There were four Indians inside, drunk and raising hell. Hathaway walked in. The Indians took one look at him and just laughed. So he cracked two of them across the shins with his nightstick. That's the best place to hit a man with a nightstick: He'll jump up and down from the pain and won't have much fight left in him. If you hit him in the head, he'll likely bleed and just get mean.

Hathaway's quick show of force convinced the Indians they needed to come downtown. The thing was, Hathaway only had one set of handcuffs. So he asked all four to get in the car voluntarily. And they did, with the biggest one riding shotgun up front. Hathaway took the men to the station and booked them on disorderly conduct charges. His major reprimanded him the next day for bringing the Indians in by himself. Should have waited for backup, the major said. Should have cuffed them. But most everyone else on the 140-member department thought it was funny.

Typical Hathaway, they said.

Hathaway arrived at the old, limestone, two-story stationhouse at 5th and Jackson Street just before 3:00 p.m. and went inside as the sergeant prepared for evening roll call. Topeka P.D. divided the city into a dozen numbered quadrants for patrol purposes. Tonight, Hathaway was assigned to 45, a section of southwest Topeka that consisted of suburban homes, occasional strip malls and a handful of bars. *Nothing wrong with that*, he thought. *Should be a quiet evening.* He pulled a cold, eight-ounce bottle of RC Cola from the lobby machine, stepped out into the thick afternoon, climbed into the K9 wagon and headed south for 29th Street.

A few blocks away, up on Kansas Avenue in the heart of downtown, 48-year-old Mary Hatke was walking north from her husband's art supply store to make the daily deposit at Merchant's National Bank. An odd sensation struck her as she walked: The air was so terribly still. Not a bird sang. Not a leaf fluttered. Even the sunlight beginning to filter through the clouds seemed strange. It didn't look right. Mary made her deposit and met Wilma Gilmore leaving the bank. Wilma and her husband ran Nightingale's Ladies Ready-to-Wear across the street from the Hatkes' shop.

"Isn't it a strange day?" Wilma said as the women walked along the busy avenue.

"Why, yes. I was just thinking that same thing," Mary replied. "Much too strange. But you know, at this time of year, you can get most anything in Kansas."

The tone of Wilma's voice changed. "I feel so apprehensive, Mary," she confided. "It just doesn't feel natural."

Mary smiled and said, "I'm sure we'll be all right."

— • —

P. N. Eland didn't have a degree in meteorology like most of the younger fellows who joined the Weather Bureau after World War II. In fact, he'd been a schoolteacher before going to work for the bureau. But he'd learned from practical experience over many years, and in that way, he was typical of his generation of forecasters. A tall man with gentle eyes and gray hair, Eland was quiet in manner, steady under pressure and unfailing in his attention to detail. Thus, in mid-afternoon, he put in a call to Jean Meinholdt, the dispatcher of the Volunteer Emergency Services Team (VEST). He advised her that the group's services probably would be needed later on. VEST was made up of citizens band radio enthusiasts and the unpaid group was an integral piece of Topeka's severe weather spotter network. If heavy weather threatened, members would take up positions at various vantage points around the city's perimeter and report their observations to the Weather Bureau office.

Eland mentally checked another item from his list and stepped into the darkened radar room at the bureau office. Operators Paul Odell and Gordon Brokaw were staring into the circular screen of the WSR-3 radar console. The screen's green light cast an eerie glow as the men scanned the counties south and west of Topeka for any sign of developing thunderstorms.

Nothing yet.

Even in '66, the bulky WSR-3 radar set was a vintage piece of equipment, originally designed for the Navy. But after World War II, the Weather Bureau acquired surplus units and began deploying them at weather stations across the country. Though primitive by modern standards, the WSR-3 was a vital tool for the severe weather forecasters of its day. Like all radar, the unit fired electromagnetic pulses, or radio waves, in continuous bursts separated by millionths of a second. The pulses traveled at the speed of light, 186,000 miles per second. If they encountered an object of any density, such as a rain-filled cloud, a portion of the radio waves would bounce back to a receiver antenna. The returning pulses were amplified and the ensuing echo displayed on a cathode-ray tube.

With the advent of weather radar in the late 1940s, meteorologists gained the ability to assess in real time the altitude, direction, intensity and speed of approaching storms. This breakthrough brought an entirely new level of sophistication to severe storm prediction. Nor was it just thunderstorms that could be seen on radar. Almost by accident, the technology was shown to be effective for detecting tornadoes. On April 9, 1953, electrical engineer Donald Staggs of the Illinois State Water Survey in Champaign was operating an APS-15A radar set originally designed for use aboard U.S. Navy aircraft. Staggs was preparing for an upcoming test designed to determine if the unit could measure rainfall amounts.

As it happened, a severe thunderstorm was passing about 25 miles to the north of Champaign. Staggs watched and took photographs as a curious, hook-shaped echo formed on the back edge of the storm's radar signature. He subsequently learned that a tornado had touched down and followed the same path the hook had taken across his radar screen.

Researchers at the Agricultural and Mechanical College of Texas (later Texas A&M) confirmed the validity of the hook echo later that spring, and a highly effective statewide radar network was set up across Texas in 1955 to provide early warning of tornadoes. By the late 1950s, radar operators nationwide were being trained to identify the distinctive radar signature, which was formed by radio waves bouncing off the rain, hail, dirt and debris wrapping around the twister. The Weather Bureau soon decided that the presence of a hook echo was evidence enough to issue a tornado warning.

In the Topeka radar room, Odell, Brokaw and Eland watched as amorphous shapes of green light began to appear and grow in size and intensity with each sweep of the beam. The center of the low-pressure system was approaching Junction City, about 80 miles west of Topeka, and storms were beginning to pop up ahead of the low. Shortly after 3:00 p.m., the bureau office in Concordia received a report of a tornado on the ground west of Alden, Kansas. A tornado warning for Ellsworth, Saline and McPherson counties in the central part of the state was issued a few minutes later.

Very quickly, a squall line of thunderstorms formed literally out of thin air across a wide area of central Kansas and began advancing steadily eastward. In Topeka, the warm front that slowly had been working its way north finally rolled in at about 4:30 p.m. The sun broke through and burned away the last of the overcast, and the warm, damp air bottled up behind the front cascaded into the city. The day quickly became oppressive and would grow more so. Because layers of even warmer air had moved in aloft, the air near the surface was trapped and unable to rise. The temperature climbed to 75 degrees, and the air became increasingly unstable in the heat of the afternoon sun. From a meteorological perspective, the atmosphere near the ground was akin to gasoline vapor.

By 5:30 p.m., Eland and his team had their hands full. Storms were popping up all over northeastern Kansas. One particularly large thunderstorm, 20 miles in diameter, was reported moving northeast at 5:45 p.m. toward Wakefield, just west of Fort Riley and about 90 miles from Topeka. The storm already had a history of producing tornadoes, and Eland quickly typed out a warning for the area in the path of the storm, which included the city of Manhattan.

In Topeka, storm clouds were starting to gather in the southwest as machinist John Meinholdt left his father's welding shop in North Topeka. Meinholdt, 32, was married, the father of two and a member of VEST, the volunteer CB spotter's organization. His wife, Jean, was the group's dispatcher. The CB radio under his dashboard crackled and Jean's voice came on. She told her husband that all of the group's spotting points south and west of the city had been manned save one: a prominent hill on the southwest edge of town known as Burnett's Mound.

"10-4. I'll take it. I'll check in when I get there. Out."

Meinholdt made a U-turn in his Ford Falcon Ranchero pickup on Topeka Boulevard and headed south. He'd deployed as a spotter dozens of times since VEST was formed nearly 10 years before. Generally, you took up a position, monitored the clouds, reported the information and stayed at your post until the danger had passed. Sometimes, it would be as late as midnight. Nine times out of 10, the storms would roll through without producing a tornado. And tonight probably would be no different.

But this particular situation was going downhill fast. New reports were coming in to the Weather Bureau office; a tornado had spun out of the Wakefield storm and apparently struck Manhattan just before 6:00 p.m., causing extensive damage both to residences and to the Kansas State University campus. No report on casualties. In the radar room, Odell and Brokaw watched a blob of light southwest of Topeka grow larger with each radar pass. Another storm was forming along the boundary of the warm front and the low-pressure system, this one much closer to the city.

The sun was still out, though, as 10-year-old Teri Huffman and her 12-year-old sister, Tami, reveled in the late-afternoon light with the other kids on the block, yelling, chanting, jumping rope and playing hopscotch. The Huffmans lived on Southwest 30th Street, just south of the busy intersection of 29th Street and Gage Boulevard and not far from the high hill known as Burnett's Mound. The Huffmans' three-bedroom, slab home was in a new subdivision called County Fair Estates. Tami, the older girl, was tall and gangly with curly hair. Her sister, Teri, was impish. She had a little bob haircut and looked just like Scout from the movie *To Kill a Mockingbird*.

A friend's mother cupped her hands and yelled from the front stoop to the children playing in the quiet street. "Teri and Tami! Your mother called! She wants you to come home right now!"

The girls looked at each other incredulously, then slowly turned and trudged up the block. Their mother was waiting in the yard.

"You kids come inside," Joanna said curtly.

"But, Mom! Everyone else is still playing! Why do we have to! It won't be dark for a while!"

"Never you mind. Just come in the house. We'll eat in a few minutes."

"Oh, Mom . . ."

The girls slunk into the house, resigned to their fate, but then brightened at the prospect of watching *Batman* after dinner.

It had been a strange day for Joanna Huffman. All afternoon, the 32-year-old homemaker had felt an emotion — if that's what you want to call it — that she'd never experienced before. It was an odd, unsettling sensation that something wasn't right. The feeling was powerful, disturbing and constant in the pit of her stomach. Years later, the only way she could describe it was as a sense of impending doom. It had nothing to do with the tornado watch, as far as she knew. You had those all the time in Kansas. And in any event, the sun was out and the wind was still. It had nothing to do with anything at all. It was just a feeling. But at least her husband, Harold, had arrived home from Goodyear, where he worked as a computer analyst. And the kids were in the house. So Joanna shook off the nameless dread and began to prepare dinner.

—  •  —

It's odd, though, how premonitions can present themselves. Across town, Kathryn Cushinberry was still pondering something she'd heard three days before. Kathryn had been in church that Sunday with her husband, Grant, and their four children. The family attended Lane Chapel on Harrison Street. The church was part of the Colored Methodist Episcopal denomination, a branch of Methodism launched by freed slaves after the Civil War. More than 150 people were in the chapel as Rev. J. P. Turner stepped up to deliver his sermon.

Turner was a tall man in his 40s. He stood behind the pulpit and pointed toward the assembled group. Then he swept his finger across the entire congregation, moving steadily from one side of the sanctuary to the other, saying not a word. He did not blink and seemed to lock eyes with every man, woman and child in the church. Then he spoke. His voice was deep and his elocution commanding and precise.

"Hear me now . . .

"You'd better make ready.

"You'd better fast.

"Something *drastic* is coming!"

There was a rustle in the church as people cast puzzled, sidelong glances at one another or shifted nervously in their seats. Turner said no more about the matter. But his words haunted Kathryn. *What in the world was he talking about? What could be coming?* Plus, she had a more practical question:

*How long are we supposed to fast?*

—  •  —

From the southwest, low, boiling clouds moved in over the city. The sun was quickly obscured, although enough diffuse light filtered through to paint the sky an unnatural, yellowish green. At the surface, the air was dead calm. As thunder clapped and growled in the distance, Topeka suddenly seemed caught in a strange netherworld between light and darkness. Across the city, people stopped to gaze up at the spectacle. To 13-year-old Irma Hillebert, standing on the campus of Washburn University, the sky looked completely unnatural, like the atmosphere of a distant planet. The air itself seemed to crackle with potential energy.

John Meinholdt turned off Topeka Boulevard and flogged the little Ranchero as he pulled onto I-470. He could see the purple-black mass of a storm in the distance, beyond Burnett's Mound. A minute or two later, he swung off the interstate at the Gage exit, descended the ramp and turned left on Gage Boulevard beneath the underpass. Gage followed the center of a shallow valley that stretched from the Shunganunga (pronounced "Shun-Ga-Nun-Ga") Creek to the base of Burnett's Mound. Across Gage to the west of the ramp were the pastel homes of the County Fair Estates subdivision, crowded between the interstate and 29th Street a quarter mile to the north. On the other side of Gage, to the right of the ramp, was a Texaco service station and small strip mall with a 7-Eleven, a liquor store and a dry cleaner. A little further east were the sprawling Embassy Apartments. The complex encompassed three separate buildings — the Embassy, the Huntington and the El Dorado. The Embassy and the Huntington were square, two-story buildings with long interior balconies centered on an open courtyard and pool. They housed some of the newest and most luxurious apartments in town, and the entire compound stretched from the interstate nearly to 29th Street. Beyond the apartments to the east, new homes of the Prairie Vista subdivision stairstepped up a long, low ridge that paralleled the valley.

Meinholdt emerged from the underpass on the south side of the interstate. To his right, Burnett's Mound formed the head of a hogback ridge that sloped back and down and away to the south. Thus, the ideal spot for observing weather moving in from the southwest was not on the mound's summit but at the southernmost edge of the ridge, four-tenths of a mile south of the mound proper. Thirty-fifth Street headed straight up the shoulder of the ridge beyond the overpass. Then a switchback gravel road split off to follow the contours of the hill to the saddle. Meinholdt downshifted as he swung the Ranchero onto the switchback. At the top, he radioed that a major storm was approaching from the southwest at a bearing of 210–260 degrees.

Dave Perkins, a VEST radio volunteer stationed at the Weather Bureau office, relayed Meinholdt's message to Eland and his staff. At 6:50 p.m., Eland pounded out a bulletin on the weather wire:

HEAVY THUNDERSTORMS ARE MOVING INTO THE WESTERN EDGE OF THE TOPEKA AREA. THESE THUNDERSTORMS WILL LIKELY CONTAIN HARD RAIN, WHICH WILL AFFECT HIGHWAY TRAVEL. THE STRONGER CELLS WILL POSSIBLY PRODUCE HAIL AND MAY CONTAIN QUITE STRONG WINDS. GUSTS TO 80 MPH WERE RECORDED IN THE MANHATTAN AREA AS THE THUNDER-STORMS MOVED EASTWARD DOWN THE KANSAS RIVER VALLEY. A PILOT REPORTED A POSSIBLE FUNNEL CLOUD 8 MILES EAST OF MANHATTAN MOVING EAST AT 6:17 PM CST.

Near the small town of Dover, 20 miles to the southwest, Lester Osburn was watching the sky. The worst of the rain had passed his farm, and although a little pea-size hail was still falling, the sky was beginning to clear. Then Osburn watched as two air masses, each marked by roiling black clouds — one from the southwest and one from the northwest — seemed to collide just to the east. From the ensuing turbulence, a slender white funnel emerged. A second funnel appeared moments later, also white and very near the first. After a few minutes, the two merged into a much larger, still-white twister and dropped hard to the ground. Osburn later recalled that the clouds above the tornado were "boiling like an A-bomb mushroom." He dashed to the phone, reached the emergency operator and reported a tornado on the ground 4 miles south of Dover, moving northeast toward Topeka.

The sun was shining brightly in the west.

# CHAPTER THREE

# Facing the Monsters

As the roar drew closer, Inge Nicely shut her eyes and squeezed Angie tighter in the cramped, musky darkness of the crawl space. The sound wasn't like a freight train. It was like a thousand freight trains, and in a moment, every one of them was right overhead. Inge squeezed Angie so hard, it occurred to her later that she could have suffocated her daughter. Then the sound finally began to abate. Three or four minutes had passed since Glenn Nicely shoved his wife and daughter into the crawl space at Glenn's mother's house. When the noise finally stopped and Inge opened her eyes, she could see that Angie was okay. But blue sky was visible through the crawl space opening. The house and garage were gone.

Inge set her daughter aside and cautiously pulled herself out through the hole. Only one kitchen wall stood. No sign of her husband or mother-in-law. She stood up. Angie started climbing out behind her, but Inge instinctively pushed the little girl back. Then she heard a guttural scream. She stepped toward it, across one of the shattered garage doors, which now lay where the kitchen had been. Glenn's voice was muffled under the rubble. "You're stepping on me! Get off! Get off! Get me out of here!" He was buried beneath the door and limestone rocks from the collapsed chimney. Inge tried to lift the stones but could not.

She immediately noticed a pervasive stench, a fetid blend of the many substances the tornado had gathered on its journey so far: mud, grass, pond water, manure, slaughtered animals, wood, soaked Sheetrock, food.

Inge gagged and looked around. Glenn's mother lay a dozen feet north of the garage. She was perfectly encased in concrete blocks, almost as if the wind had carefully erected a low protective wall around her. A heavy, old, hand-crank washing machine had ended up on top of the blocks, and Inge, all 110 pounds of her, somehow managed to throw it aside. Mrs. Nicely was conscious, her eyes wide open. She lay on her back. Her curlers were dusted with hundreds of tiny shards of glass and they glittered like diamonds in the slanting rays of the afternoon sun. She said her hip hurt when she tried to move. And there was a strange, half-inch-deep crease that ran nearly the length of her lower leg. Whatever struck her didn't break the skin. But it must have hit hard to leave a dent like that.

The silence was so profound, Inge thought for a moment that perhaps she'd gone deaf. No birds sang. Not a leaf rustled, for there were no more leaves or branches or trees. Glenn yelled again. And then, from somewhere deep in the rubble, the telephone rang. How could it be? Inge made a halfhearted attempt to find the phone but could not.

Behind the house, where Glenn and Inge's house trailer had been, only the trailer's chassis remained. Inge immediately thought of Tommy, the Siamese cat, and Mitzi, her beloved little dog. They were last seen inside the trailer — current whereabouts, God only knew. But undoubtedly dead. Up Auburn Road, 100 yards to the north, rubble from the neighbors' house — the Wolfs — was blasted across the highway as if shot from a cannon. In the Nicelys' yard, the mighty pines were gone and a smaller tree nearby had snapped off about six feet up. Glenn's sister's car was skewered on the tree's sharpened spike, right side up, like an olive on a toothpick.

Everything was dreamlike. People were running up and yelling.

"Are you folks okay?"

The man from Maine and his friend who'd watched the tornado

pass before them were among the first up the drive. "The horses! You should have seen it! The tornado lifted 'em right over the road! I think they're okay, though! They just set down and took off!"

The strangers quickly pulled Glenn from the rubble. The hot water heater had ruptured and scalded his face. Glass from the garage door windows had peppered his back and his arms were cut and bleeding. But he could stand and he was walking. A few minutes later, Glenn's father pulled up in his station wagon. The men carefully placed Mrs. Nicely on a door and loaded her into the back of the wagon. Glenn and Inge and Angie climbed in. The family took off for the hospital in town.

— • —

For sheer, concentrated violence, nothing in nature comes close to a tornado. Severe thunderstorms can pack damaging, straight-line winds in excess of 100 miles an hour. Hurricanes must top 155 miles an hour to achieve Category 5 status, the most severe designation. But the wind speeds of the nastiest tornadoes can be more than twice that.[1] Worse, tornadoes possess a kinetic arsenal seemingly designed solely for wreaking havoc along the surface of the Earth. The tornado's spinning vortex creates torque, which exerts a violent pushing, pulling and twisting motion in a way that straight winds cannot. Hence, the bony fingers of a tornado can easily enter and explode houses; pry apart anchored or attached wood and steel; and roll, toss or twist cars and other heavy objects.

Compounding this circular, buzz-saw effect is the surging updraft at the center of the vortex. Because of the enormous suction produced by the updraft, surface air rushes to meet the twister like water racing down the drain. This air is pulled up through the tornado in a spiraling, geyserlike column. The updraft, which can be accelerating vertically at 100 miles an hour or more, grabs objects torn lose by the rotational winds and propels them aloft. Here they essentially become weightless for periods of time as they bounce along inside the updraft or slide outward into the spinning column.

This debris provides the storms with yet another weapon: Much of the material caught in the vortex eventually flies out of the tornado like gravel shot from a spinning tire. The centrifugal force accelerates objects, turning two-by-fours, nails, glass, telephone poles, tree limbs, chunks of concrete, steel beams and automobiles into deadly missiles. The result is a hammering, 360-degree barrage of shrapnel firing from the tornado and extending the storm's destructive reach well beyond the immediate path of the twister.

Some tornadoes also produce so-called suction vortices, or mini-tornadoes, that swirl and rotate within the main funnel. Like baby dinosaurs engaged in a feeding frenzy at the foot of a parent, suction vortices can greatly exacerbate the tornado's destruction as they crisscross the main damage path. With wind speeds equal to or greater than those of the main funnel, suction vortices are hyperdestructive and explain why one house within the damage path may emerge relatively unscathed while the one beside it is flattened.

Some or all of these mechanisms are, to a greater or lesser extent, at work as the tornado moves forward at ground speeds ranging from 10 to 65 miles per hour. The tornado's forward motion adds yet another variable to the complex formula of destruction. The winds on the right, leading edge of the twister are accelerated by the combined effect of the tornado's lateral progress and the counterclockwise rotation of the funnel.

The tornado's destructive abilities have been well described, thanks in large part to Tetsuya (Theodore) "Ted" Fujita. In 1971, Fujita, then a University of Chicago meteorology professor, developed the now-famous Fujita Scale. Because tornadic winds are too dangerous to measure in real time, Fujita focused instead on the physical evidence left in the twister's wake. He was influenced in this by the unusual work he'd done as a young physics professor in Japan immediately after World War II. Fujita and a group of students were asked in late 1945 to conduct a survey of the damage caused by the atomic bombs dropped on Hiroshima and Nagasaki.[2]

The Fujita Scale was introduced in 1971 and assigned one of six progressively more intense designations to tornadoes based on the damage they caused. In 2007, the F-Scale was modified to provide greater consistency in damage assessments, and today is known as the EF-Scale (EF stands for Enhanced Fujita). An EF-0 tornado, with wind speeds not exceeding 85 miles per hour, causes light damage: Sign boards are pushed over, shallow-rooted trees are knocked down and branches are snapped from larger trees. EF-0s account for about 43 percent of the 883 tornadoes that strike the United States, on average, each year.[3]

The EF-1 tornado is a little stouter. With winds of between 86 and 110 miles per hour, an EF-1 will peel off roofing material, push mobile homes off foundations and shove cars from the road. The EF-1 accounts for 33 percent of all U.S. tornadoes.[4]

Wind speeds and resulting damage increase dramatically with higher Fujita ratings. Fortunately, the likelihood of these monsters occurring also falls off as the intensity level climbs. An EF-3, for instance — with winds of between 136 and 165 miles per hour — will uproot whole forests, lift roofs and derail trains. Yet it will occur in only about 4 percent of tornadoes.[5] Similarly, EF-4 tornadoes, with wind speeds of between 166 and 200 miles per hour, happen just 1 percent of the time.[6] EF-4s can level well-constructed houses, blow structures with weak foundations some distance and generate large missiles from debris.

At the top of the EF-Scale is the EF-5. Although these storms represent only about one-tenth of 1 percent of all tornadoes, that statistic is no comfort to the unfortunate souls caught in the path of the one or two EF-5s that form, on average, each year in the United States.[7] EF-5s pack winds of more than 200 miles per hour, have the potential to exceed 300 miles per hour and cause often inconceivable damage: Strong frame houses are lifted off foundations and carried considerable distances before disintegrating; trees are debarked; automobile-sized missiles fly through the air in excess of 100 yards; and steel, reinforced concrete structures are badly damaged. According to Fujita, with EF-5 tornadoes, "Incredible phenomena will occur."

Like tornadoes themselves, the storms that spawn them have been the subject of scrutiny and speculation for centuries. In the broadest sense, severe thunderstorms are a leveling mechanism that temporarily restores stability to the atmosphere in response to a buildup of heat and moisture. Weather is an enormously complex system with a single driving force — the energy of the sun — at its core. Differences between higher and lower temperatures compel air masses to move, collide, mix and eventually achieve a period of equilibrium, before new forces impinge upon them and the cycle begins anew.

Wind, clouds, rain, snow, hurricanes and tornadoes all represent various permutations in nature's never-ending, but ultimately doomed, pursuit of long-term stability. The factors that affect this quest are many: Earth's annual journey around the sun; its daily rotation on its axis and the resulting phenomenon called the Coriolis effect, or the bending of wind as it moves between air masses; the heating and cooling of land and water; the friction that develops as wind moves across terrain; the physics of energy transfer from water to vapor and back again; and gravity itself — all play a role in shaping a system of staggering size, intricacy and possibility. And while the atmosphere can never completely achieve the constancy it seeks due to the steady flow of energy from the sun, it is remarkably successful at balancing competing forces over time and thus maintaining a livable climate on Earth.

Behind the weather's almost mystical complexity lies a cause-and-effect chain often described as the "butterfly effect," which presupposes that small variations of an initial condition (such as a butterfly flapping its wings) can, under the right circumstances, work their way through the system to produce huge changes or outcomes (such as a hurricane or tornado). Whether a butterfly's wings can actually trigger a cataclysm is a matter of conjecture. But the metaphor is useful in illustrating the progressive, connected nature of all weather phenomena, from brief summer squall to arctic cold snap.

With tornadoes, that chain depends on just the right mix of circumstances and conditions. Most tornadoes — and nearly all the strongest and most violent ones — are spawned by supercell thunderstorms. Across the Great Plains and the Midwest, supercells frequently emerge as large, isolated and enigmatic beasts that feed on warm, moist air. Like their less-severe cousins, typical thunderstorms, supercells are born when moisture-laden air begins to rise rapidly into areas of lower pressure and cooler air. The subsequent updrafts create cumulus clouds, with their distinctive, cotton-like appearance. Once the water vapor cools to the appropriate temperature, the water condenses into rain.

This cycle is the basic mechanism for all precipitation. What makes the supercell different is the strength and rotation of the updraft. The updraft's velocity is a reflection of the differences in temperature and pressure between the warm, heavy, damp air near the ground and the cool, lighter, drier air above. The greater the differential, the greater the atmospheric instability and the more explosively the air rises. In storms that form as powerful low-pressure systems collide with pools of warm, moist air, it is not unusual for the updraft to shoot up 50,000 feet to the tropopause, or the edge of the lower atmosphere. Here the energy-laden vapor slams into a ceiling of stable air at the base of the stratosphere and spreads out like wet concrete to form the ominous, overhanging cliff of the anvil cloud.

Updraft rotation, or its meteorological term, vorticity, is the other key ingredient in the creation of the supercell and its progeny, the tornado. Circulation within the storm can begin in a benign fashion. For example, a southwesterly breeze may be blowing along the surface on a sunny, humid spring day. But 1,000 or 2,000 feet aloft, the wind is blowing from a different direction at an equal or greater speed. Like two hands rolling a pencil, countervailing winds — called shear — begin to shape a horizontal tube of rotating air. As the updraft begins to strengthen, the rising air grabs this invisible tube, not unlike someone lifting the middle of a Slinky, and raises it to the vertical position.

With the rotating updraft in place, a high-speed conveyor has been established to feed vast quantities of fuel in the form of warm, moist air directly into the storm.

Fully organized, a supercell is a highly efficient, self-sustaining heat engine designed to gather excessive quantities of warm, moist vapor near the surface and convert it to rain and cooler air. With boiling dark clouds and a towering anvil, blinding rain, pelting hail, cataclysmic lightning, shattering thunder and howling winds, the supercell — quite apart from its role as parent to the tornado — can be one of the most awesome and powerful spectacles on Earth.

Its killer offspring, the tornado, is conceived deep within the storm's turbulent womb. Around the updraft, a broader, counterclockwise circulation can sometimes begin as the updraft gathers strength. This rotation, called a mesocyclone, spins faster and tighter and eventually can elongate to nearly the full height of the storm, from the anvil nearly to the ground. At the same time, winds aloft on the back side of the storm — sometimes originating in the jet stream, sometimes coming in at lower altitudes — plow into the updraft column. Because of the extreme intensity of the updraft, the flow of the lateral winds is blocked. As a result, these currents are diverted downward to form a cascading downdraft.

It is along the volatile boundary between the rear-flank downdraft and the mesocyclone rotation that the tornado is formed. Typically, the bottom of the spinning mesocyclone will drop from beneath the low cloud deck on the back side of the storm like a massive, rotating freight elevator. This formation is called the wall cloud, one of the many tornadic features identified by Fujita. The funnel, a twisting column of water vapor, then emerges and, just as often as not, drops to the ground. Once touchdown takes place, the earth impedes the free flow of air back up into the funnel. The tornado pulls harder and faster, like a vacuum hanging up in thick carpet, in an attempt to feed the voracious low pressure above.

Many aspects of tornado formation, or tornadogenesis, remain only dimly understood. Despite scientific advances through the last half of the 20th century, specific cause-and-effect equations encompassing fluid dynamics and atmospheric physics have yet to be worked out. The fact is, scientists still don't know everything that occurs behind the supercell's mysterious curtain or why some of these storms spawn tornadoes but most do not.

Yet if the details remain sketchy, nature has repeatedly demonstrated the general conditions in which tornadoes are likely to form.

And at no place on Earth do these circumstances present themselves with more vigor or frequency than on the plains and prairies of the central United States. Unbounded by natural barriers, advancing air masses turn the vast amphitheater of the plains into a battlefield in the spring and summer months. Cold, dry air plunging south from Canada collides with warm, humid air rising up from the Gulf of Mexico to create the potent, unstable mix required for severe thunderstorm formation. In many cases, rotating low-pressure systems moving out of the Southwest work like giant waterwheels, extracting humid air from the Gulf and cooler air from the north and pulling both together at the center of the low.

Other geographic features contribute to the prevalence of tornadoes in the country's midsection. Warm, dry air from the desert Southwest can move in aloft and form what amounts to a temporary ceiling or cap, several thousand feet above the warm, humid air near the ground. This inversion creates a lid that prevents the high-octane, moist air from naturally rising. As a result, the air near the surface continues to heat and expand like boiling water in a pressure cooker until it finally blows through the inversion to reach the cooler air above, thus creating the violent updraft of a nascent supercell.

In another scenario, winds whipping east from the Great Basin and the Northwest are diverted upward as they pass over the Rocky Mountains. This cools the air and wrings out its moisture. The colder, drier air moves over the plains on top of warm, moist air at lower levels, thus setting up the all-important temperature gradient and cocking the hammer for a severe weather outbreak.

Tornadoes, of course, are by no means limited to the Great Plains. They can and do occur in every state, and for that matter, in nearly every region of the world. Killer storms are common in the Deep and mid-South. One of the worst in U.S. history moved straight up the Mississippi River near Natchez, Mississippi, on May 7, 1840. More than 300 were killed, including many caught on the open water in boats.[8] Another killer ripped through the Worcester, Massachusetts, area in June of 1953, claiming 94 lives.[9] Florida, for its part, is regularly bedeviled by tornadoes. That state ranked behind only Texas and

Oklahoma in the average number of tornadoes per year (44) between 1953 and 1989, according to Storm Prediction Center statistics.[10]

Yet for frequency and intensity, a diagonal swath of the central United States known as Tornado Alley remains the most prolific tornado breeding ground in the world. The region's boundaries are amorphous. But most meteorologists generally consider Tornado Alley to encompass portions of six states, stretching from north-central Texas northeast through central Oklahoma, into the eastern third of Kansas, across the southeast corner of Nebraska, through the northwest corner of Missouri and into central Iowa. It's along this corridor that all the ingredients for tornado-producing storms habitually converge. Texas, Oklahoma, Kansas and Nebraska alone accounted for more than 9,300 tornadoes during the 36-year period ending in 1989.[11] That's about 260 per year. In Texas, Oklahoma and Kansas, the combined death toll from tornadoes through the same period was 872, or about 24 per year.[12]

In terms of intensity, no state has faced more EF-5 tornadoes than Kansas, with 16 recorded between 1880 and 2008. Iowa and Texas are next with 10 each, followed by Oklahoma with nine and Nebraska with six.[13]

Native Americans always contended with the sudden terror of the tornado. But as settlers poured into the West after the Civil War, tornadoes became a mysterious, horrific new fact of life for a growing number of Americans. Fortunately, science was searching for answers. One individual in particular worked relentlessly in the late 19th century to better understand and predict tornadoes. Today, we can only wonder what might have been had his efforts been taken more seriously in his day. For if ever there was a man ahead of his time, it was John Park Finley.

The son of a farmer from Ypsilanti, Michigan, Finley was born in Ann Arbor on April 11, 1854. He enrolled in Michigan State Agricultural and Mechanical College, now Michigan State; studied meteorology and agriculture; and in 1873, earned a Bachelor of Science degree.[14] With letters of recommendation from his college professors, Finley enlisted in the Army and won assignment to the prestigious

U.S. Army Signal Corps, the predecessor of today's National Weather Service. Finley was detailed to Fort Whipple, Virginia, and trained in multiple disciplines, including telegraphy, signaling, electricity and meteorology.

In May of 1879, the 25-year-old was ordered west to conduct a survey of damage resulting from a tornado outbreak that had struck portions of Kansas, Missouri, Nebraska and Iowa. Over a 20-day period, Finley traveled more than 500 miles by horse and buggy throughout the damaged area. He compiled a wealth of data, including eyewitness accounts, calculations of tornadoes' speed, grim observations of some of the 42 killed and damage assessments very much like those Fujita would base his tornado scale on nearly 100 years later.[15]

Private Finley's hardbound, 116-page report included numerous drawings and maps. Finley even speculated on the cause of tornadoes, accurately suggesting that "marked contrasts of temperature and moisture invariably foretell an atmospheric disturbance of unusual violence . . ." [16]

His superiors were impressed with the young man's work and Finley was allowed to continue his tornado studies. He next gathered old records on tornadoes, some dating to the late 1700s, and put together a seminal report titled "The Character of 600 Tornadoes." The report represented by far the most comprehensive survey of tornadoes up until that time and included tables, maps and a list of rules for forecasting tornadoes.[17] Finley subsequently convinced his superiors that an entire tornado season, not just individual storms, should be studied in detail with an eye toward predicting the storms. They agreed, and in 1882, Finley set up shop in Kansas City, Missouri, to oversee the effort. Through the spring of '82, Finley traveled extensively across the country's midsection, enlisting a network of field spotters to report severe weather information back to the Kansas City office.[18]

After a major tornado outbreak killed hundreds across the South in February 1884, Finley began making experimental and — given the tools available at the time — relatively successful predictions regarding the potential for tornado-producing storms over large sections of the country. In so doing, he became the first meteorologist to accurately predict conditions favorable to the formation of tornadoes, with 28 of his 100 predictions verified.[19] Through 1884, Finley continued to refine his prediction models and increase his tornado spotter network, which eventually totaled more than 2,000 volunteer reporters.[20]

At least one supporter, astronomer Edward S. Holden, urged action regarding Finley's groundbreaking efforts. Holden suggested that the Signal Corps use telegraph lines to establish a warning system capable of reaching towns and households in tornado-prone areas. He proposed that wires be strung throughout communities and bells installed in every house. An alert could be centrally activated to warn of heightened tornado risk. Holden even recommended that cannons be fired to warn people outdoors.[21]

Though perhaps less than practical, Holden's ideas nonetheless underscored the need for some type of comprehensive tornado forecasting and warning system. But the Signal Corps would have none of it. Officials were worried that tornado predictions would spark widespread panic. As a result, the organization in 1885 banned the use of the word "tornado" in weather forecasts. In an official report two years later, the chief signal officer justified the decision by claiming that "the harm done by such a prediction would eventually be greater than that which results from the tornado itself."[22]

With the ban, Finley and his efforts quickly fell from favor. He was pulled from tornado research and shunted to a bureaucratic siding within the corps. He nonetheless managed to produce a second comprehensive book on tornadoes in 1887 that included a section on what the public could do to protect themselves from the threat.[23]

Responsibility for meteorological studies and forecasting shifted from the Army to the Department of Agriculture in 1890 with the creation of the United States Weather Bureau. But instead of prompting a reexamination of the tornado forecasting ban, the change effectively codified the prohibition as part of bureau doctrine. In 1899, Cleveland Abbe, influential editor of the American Meteorological Society's *Monthly Weather Review*, asserted that given the minimal risk of individuals actually encountering a tornado, the government had "no right to issue numerous erroneous alarms. The stoppage of business and the unnecessary fright would in its summation during a year be worse than the storms themselves." Abbe absurdly went on to claim that "there is no material advantage to be derived from any, even the most perfect, system of forewarnings and attempts at protection," given the total and absolute destruction caused by a tornado.[24]

Tragically, this head-in-the-sand approach would stand as official government policy for the next 60 years. It is true that tornado forecasting was — and remains — extremely tricky and that early in the century, the tools we take for granted today (computers, radar and weather balloon soundings, to name a few) didn't exist. And Finley didn't help his cause by exaggerating his successes; critics argued that Finley's forecasting prowess was a statistical mirage.[25] Nonetheless, it now seems unconscionable that a greater effort wasn't made to build on his pioneering work. Consigned to the dustbin of science by the weather bureaucracy and leading meteorologists, tornado research, reporting and prediction effectively ground to a halt.[26]

Tornadoes, however, observed no such moratorium and continued to visit death and destruction on farms, towns and cities across the country. In 1899, the same year Abbe claimed that warnings were worthless, a tornado formed over Lake St. Croix, Wisconsin, and moved 15 miles northeast toward New Richmond. The Gollmar Brothers Circus was in town and hundreds of people were caught in the open when the twister struck. Virtually the entire community was destroyed; 117 people were killed and about 200 were injured.[27]

Nine years later, multiple tornadoes swept across Louisiana and Mississippi and killed more than 300. On June 5, 1916, 18 killer tornadoes struck Arkansas. The outbreak remains the record for the most killer storms in a single state on a single day. In 1920, 11 tornadoes killed at least 20 people each.[28] And on March 18, 1925, the worst tornado disaster in U.S. history unfolded near the confluence of the Ohio and Mississippi rivers. A twister one mile wide doing 60-plus miles an hour gouged a 219-mile path of destruction across portions of Missouri, Illinois and Indiana.[29] The tornado was on the ground for an unheard-of three and a half hours[30] and struck at least 19 communities, wiping four entirely off the map. A total of 695 people died that day, including 69 students in nine schools.[31]

The annual assault continued through the 1930s. Over two days in April 1936, for example, separate tornadoes in Tupelo, Mississippi, and Gainesville, Georgia, killed 216 and 203 people, respectively.[32]

Despite the grim toll tornadoes racked up through the early 20th century, it took World War II to finally spur the federal government to action. In 1940, the Weather Bureau began providing "severe local windstorm warnings" (a euphemism for tornadoes) to munitions plants and military airfields in tornado-prone areas. The facilities themselves established networks of spotters, sometimes armed with two-way radios, to provide direct warning when destructive storms were imminent. The system worked well, and after the war some communities in Kansas and elsewhere continued to operate spotter networks.[33]

Yet even with the initiative's success, the Weather Bureau remained unwilling to actively pursue anything more than isolated and experimental prediction and warning efforts. Francis W. Reichelderfer, chief of the Weather Bureau, reiterated the prohibition against tornado forecasting in 1943. He apparently was concerned that the agency would look bad if tornadoes were forecast but did not occur. The bureau also believed that business and industry would suffer if citizens changed their behavior due to fears about the weather.[34]

Fortunately, the Weather Bureau's hand was about to be forced by two young Air Force officers in Oklahoma. Capt. Robert C. Miller, 28, was a trained meteorologist who had served as a weather officer in Dutch New Guinea during the war. Maj. Ernest J. Fawbush, 33, was an expert on Alaskan weather and the commanding officer of the Weather Station at Tinker Air Force Base outside Oklahoma City.[35] In early March of 1948, Miller was assigned to Fawbush's command. Tinker, named for an Oklahoma bomber pilot lost in the war, was the nation's largest aircraft repair and maintenance depot. Approximately 2,000 planes were stored at the base, including numerous mothballed B-29 bombers and P-47 fighters.[36]

Miller was a California native with no previous experience observing or predicting Midwestern weather. He was working the late shift on the evening of March 20. Studying the charts, Miller concluded that aside from gusty winds, the night would be uneventful. But shortly after 9:00 p.m., weather stations to the southwest began reporting thunderstorms moving toward the base. Miller and a co-worker confirmed the fast-moving storms on radar and issued a high-wind warning for the base, although it came too late to allow for aircraft to be secured. At 9:52 p.m., a chilling message came in from Will Rogers Airport, seven miles west-southwest of the base. The airport reported heavy thunderstorms, wind gusts of up to 92 miles per hour and a "TORNADO SOUTH ON GROUND MOVING NE."[37]

Miller watched dumbstruck as an enormous funnel materialized through the lightning flashes and moved diagonally across the base. When it was over, numerous buildings were wrecked, 50 planes were destroyed and 50 more were damaged. The property loss exceeded $10 million.[38] Six people were injured, including air traffic controllers struck by flying glass when the windows in the tower blew out.[39]

Five Air Force generals flew in from Washington, D.C., the next morning to assess the damage and investigate the circumstances surrounding the storm. Fawbush and Miller were called on the carpet. According to Miller, the generals' questions were "well put, concise and fair." Fawbush, he said, described the difficulty involved in forecasting tornadoes and the resulting reluctance of weather services to issue public warnings. The generals concluded that the storm was an act of God and could not have been forecast. Nonetheless, they urged the meteorologists to try to find ways to warn the public about impending severe weather.[40]

Attending the meeting was General Fred S. "Fritz" Borum, the commanding general of the Oklahoma City Air Materiel Area. Borum had a reputation as an innovator. Afterward, he pushed Fawbush to follow up on the generals' suggestion and investigate the feasibility of forecasting tornado-producing storms.

"Major Fawbush had been interested for some years in such storms and I had become 'most interested' overnight,'" Miller wrote years later in an unpublished manuscript. "I was most fortunate in being selected to aid in the investigations."

For nearly three days straight, Fawbush and Miller pored over every tornado-related document they could lay their hands on. They studied charts and maps and compared data points and patterns associated with previous tornadic thunderstorms, including barometric pressure, temperature, humidity, wind speed and direction. By the time they were finished, the two had developed a checklist of six conditions they believed needed to be present for tornadoes to develop.[41]

The next day, while studying the morning charts, the meteorologists were alarmed to see that the weather patterns of March 25 bore a striking resemblance to conditions present on the morning of March 20, the day the tornado had hit the base. General Borum was alerted, and after hearing the weathermen's assessment, he asked if they intended to issue a tornado forecast for Tinker. Fawbush and Miller demurred. Borum consequently suggested that they issue a forecast for heavy thunderstorms.

The day wore on and storms began to gather. A squall line 100 miles long had formed about 60 miles northwest of the base and was moving toward Tinker at 27 miles an hour. Again Borum was notified, and again the general put the question to the weathermen: Were they going to issue a tornado forecast or not? According to Miller, Borum pointedly noted that "if you really believe this situation is very similar to the one last week, it seems logical to issue a tornado forecast."

Fawbush and Miller stalled. They pointed out the infinitesimal likelihood of two tornadoes hitting the same location in such a short period of time. They added that no one in modern times had ever issued a site-specific, operational tornado forecast. But Borum was insistent.

"You are about to set a precedent," Borum responded.[42]

And so it was that the historic warning, for the 5:00 to 6:00 p.m. time frame, went out at 2:50 p.m. on March 25, 1948. Borum immediately began implementing a tornado safety plan he'd developed, which included hangaring aircraft, securing loose objects, diverting incoming air traffic and moving base personnel to safe areas.

Fawbush and Miller, meanwhile, lamented their predicament, given the near-impossibility of another tornado hitting the base. "I could see it now, a sure 'bust' and plenty of flack thereafter," Miller wrote. "I wondered how I would manage as a civilian, perhaps as an elevator operator. It seemed improbable that anyone would employ, as a weather forecaster, an idiot who issued a tornado forecast for a precise location."

His concern seemed justified. As the squall line moved closer, it became clear that the storm didn't pack nearly the punch of the one five days earlier. This time, the weather personnel at Will Rogers Airport reported a light thunderstorm with 26-mile-an-hour winds and pea-size hail.

"That did it," Miller wrote. "I abandoned ship, leaving a grim Major Fawbush to go down with the vessel."

From his home nearby, a depressed Miller watched the storm come in until rain obscured his view. A little while later, he turned on the radio and was annoyed to hear an "urgent news bulletin" about a "destructive tornado at Tinker Field."

"Good grief," Miller recalled. "I thought, 'They're still talking about last week's tornado'—but why break into the news?"

Miller tried to phone the base but the lines were dead. Jumping into his car, he sped toward the weather station with a "strange, unbelieving excitement rising." Miller arrived at Tinker to find destruction everywhere and emergency crews scrambling to restore power and clear the runways. At the weather station, a "jubilant" Major Fawbush described how a funnel had formed and dropped to the ground as the line of thunderstorms passed over the airfield. The twister, which struck at 5:58 p.m., lasted just three or four minutes. Only one person was slightly injured, but 84 B-29s and P-47s were damaged and 35 were wrecked beyond repair.[43] The property damage totaled $6 million, $4 million less than the previous storm.

"General Borum's Tornado Disaster Plan had been just as successful as the first operational tornado forecast," Miller wrote. "We became instant heroes and, in my case, the rest of my life would be intimately associated with tornadoes and severe thunderstorms."

Tornado prediction evolved quickly from this auspicious beginning. Fawbush and Miller continued to hone their forecast methodology and continued to score successes. In the 14 months ending in May 1950, the duo accurately predicted tornadoes in 31 of 34 separate warnings issued for areas of Oklahoma, Texas, Alabama and Georgia.[44] Unfortunately, the warnings were limited to military bases. But civilians soon caught on to the forecasts, and news of the alerts would spread rapidly by word of mouth in the communities around military facilities.

Astonishingly, despite Miller and Fawbush's success, the Weather Bureau continued to cling to its prohibition against tornado prediction. Reichelderfer, the director, remained convinced that tornadoes were too difficult to forecast, that erroneous predictions would reflect poorly on the bureau and that the general public would panic if the bureau began issuing warnings.[45] But by 1952, public pressure on the agency had reached a fever pitch. Radio stations in Oklahoma routinely broadcast the leaked Air Force warnings, and the media repeatedly castigated the bureau for its timid stance. The state's congressional representatives eventually jumped into the fray and urged the Weather Bureau office in Oklahoma City to cooperate with Fawbush and Miller's newly created Severe Weather Warning Center.[46]

The bureau finally relented in the face of withering criticism and began issuing its own tornado predictions in March of 1952. The forecasts proved reasonably effective, and by 1954, the Weather Bureau had established a Severe Local Storms Forecast Center in Kansas City to focus exclusively on tornado forecasting. Thus ended the bureau's long and disgraceful era of ignoring the dangers posed by tornadoes and leaving at-risk citizens to their own devices. Before long, local Weather Bureau officials up and down Tornado Alley were scrambling to make up for lost time, working to devise systems to warn the public and boost awareness of tornado safety.

# CHAPTER FOUR

# The Legend of Burnett's Mound

Every community has its legends and Topeka, Kansas, in 1966 was no different. The most potent of these involved Burnett's Mound, the high hill on the southwest edge of the city. The story surrounding the hill, tornadoes and the Indian chief for whom the mound was named drifted down through the decades to cast a long shadow over the events of June 8, 1966.

This particular legend had its origins in the collision of cultures that marked westward expansion in America. As much as any state, Kansas helped cement the heroic saga of the West in the collective memory of the American people. Through the 19th century, explorers, trappers, buffalo hunters, mule skinners, soldiers, sodbusters, pioneer women, gunslingers, railroad builders, cowboys and lawmen all turned in larger-than-life performances on the dangerous and unforgiving stage of Kansas. The power of their life-and-death drama lingers still. And it's a true tale, as far as it goes.

But there was always another side to the story.

Through Indian eyes, white encroachment was a nightmare of sickness, death, humiliation and unrelenting land grabs that squeezed tribes onto ever-smaller parcels of inferior ground, often hundreds or even thousands of miles from their ancestral homes. At no place in the mid-19th century was the impact of these dislocations more evident than in Kansas Territory and future Oklahoma to the south. In Kansas, the catastrophe was twofold: Not only were native civilizations put to flight by advancing whites, but the territory also served in the early days as a dumping ground for entire indigenous populations run out of Ohio, Indiana, Michigan, Wisconsin and Illinois.

First contact between whites and Native Americans in Kansas involved the Spanish, who came out of the Southwest in search of Quivira, one of seven mythical cities of gold supposedly located somewhere north and east of Tiguex, or modern-day Albuquerque. An ambitious colonial governor named Don Francisco Vasquez de Coronado led a party of conquistadors north in the spring of 1541 to find the fabled metropolis. They arrived on the grasslands of central Kansas in late June. But they didn't find Quivira, gold or even rumors of gold. Instead, they discovered the Wichita nation, a 4,000-strong tribe of farmers and hunters who had lived in earthen huts along the Arkansas River and its tributaries for at least 500 years.[47]

The French came next, pushing down from Canada to establish trading relationships with the native people of eastern Kansas, primarily the Pawnee, the Osage and the Kansa. The Kansa, whose name meant "People of the South Wind," were buffalo hunters and sustenance farmers who'd drifted in from the east in prehistoric times. In 1702, a French official put the Kansa population at about 5,000.[48] The French plied the tribes with gifts and trade goods: blankets, flour, clothing, weapons, gunpowder and brandy. The Indians, in turn, provided the French with furs and slaves, the latter mainly Comanches and Plains Apaches taken in western Kansas.[49]

The years rolled on, the bonds of mutual dependency drew tighter and the slow asphyxiation of Native American society advanced. Ruin for the Indians was accelerated by the diseases carried by the Europeans. With no natural immunity, tribes were ravaged by influenza, cholera, measles, whooping cough and smallpox. Exposure only increased after France sold the Louisiana Territory to the newly independent United States in 1803.

As Americans trickled and then flowed into the plains, Kansas would become a central battleground in the grinding conflict with the Plains Indians. Yet it was an earlier struggle between Native Americans and whites — this one played out along a now-long-forgotten

Western frontier — that gave rise to the most enduring legend associated with Topeka and the tragedy of June 8, 1966.

For decades, the Algonquin or Woodland nations of the Great Lakes region — the Chippewa, Ottawa, Huron, Potawatomi, Winnebago, Kickapoo, Fox, Sac and Illinois — battled tenaciously to hold their ancestral homelands against the advancing tide of white settlers. To thwart the Americans, or "Long Knives," as they called them, the Indians aligned first with the French and then with the British. One of the Algonquin tribes, the Potawatomis, was particularly determined to resist white incursion. The Potawatomis lived throughout what was then known as the Old Northwest, in an area that would become southern Michigan, eastern Wisconsin, northern Illinois and Indiana. At their peak, they were perhaps 6,000 strong.[50] They were hunters, fishermen and farmers, and they organized themselves in loose confederations in which chiefs led more by consensus than decree.[51] With shaved heads and painted faces, the Potawatomis were ferocious in battle.

But the Americans were relentless and more numerous. After it became clear that the white world was rapidly overtaking the Algonquin peoples, a Shawnee prophet, Tenskwatawa, and his militarily minded brother, Tecumseh, worked to unify the often-feuding tribes east of the Mississippi into a single hammer that could crush the Americans once and for all. Thus, when the United States again went to war with the British in the War of 1812, Tecumseh seized the opportunity to align with the English and drive the Americans from Native lands. Sixty years before Sitting Bull united the Lakota and Northern Cheyenne to defeat Custer at the Little Bighorn River, another charismatic Indian leader rallied his peoples for a final stand.

Savage battles, skirmishes and depredations on both sides raged up and down the frontier. Proving again to be a savage foe, the Potawatomis were awash in bloodshed. But at the climactic Battle of the Thames in Chatham, Ontario, an army of 3,500 under William Henry Harrison — the governor of the Northwest Territory and future U.S. president — crushed British and Indian combatants. Tecumseh was killed in the fighting.

With Tecumseh's death, the Indian confederacy shattered and any hope of holding back the Americans vanished for good. An armistice was reached between the United States and the Indians. Harrison, however, initially refused to make peace with the Potawatomis. He called them "our most cruel and inveterate enemies."[52]

After 50 years of nearly continuous bloodshed, government negotiators spoke of friendship and peace. Money, gifts and whiskey changed hands. Treaties were drafted with solemn, ceremonial pomp and authority. And the tribes, one by one, signed away their birthrights. They had little choice. Game was diminishing, the fur trade had declined and often-violent friction with white settlers was unrelenting. Metea, a Potawatomi chief, lamented that whites were coming into Indian land so fast that "the plowshare is driven through our tents before we have time to carry out our goods and seek another habitation."[53]

The Indian Removal Act of 1830 cleared the way for the final chapter in the conquest of the eastern tribes. Through treaties, coercion, bribes, duplicity and threats, Indians east of the Mississippi River were relocated to lands farther west. The tribes in the south — Cherokee, Chickasaw, Choctaw, Muscogee-Creek and Seminole — traveled the infamous "Trail of Tears" to what would become Oklahoma. Tribes from the Old Northwest came to Kansas Territory. In 1834, virtually the entire West was designated as "permanent Indian country." Trade with the Indians was to be strictly regulated and white settlement forever banned.[54]

More than 10,000 eastern Indians eventually were removed to Kansas.[55] Delaware, Shawnee, Wyandot, Miami, Shawnee, Kickapoo, Potawatomi, Chippewa and Ottawa: Tribes that had fought to hold on to the Old Northwest now found themselves crowded into reservations in arid, windswept Kansas Territory, far from the woods, rivers and lakes of their homes.

They drifted west like ghosts, in small groups and large, on foot and by riverboat. In early September 1838, a group of about 850 Potawatomis were forced out of northern Indiana under the watchful eyes and guns of a military escort.[56] Their destination was Kansas.

Among this band was a 26-year-old chief named Nan-Wesh-Mah, better known as Abram Burnett. He was probably as close to royalty as the Potawatomis had. His great-great-grandfather was Chief Nanaquiba, a renowned and respected Potawatomi chief who'd fought beside the French. His grandfather, Chebaas, and his great-uncle, Topinabee, were war chiefs who had led their people against the Long Knives.

After his biological father passed when Nan-Wesh-Mah was young, the boy was adopted by a mixed-blood man, Abraham Burnett, and his name was changed to Abram Burnett. Abraham Burnett's father, William, had been a prominent white trader from New Jersey who'd established himself among the Potawatomis in southern Michigan after the Revolutionary War.[57]

The Potawatomis' two-month trek from Indiana to Kansas was brutal. The Indians suffered greatly from dehydration in the heat and dust of late summer.[58] The food provided by the government was wretched. Worse, a typhoid epidemic sweeping across southern Indiana and Illinois infected the exiles as they slowly passed through. More than 300 fell sick.[59] By the time the group reached Kansas, 40 had died, including numerous children and newborns.[60] The journey would become known as the "Trail of Death" among the Potawatomis.

In Kansas, the Indians settled initially along the Marais des Cygnes River around Osawatomie, near the Missouri border. Then, in 1848, Chief Burnett and others moved to a permanent Potawatomi reservation further north, about 70 miles west of Kansas City. The new reservation was a swath of prairie roughly 30 miles square on the edge of the plains, near where the Oregon Trail and California Road crossed the Kansas River.[61] A ferry had been established at the river crossing six years earlier by two French-Canadian brothers, Joseph and Ahcan Papan.

Chief Burnett was, by any standard, an educated man. Among Native Americans, he was exceptional. Born in 1812, he attended Indian schools in Fort Wayne, Indiana; Carey, Michigan; and Bear-swallow, Kentucky. The schools in the Northwest were organized by the Reverend Isaac McCoy, a Baptist minister who — for better or worse — dedicated his life to civilizing Indian tribes. Young Burnett evidently was a bright child. At 10 years old, he served as McCoy's interpreter in the reverend's travels among the Potawatomis. McCoy held the boy in high esteem.[62]

Bridging the white and Indian worlds was a role Burnett was destined to play throughout his life. He negotiated and signed a number of treaties with the Americans on behalf of the Potawatomis. His first wife was Indian, but after she died, Abram married a young German emigrant, Mary Knoffloch, in 1842.[63] And though he wore white man's clothes and had been educated in Christian theology, Abram continued to follow the traditional and religious ways of the Potawatomis.

One thing about Chief Burnett: If you ever saw him, you didn't forget him. The chief tipped the scales at 450 pounds, had a large, round face, and often wore a frock coat and a tall, wide-brimmed, black felt hat. Despite his girth, he was a man of great strength. Once, a stranger passing through the territory stopped at Burnett's cabin. The stranger weighed 300 pounds and had a reputation as a strong man. He challenged Burnett to a contest of strength. The chief pointed to a huge rock nearby and told the man to lift it. After a struggle, the man managed to get the rock off the ground. Chief Burnett then told the man to sit on the rock. Once the stranger was seated, the giant Indian calmly walked over and lifted the rock with the added weight of the man.[64]

Burnett built his cabin on the open prairie, a few miles southwest of the ferry on the Kansas River and just north of the Shunganunga Creek, a meandering, timber-lined stream that drifted northeast before flowing into the Kansas River.[65] A half mile beyond the creek, due south of Burnett's cabin, was a treeless, cone-shaped, rock-strewn hill. The prominence rose 265 feet above the Shunga Valley and commanded the countryside for miles around. The hill consisted largely of limestone and shale, remnant materials of an ancient seabed from 40 million years earlier and testament to the vast inland ocean that once covered the central plains. The mound itself was relatively young, carved from the long-dry ocean floor by glaciers that stabbed southward during the last ice age, 600,000 years before.

Supposedly, a tragedy took place soon after the Potawatomis were relocated to northeast Kansas, and from it, the legend of the mound was born. No proof of the tale's veracity exists; no written documentation has been found. Yet the story's resonance among both Native Americans and whites down through the years suggests some basis in fact. The tale, as told by an ancient Potawatomi to a couple of boys playing on the mound early in the 20th century, went something like this: One day, the weather took a dark and foreboding turn. A storm came up and a tornado, or "crazy cloud," dropped from the sky, touched the ground and roared straight for a Potawatomi camp. When it was over, many Potawatomis lay dead. The casualties were mourned and, in keeping with Indian tradition, buried atop the hill to be that much closer to the heavens. As part of the burial ceremony, a medicine man asked the Great Spirit to bless the hill and forever protect the surrounding region from tornadoes. The Great Spirit granted this request, it was said, providing that the burial site was never disturbed. The hill became known as Burnett's Mound.[66]

Whether Chief Burnett was involved in the burial ceremony is unknown. But it seems possible, given the proximity of the hill to his cabin site and his role as a ranking chief. In any event, life for Burnett and his wife, Mary, slowly improved as the years unfurled. Mary had come from Germany when she was eight and was "stocky built and low, a good woman and a fine cook." The couple eventually had six children.[67] Burnett farmed the ground near his cabin. But his real calling was livestock trading. And for that, he was in the right place at the right time. Settlers lured by rich land in California and Oregon Country had begun pushing west from Independence and Westport, Missouri, in the early 1840s along a trail that cut across northeast Kansas to the Platte River in the Nebraska Territory. The wagon trains grew more numerous through the '40s, and after gold was discovered in California in late 1848, a flood tide of emigrants surged west through the territory. The ferry manned by the wily Papan brothers did a booming business, floating wagons across the wide Kansas River at $4 per wagon. The crossing was a week or so out from the jump-off in Missouri. Emigrants would camp near a grove of locust trees on the open plateau above the river to await their turn to cross.

Shrewd trader that he was, Chief Burnett would send one of the young Potawatomi braves to the wagon train camps. The Indian would walk among the settlers' livestock, examine the horses and oxen, and shake his head or make a long face. The nervous pioneers — many of whom probably hadn't encountered a "wild" Indian before — would finally ask him what he was doing.

"You're never going to make it across the Great American Desert with animals like these," the brave would say. Fortunately, he'd point out, good livestock was available nearby. He'd direct the settler to Burnett's cabin. Burnett would then offer to sell the emigrant fresh horses or oxen, albeit at extremely high prices. The traveler would protest vehemently. "Why, that's highway robbery," they'd say. "That's five times what a horse cost me in St. Louis!"

"Then go back to St. Louis and get another one," Burnett would reply, although he might lower his price if the emigrant agreed to trade in his existing animal. Burnett would then graze the horse or ox for a week or two behind his cabin and sell it to the next wagon train that came through. And in this way, the chief grew rich and survived in the white man's world.[68]

That world was about to roll over the Indians of Kansas. In 1854, Congress ignored its earlier prohibition against white settlement on the plains and opened Kansas Territory to homesteaders. The move was designed to ease a growing sectional impasse over whether new states coming into the Union would be free or slave. In Kansas, Congress decided, settlers themselves would vote to determine if the territory's allegiance would be to the North or the South.

What followed was a bloody free-for-all. Pro-slavery Southerners and anti-slavery Northerners quickly poured into the territory in an attempt to gain the upper hand. Many of the Southerners came from neighboring Missouri, which had become a slave state in 1821. In the North, particularly Boston, emigration to Kansas became a cause célèbre, not unlike joining the Freedom Riders or voter registration drives in the Deep South 100-odd years later. Groups were organized to move en masse to Kansas.

Rival bands threw up towns across eastern Kansas Territory: the abolitionists in Lawrence and the slavers in Lecompton and Atchison. In between, clashes became common. When the vote to choose a territorial legislature was held in the spring of 1855, it was a fiasco: Heavily armed Missourians poured over the border, stuffed the ballot boxes and defied authorities to stop them. Both sides prepared for the worst. John Brown and his boys came from New York State, armed to the teeth. Southerners grew evermore incensed with the "nigger-loving abolitionist sonsofbitches" pouring into the region. Violence flared. Towns were sacked, homesteads burned and men on both sides stabbed, shot and bludgeoned for their beliefs. For all practical purposes, the embers of civil war ignited along the Missouri-Kansas border long before Confederate guns stoked the blaze in Charleston Harbor in 1861.

Amidst this danger and chaos, nine strangers made their way up the Kansas River from Lawrence in December 1854 to find a suitable location for a new free-state town. Several had been to the area surrounding Papan's Ferry before, and it seemed as good a place as any to start. Traffic to the ferry would support trade and commerce. Good timber was in ample supply along the river, and the rolling, open ground to the south offered room to grow.

When the question of what to call their new community came up a few weeks into the adventure, the group mulled various possibilities before settling on Topeka. The word, pronounced "Tah-PE-Ka," was the Kansa name for the area. Literally it meant "a good place to grow potatoes," a reference to the wild tubers that grew in abundance in fertile bottomlands along the river.[69]

Progress came quickly. Within a year, a two-story hotel had been built.[70] Steamboats came up the river, disgorging Northern emigrants and picking up agricultural goods.[71] The town found purchase. Property values soared; the founders made their money (which, of course, was a primary aim); new stores, hotels and homes went up; and by

1859, just four years after its founding, Topeka boasted a population of 700 people.[72]

Statehood for Kansas came on January 29, 1861 — the 34th in the Union. The war that had begun along the Missouri-Kansas border erupted nationally a few months later and in the region that had spawned the first violence, the conflict became even more personal, savage and bitter. Bands of Kansans known as Jayhawkers prowled the countryside, raiding Missouri towns and farms and indiscriminately killing, looting and plundering. Missouri Bushwhackers crossed into Kansas and did the same. Many times, it was hard to tell who was who. North or South? Yank or Reb? Give the wrong answer to a group of armed riders on a lonely road and you'd be dead just like that. Topeka was far enough from the border that the worst of the marauding missed the young town. But at sunrise one August morning in 1863, more than 300 Missouri guerrillas led by a blond-haired, blue-eyed killer named Bill Quantrill fell on Lawrence, the hated abolitionist stronghold 30 miles east. The raiders burned the town and proceeded to slaughter just about every man and boy they could find. Nearly 200 died.

When the long war was over, Kansans made an uneasy peace with Missouri and then turned their gaze back to the West. Topeka boomed. Construction began on a majestic state capitol building in 1866. An estimated 400 structures, many of them brick and stone, went up in 1868 alone.[73] Ex-soldiers, Union and Confederate, came to homestead on the prairie. And freed slaves came, too. The former slaves were called Exodusters, as in exodus, and many settled in the shanties of Tennesseetown on the edge of the growing community.[74]

One familiar figure on the muddy streets of Topeka was Chief Burnett. He'd take his wagon into town once a week to trade horses and buy supplies, his wide girth covering the entire seat of the buckboard. On Kansas Avenue, Burnett would attend impromptu horse races. Sellers would "prove" their horses for would-be buyers by racing from the watering tank at 6th and Kansas.[75] Before or after a race, Burnett might mutter something about a particular animal. Because he was by now a legendary judge of horseflesh, all in attendance would strain mightily to hear Burnett's words.

At one point, the renowned chief was invited to address the Kansas legislature, though the subject of his speech has not survived. As he approached the podium, several people made cutting remarks. One man pointed at the chief and snickered, "Heap Big Injun." Burnett gave his speech, which was well received, then pointed to the man who'd made the comment and said loudly, "Heap Damn Fool."[76]

As for his habits, it was said the chief was a voracious reader of newspapers, and supposedly he never missed a show when the circus was in town. He also was fond of dancing and was, by all accounts, graceful for a man of his size.[77]

But Burnett liked his whiskey. It was the curse of the Potawatomi and many other tribes. Burnett's great-uncle Chief Topinabee (pronounced "Top-In-A-Bay") had fought alongside Tecumseh before making peace with the Long Knives. At a treaty ceremony in Chicago in 1821, an angry and impatient Topinabee growled at the chief negotiator for the Americans: "We care not for the land, the money or the goods. It is whiskey that we want — give us whiskey."[78]

Burnett would frequent some of the 15 saloons along Kansas Avenue, often conducting his horse-trading business with a jug in hand. Contemporaries recalled that his demeanor toward strangers was dignified reserve, but with intimate friends he was cordial and communicative. One article from 1896 reported that, though stoic when sober, Burnett would often weep when drunk.[79] Perhaps he was recalling the faces of the dead on the long march to Kansas or the lost lands of his youth.

In any event, Burnett would frequently get so drunk he'd pass out. Friends devised a ramp to roll his massive, unconscious form into the back of his buckboard, and his mustangs would always find their way back to the cabin on their own. The chief had a system worked out with his wife, Mary: If, after a night on the town, he regained consciousness by the time he arrived home, he'd toss his hat through the cabin door. If the hat didn't come back, Burnett was welcome to come in. But if the hat flew back out the door, he kept his distance and slept in the wagon. Mary apparently had quite a temper and supposedly was the only person Burnett feared.[80]

The chief finally died on June 14, 1870. He was 59. The obituary noted that Burnett was "a steadfast friend of the Union" during the war, and in his business relations, "strictly upright and honorable."[81] He was buried along a branch of the Shunganunga, about a mile and a half west of the mound that bore his name. Rumors abounded after his death that Burnett had accumulated great wealth, and treasure seekers dug many holes on the mound and around the cabin after Mary remarried and moved to Oklahoma. They even ripped the old cabin apart looking for gold. But all the greed was in vain. No gold was found. One newspaper article reported that holes were still visible around the cabin site as late as 1928.[82]

Burnett's passing came as civilization rapidly closed in on the Plains Indians. The railroads were bootstrapping themselves across Kansas in the late 1860s and '70s, opening the western part of the state to settlement. Buffalo hunters passed through Topeka to slaughter the mighty herds for hides, for meat to feed the railroad workers, for bone meal and simply for sport. Cattle towns sprang up at each successive railhead to meet the longhorns coming up from Texas. In the streets of Abilene, Ellsworth, Newton, Wichita, Hays and Dodge City, lawmen and gun hands like Masterson, Earp, Hickok, Cody and Holliday writ their names large in Kansas legend.

But there was no more room for the Indians. The Cheyenne, Comanche, Kiowa and Arapaho fought a hit-and-run war to defend their dwindling hunting grounds on the plains of western Kansas and eastern Colorado. In fast-growing eastern Kansas, the original inhabitants, the Kansa, were squeezed nearly into the dust. They'd already been forced off a 2-million-acre reservation set aside for them in 1825 and been relocated to a 20-square-mile reserve near Council Grove along the old Santa Fe Trail. But by 1869, the railroad was coming across reservation land and illegal squatters were streaming in, breaking the virgin prairie, cutting down timber and bringing in livestock. Although the Indians protested, nothing was done. Finally, in 1872, the U.S. secretary of the interior came to Council Grove to inform the Kansa that they must relocate yet again, this time to a new reservation in modern-day Oklahoma. The Indians opposed the move. But short of a suicidal war, they could do nothing to prevent it. And so, after a final, government-approved buffalo hunt in western Kansas, 600 remaining Kansa made the trek south to Indian Territory in June of 1873.[83]

The eastern nations fared no better. Squatters, speculators, town promoters and railroads tore at their lands like wolves ripping the flanks of a buffalo. The pressure became too great. By 1873, the government had dismantled virtually all the reservations that had been established in Kansas following the Indian Removal Act of 1830 and moved the eastern tribes again, this time to Oklahoma Territory.[84] A small group of Potawatomis refused to go, however, and somehow managed to hang onto a portion of their reservation north of Topeka.

A Kansa chief, Al-le-ga-wa-ho, undoubtedly spoke for thousands when he told a federal official, "You whites treat us Kansa like a flock of turkeys; you chase us to one stream, then you chase us to another stream — soon you will chase us over the mountains and into the ocean . . ."[85]

The West couldn't be wild much longer. Topeka was booming. The city's population had reached 15,500 by 1880. An iron bridge was built across the Kansas River. Pennsylvanian Cyrus K. Holliday, the leader of the nine pioneers who had founded the town back in the winter of 1854, went on to establish a new railroad company and the first tracks were laid in 1868. By the 1880s, the Atchison, Topeka and Santa Fe Railway was thriving. As track gangs pushed southwest to California, the fortunes of Topeka and the railroad became inexorably linked.

So rapid was Topeka's growth and so vibrant its commercial activity that the city for a time became known nationally as "the Boston of the West."[86] Industry prospered, and residential neighborhoods spread south and west from the plateau above the river, slowly filling in the gentle, rolling watershed of the Shunganunga Creek. By 1889, the city boasted 42 miles of electric trolley rails.[87] Construction on the state capitol, which had begun 37 years earlier, was finally finished in 1903. The massive limestone building towered over downtown, its stern, copper-clad dome reaching 304 feet into the blue Kansas sky. Nine men died putting the building up.

The new state had a motto: *Ad Astra Per Aspera*, or "To the Stars Through Difficulties." The slogan captured the troubles that habitually afflicted Kansas as well as the inhabitants' stoic determination to ride them out. In those early days, it almost seemed as if Kansas had become some kind of diabolical laboratory designed to test how much adversity human beings could stand. Along with the bloodshed and anarchy of the war, Mother Nature frequently delivered knock-out blows: Drought, flood, blizzard, prairie fire, hail and wind all were regular events. In the 1870s, swarms of grasshoppers swept in from the west and raced down the Kansas River valley, obscuring the sun for hours and stripping every tree, plant and crop in sight.

Tornadoes also made their presence felt. A tornado struck Tennesseetown, the ex-slave community, in the spring of 1897, and another hit just north of the city in the community of Elmont in 1917, killing nine people and causing extensive damage. The city itself, however, was spared any direct hits. An article in the *Topeka Daily State Journal* on May 20, 1922, explained the reason. The headline read: "Tornadoes Are Unknown in Topeka and Vicinity Due to Bends in River."

According to the story, town father Cyrus Holliday had studied meteorology in college in Pennsylvania and had made a point to learn as much as he could about storms and "wind formations." Upon scouting out the location for the new town, Holliday "carefully decided that owing to certain bends in the river, the slope of the valley, and the height and location of the surrounding hills, it would be impossible for a tornado to touch the site."

Holliday's theory was, of course, sheer nonsense. A tornado's formation and trajectory are unaffected by geographic features, be they hills, valleys or even "bends in the river." But coming at a time when tornado forecasting was officially banned by the Weather Bureau, the article undoubtedly gave comfort to many.

Topeka continued to grow with the new century. War came in Europe, Wall Street crashed and the Great Depression settled in.

A few Topekans gained notoriety in those years: Charles Curtis, a mixed-blood Kansa Indian, became a U.S. senator and eventually vice president under Herbert Hoover. Several years later, in 1936, Kansas governor Alfred M. Landon became the Republican presidential nominee. Running against Roosevelt, he was crushed in the general election and won only Maine and Vermont.

With the coming of World War II, Topeka gained an institution that would help shape the city's character and fuel its economy for the next 35 years. Less than a month after Pearl Harbor, the Army began building an airfield on farmland three miles south of the city. By late '42, aircrews were arriving in Topeka to take possession of B-17s and B-24s fresh off assembly lines in Wichita and Omaha. The airmen would undergo 30 days' transition training at the base before deploying to Europe and the Pacific. By early 1945, new B-29s and their crews also were converging at the airfield before flying to the Pacific. One of the first aircraft commanders to receive his sleek, silver Superfortress was Lt. Col. Paul W. Tibbets Jr. Tibbets would make history with the "Enola Gay" by dropping the atomic bomb over Hiroshima on August 6, 1945.[88]

The Strategic Air Command (SAC), the Air Force unit charged with America's bomber- and ballistic-missile-based nuclear defense, took control of the airfield in 1948. The facility was renamed Forbes Air Force Base in honor of Maj. Daniel H. Forbes, a Topeka test pilot killed while test-flying the XB-49 Flying Wing bomber near Muroc Dry Lake, California, in June of that year.[89] By 1961, the height of the Cold War, Forbes was home to B-47 nuclear bombers and was the second-largest SAC base in the country behind Westover AFB in Chicopee Falls, Massachusetts. Nearly 8,000 officers, airmen and employees were assigned to the facility. The total base population, including dependents, was 21,000, and annual payroll reached $20 million.[90] Along with a vast number of aircraft, Forbes also supported nine Atlas E intercontinental nuclear missiles dispersed in hardened silos in the countryside around northeast Kansas.[91]

One of the airmen who came to Topeka courtesy of the U.S. Air Force was a radar specialist named Tom Noack. The bantam-weight

Noack, a native of Antioch, California, was of Italian and German stock and had curly dark hair and a friendly smile. He arrived at Forbes in '56 and soon after, met a fiery, red-headed, local Scotch-Irish girl, Connie Lee McCall, at Charlie Hall's dance hall in North Topeka. The two were married in May of 1958 and Noack was discharged that fall. He entered the electrical workers' apprentice program and was hired on by an electrical contracting company owned by Connie's dad. There was no shortage of work for the building trades in Topeka. Housing was scarce for returning servicemen and their families. New subdivisions were springing up along the expanding fringe of the city.

Growth was particularly strong in southwest Topeka. In October 1960, a bypass for through traffic on busy I-70, known as I-470, was opened along Topeka's southern flank. As it happened, the four-lane passed directly below Burnett's Mound. Homes quickly filled in around the highway, and Noack found himself wiring houses in the new County Fair Estates subdivision, just north of the interstate. The neighborhood's three-bedroom ranches — painted in soft pastels of blue, yellow, green and brown — were nothing fancy: Most were on slabs, some were bi-levels with walkout basements and only a few had full basements. But they were brand-new, attractive and cheap. Tom and Connie had a son by now, and they liked what they saw, paying $14,500 for a ranch on a quiet cul-de-sac. The house, on Southwest Twilight Drive, was near the middle of the subdivision and a long touchdown throw from the interstate.

Another construction project got under way nearby that year. One early summer day, June 7 to be exact, a startling sight appeared on the shoulder of Burnett's Mound. Bulldozers, front-end loaders and dump trucks were busily excavating an enormous section of shale and rock from the eastern side of the mound. The city had its needs: To ensure sufficient water supply and pressure for new homes, businesses and motels in the area, the water department had decided to take advantage of the mound's height to construct a 5-million-gallon water storage tank on the hill.

Approximately 35,000 cubic yards of dirt were removed to grade a site for the reservoir. In the process, the symmetrical, cone-shaped appearance of the ancient mound was irrevocably destroyed. That Indians supposedly were buried on the mound was well known locally, and officials took pains to assure Topekans that no bones, human or otherwise, had been found during excavation. Even so, rumors swirled that human remains had in fact been recovered but that the city had hushed it up to quell controversy.

The water tank itself was designed by a Topeka engineering firm, Servis, Van Doren & Hazard. It was a low, circular affair — 184 feet in diameter and about 25 feet tall — and assembled from reinforced steel plates. When work on the reservoir was finished in the spring of '61, the tank was not exactly an aesthetic marvel, despite a finish coat of light blue paint. Vaguely resembling a ribbed hockey puck, the squat, brooding giant frowned down on the city like a cold and indifferent monument to progress.

Aesthetic issues, of course, were not a primary concern for city officials. The tank served an important purpose by ensuring adequate fire protection for the growing subdivisions in the southwest part of town. Even so, the reservoir didn't sit well with many Topekans. Tom Noack, for one, didn't like the idea of anything being built on Burnett's Mound. Though a newcomer to Topeka, he was aware of the legend surrounding the mound, about how Indians were supposedly buried there and how the hill would protect the city from tornadoes, as long as it was not disturbed. Noack had no special affinity for Native Americans. But it seemed disrespectful to erect the mammoth tank on sacred ground. In the back of his mind, Noack wondered if the city wasn't tempting fate.

He was not alone. Ted Mize grew up in Topeka and was in the construction business with his father. He lived far from Burnett's Mound at the city's eastern edge, along 6th Street or Highway 40, which was the old Oregon Trail. Mize had heard the legend of the mound since he was a boy. After the tank went up, he said, there was considerable talk among locals about the wisdom of the project.

"People made comments. There were a lot of nervous jokes about how the powers that be had fouled up, that they'd violated the mound and that we were in for it now," he said. Like Noack, Mize didn't think it was right to build on the hill. "It was sacred, like a cemetery," he said. "We weren't supposed to bother the mound."

# CHAPTER FIVE

# The Guardian

Despite the misgivings of some about the wisdom of erecting a massive steel reservoir on Burnett's Mound, most Topekans didn't give the city's austere new landmark a second thought. For many, the tank's presence did nothing to diminish the belief — or at least the hope — that the mound would protect Topeka from tornadoes. This conviction was more widely held than ever by 1966, although the legend of the mound had morphed somewhat with retelling through successive generations. Most now assumed it was Chief Burnett who was buried on the mound, not a group of Potawatomis, and that it was Burnett's spirit that guarded the city, not the Great Spirit. Others believed the hill itself would physically deflect tornadoes away from Topeka, like some kind of giant shield. This view was akin to the cockeyed meteorological assertions made in the 1922 newspaper article about "bends in the river" protecting the city from tornadoes. Like that claim, this one had no basis in fact.

Still, Topeka was far better equipped to deal with tornadoes than most other communities across the plains. For that, the city could thank one man: Richard Albert Garrett, meteorologist-in-charge of the Topeka office of the U.S. Weather Bureau. Lean, angular and sporting a rakish, Errol Flynn–style mustache, the balding, bespectacled, pipe-smoking Garrett looked every inch the career government scientist that he was. In the summer of 1949, the 43-year-old had arrived to take charge of the Topeka Weather Bureau office, which was responsible for providing forecasts for a 17-county region in the northeastern part of the state.

Garrett had big shoes to fill: He replaced Snowden "Frosty" Flora, a legend in Kansas weather circles. Flora had held the top post in Topeka for more than 40 years and was well known for his radio weather reports to farmers across the state. In 1953, Flora even authored a landmark book, *Tornadoes of the United States*. It was the first general interest book on tornadoes since John Park Finley's groundbreaking work in the late 19th century.

But Garrett was formidable in his own right. He'd attended the University of Colorado before joining the Weather Bureau in 1927. And except for a brief hitch as a forecaster with Trans World Airlines in the mid-1930s, he'd been with the organization ever since. Garrett had seen just about every kind of weather the United States could dish out, with stints in Santa Fe, Denver, Portland, San Francisco, Oakland and Cleveland. Before transferring to Topeka, Garrett spent six years as supervisor of the international aviation division at LaGuardia Airport in New York City. He was an expert on aviation forecasting and had even briefed aviator Amelia Earhart once. A photograph of the two together was one of his prize possessions.

Transferring to a relative backwater like Topeka at the apex of his working years didn't seem like the wisest career move, and Garrett initially was reluctant to leave New York. But the people of Kansas were clamoring for a native Kansan to replace Flora and Garrett fit the bill. He was born in 1906 on a farm in Osborne County near the community of Downs, about 200 miles west of Topeka. At age 15, he'd moved to Canon City, Colorado. Garrett worked on the family farm, and then, after high school, he became something of a roustabout, finding employment at a dairy farm, at a cement factory and in the rough Colorado silver camps. Evidence of his rural, hardscrabble youth was hard to find, though, in the urbane, articulate and sometimes acerbic scientist he became.

Garrett's early years in the Topeka office were uneventful, so much so that his initial doubts about returning to Kansas seemed to be confirmed. But then, in the spring of 1951, the rains began. The precipitation was a blessing at first, as areas of Kansas had suffered through a period of drought in 1950 and many hard-pressed farmers were hungry for a good year. As May and June wore on, however, heavy storms continued to roll across eastern Kansas. The ground was saturated by early July, and creeks and rivers were filled to their banks. After a brief pause, the rain returned on July 9 and over the next five days, a deluge of between 5 and 17 inches swamped the eastern third of the state. The Kansas and its tributaries, the Big Blue, the Wakarusa and the Black Vermillion, as well as the other major rivers that drained eastern Kansas, all jumped their banks and spread into the surrounding lowlands. From west to east, rising water poured into Manhattan, Topeka, Lawrence and Kansas City as well as dozens of smaller towns and countless farms across the broad river valleys.

Before the flood receded, 40 people had lost their lives, 87,000 were forced from their homes, 186 towns in Kansas and Missouri were inundated, and nearly $1 billion in losses had been tallied in Kansas and surrounding states. The Kansas River flooded virtually all of North Topeka in a repeat of a major 1903 flood and brought much of the city's rail and industrial power to a standstill.

For Garrett, the flood underscored the need for more effective flood prediction and warning systems. His predecessor, in addition to being an expert on tornadoes, was a pioneer in the science of river hydrology, and Garrett quickly picked up where Flora left off. In time, the Topeka office emerged as a national leader in the science of calculating watershed capacity and the stages of rising rivers and streams. Garrett also developed a network of river watchers to monitor and report rising water in times of heavy rain.

Yet it would be the struggle against wind, not water, that ultimately would define Garrett's legacy. Over time, his foresight and determination in this arena would save countless lives across Kansas. And the fruits of these labors were never more evident than in Topeka on June 8, 1966.

After the U.S. Weather Bureau's 60-year ban on tornado forecasting was lifted in 1952, Garrett set to work devising a viable tornado warning system for the city. One of his first steps was to enlist citizens in rural areas outside Topeka to become weather spotters. The spotters were instructed to note the tornado's location, its distance, the time of the sighting and the direction the twister was headed, and then relay the information via collect call to the Weather Bureau office. Weather personnel would alert local radio stations for immediate broadcast to the public. Garrett also convinced two of the city's largest employers — the Santa Fe shops and Beatrice Foods Company — to blow their shift-change whistles if a tornado was approaching.

Those who were inclined to dismiss Garrett's preparedness efforts as unnecessary or alarmist received a savage wake-up call on May 25, 1955. The events of that day would lay bare the primitive state of tornado readiness on the plains and, for Garrett, would energize his work for years to come. It was a stormy Wednesday evening and tornadoes already had dropped in central Oklahoma. Shortly after 9:00 p.m., a massive tornado emerged from the clouds and sliced through the town of Blackwell in far northern Oklahoma near the Kansas line. The twister killed 20 and injured about 250. Earlier, the Severe Local Storms Forecast Center in Kansas City had issued a tornado forecast, the equivalent of a modern-day tornado watch, for a wide swath of Oklahoma and south-central Kansas. But the forecast was set to expire at 10:00 p.m. As a result, the ten o'clock news programs out of Wichita, both television and radio, reported that the danger for southern Kansas had passed.

Unfortunately, it had not, and another tornado forecast for the region quickly was issued after Blackwell was hit. But because of creaky bureaucratic procedures in the Weather Bureau, the new alert initially was routed to Denver before finally being relayed to Wichita media outlets. And by then, most stations had finished their evening broadcasts.

As a result, the 750 residents of Udall, Kansas — a Cowley County farming community 22 miles southwest of Wichita and 40 miles north of Blackwell — had no idea that out of the darkness a monstrous EF-5 was bearing down on their town. The police chief in nearby Mulvane spotted the tornado amid the lightning flashes and desperately tried to warn Udall. But the Udall Police Department had no radio. A railroad engineer likewise saw the twister and laid into his whistle in an attempt to save the city.

He could not. At 10:35 p.m., with most citizens going to bed or already asleep, the tornado plowed into Udall from the southwest and carved a path of destruction nearly three-quarters of a mile wide through the entire town. Virtually every building was destroyed. Eighty-two people died, including 22 children. Among the dead were two people in a car who apparently drowned after the tornado ripped open the town's water tower and dumped its contents on top of them. A Mrs. Le Force reported that a family of six "literally appeared out of the air" and landed in her kitchen, badly bruised but otherwise unhurt.

For Garrett and others, the Udall tornado — the deadliest in the state's history — marked a turning point. "It was a storm that brought people to their knees in terms of forcing us to bear down to do something to provide better warnings, because population density was increasing, and the risks were becoming greater," said Phil Shideler, a retired meteorologist-in-charge at the Topeka forecast office. Shideler went to work for Garrett in 1956, a year after the Udall tornado.

In a 1986 interview with the local paper, Garrett himself recalled that before Udall, his efforts to boost tornado preparedness frequently fell on deaf ears. But that changed quickly. "Plans began to jell (after Udall)," Garrett said. "I remember talking with the mayor of another small Kansas community. He told me, 'We'd heard about you and your work on preparedness. But it wasn't until I went to Udall after it was struck that I found out that our community leaders have a responsibility.'"

The bungled attempts to alert Udall underscored the Weather Bureau's dysfunctional warning protocols and reinforced Garrett's commitment to strengthen tornado defenses, not just in Topeka but statewide. To avoid a repeat of the miscommunications that had doomed so many, Garrett fanned out across Kansas to meet with the media, law enforcement and local government officials. Procedures were developed to streamline communication between weather offices and the media during severe weather outbreaks. Communities were urged to develop spotter networks like the one established in Topeka, and training courses were created to instruct law enforcement personnel and volunteer spotters about what to watch for when scanning the skies.

In Topeka, the local school district was pulled into the loop and a system devised to immediately alert the district when tornadoes were spotted. The district, in turn, would rapidly convey the information to the city's 2 high schools, 11 junior highs and 35 grade schools. Like Cold War air raid drills, tornado drills had become a regular springtime ritual for Topeka schoolchildren by the late 1950s. The procedure for both — sit in interior hallways in the duck-and-cover position — was the same.

As the years passed, Garrett succeeded in establishing coordination between a host of often competing agencies, groups and bureaucracies at the local, state and federal levels. His commitment was unrelenting.

"He was driven; he worked very hard, and he expected the same from everyone who worked for him," Shideler recalled. "So he had little patience for those who didn't want to give it their all. 'Intense' was probably the best way to describe him. But it was also true that everyone who worked for Dick had a tremendous amount of respect for him."

Garrett may have been a by-the-book government man, but he wasn't afraid of defying authority if he thought something or someone was blocking his way. In the late '50s, this independent streak would result in the addition of arguably the single most important weapon in Topeka's tornado-preparedness arsenal.

In 1950, the Civil Defense Administration had been created to help communities and citizens prepare — as best they could — for the prospect of nuclear war. The agency produced reams of public education material on all aspects of surviving an atomic blast, from pamphlets on how to build and stock bomb shelters to information on how to cope with radioactive fallout. Civil Defense also was responsible for mandating the installation of air raid sirens in cities and towns across the country to provide first warning of an inbound missile attack.

Nineteen of the powerful sirens eventually were installed around Topeka, which was considered a relatively high-risk target due to the presence of Forbes Air Force Base and the nine missile launch sites that dotted the area. Garrett and local Civil Defense officials quickly recognized that in addition to warning citizens of incoming Soviet ICBMs, the sirens could play a crucial role in alerting the community to approaching tornadoes. But national Civil Defense leaders quickly vetoed the idea. They insisted that the "wartime sirens" could only be used in the event of nuclear attack.

This was not the answer Garrett and Robert Jones, then the director of Shawnee County Civil Defense, were looking for. Both understood that the risk of tornadoes was probably much greater than the likelihood of a nuclear exchange. As a result, they ignored the prohibition from Civil Defense headquarters and began using the siren network as the centerpiece of Topeka's warning system.

And a formidable centerpiece it was. Most of the city's sirens were Thunderbolt models manufactured by Oak Brook, Illinois–based Federal Signal Corporation. Each unit consisted of a tapered, elongated, almost cartoonish-looking horn, four and a half feet long and two and a half feet square at the mouth; a chopper assembly (a circular aluminum casting with a series of holes that interrupted the airflow to produce the sound); and a blower and compressor unit located at the base of the siren to provide compressed air to the chopper and horn above.

Per federal specifications, the bright yellow sirens were mounted either on poles or on building tops at regular intervals across the city. The 240-volt units were powered by a 10-horsepower blower motor and a smaller motor for the chopper. The Thunderbolt also included a motor and gear assembly that rotated the horn 360 degrees as the siren wailed. This feature enhanced the siren's reach by projecting the sound in all directions as it turned at adjustable speeds of between two and eight revolutions per minute.

The Thunderbolt was capable of producing two types of alerts — the classic, rising-and-falling wail most commonly associated with sirens and a flat, steady, unwavering tone. It was determined that the wavering sound would be reserved for actual air raids, while the flat tone would be used for tornado warnings.

Both alerts were extremely loud. Depending on wind conditions, the siren could be heard for a mile or more, producing about 127 decibels at 100 feet. To the human ear, this is well above the level where sustained exposure can cause hearing loss and just at the point where physical pain begins. Blasting for three to five minutes straight during a tornado warning, the Thunderbolt produced an ominous, mournful roar unlike that of any other siren. The reason had to do with the fact that, for each type of alert, the siren's chopper generated a dual tone that simultaneously growled at a lower pitch and screamed at a higher pitch, thus creating a multidimensional sound in a minor chord. The result was profoundly menacing and impossible to ignore.

With a citywide network of warning sirens just a flip of the switch away, a trained spotter network in place, and local agencies, the media and the Weather Bureau finally on the same page, Topeka's tornado defense system was formidable. Yet even the most sophisticated warning capabilities were worthless if the average citizen couldn't or wouldn't respond appropriately. Hence, developing public awareness about tornadoes and the steps to take when they threatened became just as important to Garrett as building the warning infrastructure. To that end, he never turned down an opportunity to address community groups, whether it was the Kiwanis or Optimist club, a school assembly, the Chamber of Commerce or a church organization. He also worked closely with the media to get the word out. In March of 1956, Garrett was featured prominently in an 11-part series on tornadoes that appeared in the *Topeka Daily Capital*. The articles were written by reporter Jim Reed and were featured on page one for nearly two weeks. Information presented ran the gamut, from the history of tornadoes in the state to the power of the storms ("More Wallop Than the Atom Bomb," one headline bellowed); some articles stressed the importance of alerting the Weather Bureau when tornadoes were sighted, while others explained what typical tornado-producing weather was like ("hot, sticky days with southerly winds and a threatening, ominous sky.") Most important, the series included practical tips on how to stay alive when tornadoes struck.

"You must think quickly and intelligently, and move swiftly, if you are to pass through a tornado alive and unharmed," Reed wrote with grim lucidity and not a little panache. The list of tornado do's and don'ts — many drawn from S. D. Flora's book *Tornadoes of the United States* — were time-tested and straightforward. If a tornado has been sighted, go to a basement, tornado cellar, cave or underground excavation immediately; if the home has no basement, find a nearby building or home that does have a basement and make arrangements ahead of time to go there when storms approach. If caught in open country, move at right angles to the tornado's path, and if there is no time to escape, lie flat in the nearest depression, ditch or ravine. And in every instance, stay away from windows. Citizens also were urged to obtain one of the new, battery-powered transistor radios to monitor weather developments from the safety of an unfinished basement or in the event of a power failure.

Shideler, a native Topekan who worked under Garrett for more than 15 years, said the psychology of severe weather became a factor in how the Weather Bureau honed its messages to the public.

"As time went on, we realized that people reacted to storms in very different ways and that we were dealing with a wide range of emotions," he said.

Some people, for example, would become almost paralyzed by the mere possibility of tornadoes. To allay their fears, the Weather Bureau would stress that the odds of actually being struck by a tornado were very low and that people shouldn't overreact. But by the same token, they would point out that the penalty for failing to understand or address the threat could be high.

"We emphasized that people could survive even a direct hit if they did just a few simple things," Shideler said. "We would point out that if a tornado was approaching from just one mile away at the typical speed of 30 miles an hour, then they'd have two minutes to take cover, and that was plenty of time if plans were made beforehand."

Topeka schoolgirl Wanda Idlet was among those who'd developed a near-pathological fear of tornadoes. Her anxiety likely originated with stories she'd heard as a small child. Wanda's mother grew up on a farm in Circleville in northeast Kansas, and her aunt came from the Ozarks; both women told frightful tales of towns destroyed, people killed, even cattle skinned alive by tornadoes. By 1966, the fear had taken permanent root in the shy, sensitive 14-year-old. To her, tornadoes were monsters, inexplicable, savage, death-dealing beasts, and the panic would begin to rise if the air turned heavy and still in the spring. Her fears probably were magnified by the fact that she lived in a small frame home with no basement, on the northeast side of town.

Those who shrugged off warnings and remained apathetic in the face of danger represented the other end of the spectrum. People with this mindset believed the risk of tornadoes was so low that it wasn't worth worrying about. They belittled what they saw as the Weather Bureau's constant fearmongering and frequent false alarms. For them, it took events like Udall to shatter the indifference.

Most Topekans landed somewhere in the middle. They respected the storms and understood their destructive power. But they didn't allow wariness to fester into chronic fear. For many, springtime in Kansas was a little like hunting season, except that Mother Nature was the hunter and humans were the prey. People understood that a period of heightened risk existed for several months each year. But they also knew that if they paid attention to watches and warnings, used common sense and were ready to act quickly if danger drew near, they'd probably be okay.

That mentality dovetailed with the Weather Bureau's overriding message to all segments of the public: Take personal responsibility. Watches and warnings put out across the television and radio airwaves were vital tools for alerting the community to increased risk. But ultimately, it was up to the individual to monitor the situation and take action if the threat became imminent. This was particularly true for people who were planning to attend large public gatherings, such as ballgames, graduations or other entertainment events. These were a forecaster's worst nightmare. That's why Garrett and his team would stress that even though the sky may be clear and the sun shining, a tornado or severe thunderstorm watch meant the situation could deteriorate quickly. Therefore, individuals had a responsibility to monitor weather conditions and identify ahead of time an escape route or an appropriate shelter if a tornado were to approach.

By 1966, Garrett's messages had been drummed into the local population so many times and in so many ways that for most, tornado safety had become second nature, Chief Burnett's legend notwithstanding. Of course, the work in Topeka did not occur in a vacuum. Other communities across the plains made similar efforts to protect themselves from tornadoes through the '50s and '60s. But few leaders were as determined as Garrett. And few cities were as effective as Topeka in implementing a comprehensive tornado-preparedness strategy.

Garrett had done his job well. And that was a good thing.

For the hour of reckoning had come.

# CHAPTER SIX

# To the Mound

Volunteer spotter John Meinholdt parked in an open, gravel area at the crest of the ridge on Burnett's Mound and watched the supercell roll in. It came on like a black mountain sliding across an angry sea. Lightning ripped the face of it and illuminated the clouds from within to reveal the exquisite lavender cast of the storm. The sky in front of the cell was still a murderous yellow-green, and thunder boomed in the distance like the guns at Gettysburg. The temperature was falling and the wind was up. A few scraggly trees clinging to the ridgeline convulsed in the wind.

Another car was parked nearby. Meinholdt ran over to it, staying low. A young man and woman were inside. The mound was a popular place for kids to park, kiss and hang out. Meinholdt tapped on the window and told the couple they'd better go. Heavy weather coming. They thanked him and took off.

Inside WREN radio's single-story, brick studio on 10th Street, Rick Douglass, fellow disc jockey Steve Southerland and Max Falkenstein, the station manager, listened as a voice crackled through heavy static on the two-way radio. It was news director Roy Vernon, checking in from west of Topeka on weather watch. "This is 22. It's really starting to boil out here," Vernon said. "I think we need to get somebody on the mound."

"I'll go," Douglass said. "I'll take the WREN-mobile. Do I have time to grab a sandwich?"

"Yeah, probably," Vernon replied. "It's still a ways away."

Douglass called his mother and asked if she could throw a sandwich together for him. He'd swing by in a few minutes. "You be careful out there," she admonished him. "It's starting to blow here, and the sky looks just awful."

At police headquarters, dispatcher Marc Hood and senior patrol officer Lt. Robert Martin read the Weather Bureau bulletin about the approaching storm as it clattered off the wire. They agreed it was time to deploy police spotters. Hood keyed the mike and read the statement to all cars. Then he began assigning patrolmen to various vantage points along the city's southern and western flanks.

"Forty-five to the mound for weather watch."

"Roger, 45 to the mound," Officer David Hathaway responded. It was 6:55 p.m.

Meinholdt squinted against the wind as he peered across the rolling farm ground and woodlots that fell away for miles to the southwest of the ridge. The sky above him was churning and the thunderstorm was coming on in the middle distance. But well to the west, beyond the storm — under a flat, gray deck of clouds — a bright band of lighter, nearly blue sky was visible along the horizon. It was near this motionless, flat area that he first saw it: a funnel that appeared to be white, seemingly not touching the ground but hovering, perhaps 15 or 20 miles away. Meinholdt flipped open his compass and took a bearing: 260–265 degrees. He radioed the Weather Bureau.

Sue Goodin was cooking dinner in apartment 218 of the Huntington Apartments. The building was part of the Embassy complex located kitty-cornered from Burnett's Mound across the interstate. A couple of friends and neighbors had joined her. The 25-year-old Goodin grew up in town; her father ran Goodin's Florist and Nursery on Kansas Avenue. Three years earlier, Goodin had earned an education degree from Kansas State Teacher's College (now Emporia State University) in Emporia. She was teaching second grade in 1966 at Highland Park South Elementary School. With summer here, she'd started work on a master's degree at her alma mater. She commuted with a couple of teacher-friends each weekday, leaving at 6:00 a.m. to make the 90-minute drive to Emporia.

Goodin was a serious, thoughtful young woman. Her parents — particularly her dad, a World War II vet — had imprinted on her that iron work ethic so prevalent on the plains: a relentless, almost savage determination to complete the task, whatever it was, no matter what it took — to adapt, survive and prevail.

But work wasn't the only thing in Goodin's life. She was part of an eclectic group of Embassy residents who frequently socialized together. Some were soldiers or soon to be, bound for Vietnam or just returning. Others were college students at Washburn or young professionals like herself. Over bottles of wine, they'd discuss and debate the war, civil rights, LBJ, the Kennedy assassination, rock music and whether God, as some claimed, really was dead.

Tonight, Goodin was supposed to be having dinner with a sister who lived at Lake Sherwood Estates, an upscale community on a man-made lake a few miles west of Burnett's Mound. But an odd thing had happened. Goodin had driven out to her sister's at about 5:30 p.m. She was early, so she sat in the driveway in her '63 Dart and waited for her sister and family to return. She watched the lake and the sky as low, menacing clouds raced past.

Then Goodin saw a white cloud — not a tornado, but just a small white cloud — separate from the churning mass above and dip down toward the water. The little cloud moved silently like a sprite across the lake's surface and the water parted before it as if a small boat were passing. Then, just as quickly as it came down, the cloud lifted back up and melted into the sky. It was such a strange sight, like nothing Goodin had ever witnessed before. What to make of it? She had no idea. But it seemed like an apparition and it filled her with dread. She decided to skip dinner with her sister and head home. Back at the apartment, Goodin put the event out of her mind. The hamburgers were almost ready. She chatted with friends.

Meinholdt watched the funnel slowly grow larger in the distance. He again radioed the sighting and estimated the tornado's location, path and speed. "If this thing continues its present course, it will go right through South Topeka," he warned. "Sound the sirens." But as yet there was no radar confirmation, no hook echo. The bureau waited. Meinholdt, though, knew what he was seeing. In spotter training, volunteers were taught that if a tornado appears to be stationary but seems to be increasing in size, then it's probably heading straight for you.

Meinholdt remembered something else an instructor had said: Do not become mesmerized by a tornado. So awesome and unusual is the sight that many people become transfixed when confronted by one. From a distance, the tornado's roar is imperceptible and the damage it's causing is largely invisible, particularly in open country. People consequently tend to linger too long and only awaken to the danger when they realize the twister is much closer than they'd previously thought. But by then, it can be too late to get away. Meinholdt wasn't going to make that mistake.

Officer Hathaway pulled to the top of the mound. He got out of the patrol car and looked to the southwest. He was a native of Woonsocket, Rhode Island. He'd never seen a tornado before. Like many others, he'd come to Topeka through the Air Force. Hathaway had worked as an engine mechanic on B-47s before being honorably discharged in early 1956. After the service, he'd hired on at the DuPont cellophane plant, and later he managed Poor Richard's, a legendary late-night eatery downtown. But he'd been on weather watch many times since joining the department. He knew what to look for. And he saw it in the still area beyond the storm. To him, the funnel looked like an enormous, whitish-gray basket — broad at the bottom and wider at the top — slowly being lowered from the cloud above. He radioed dispatcher Marc Hood.

"Uh, this doesn't look good," he said.

Others were spotting the tornado now. Ed Rutherford lived three miles west and one mile north of Auburn. Rutherford was a news cameraman for WIBW-TV. He was a veteran hand, well liked and widely respected around town by newsmen and politicians alike for his professionalism and low-key manner. He'd been a reconnaissance cameraman in the Air Force and he was not one to get excited. In fact, according to his wife, he often grumbled that this weather warning business on television and radio was getting out of hand; it was a lot of foolishness, if you asked him, scaring people and exaggerating the danger the way they do.

So when the two-way radio at WIBW crackled, and Rutherford reported from his car that he'd just seen a tornado pass near his rural home and that the funnel was heading northeast toward the city, the station's staff paid attention. Rutherford said the tornado was nearly transparent and looked like a "sand devil, only 100 times bigger." A barn roof was swirling in the cloud, he said. Based on Rutherford's report, WIBW 580 AM station manager Jerry Holley interrupted a broadcast of the Kansas City Athletics–Minnesota Twins baseball game just getting under way from the Twin Cities to warn residents of Topeka and rural Shawnee County of the approaching danger. A minute or two later, at 7:01 p.m., WIBW-TV broke into *Lost in Space,* and newsman Bill Kurtis stepped in front of the camera to calmly alert viewers of a tornado on the ground and heading for the city.

From up on the mound, it was still difficult to tell if the tornado was actually touching down or not, as the space between the base of the twister and the ground was indistinct and blurred. But there was no doubt that it was getting larger against a widening backdrop of whitish sky.

Hathaway radioed in. "Forty-five calling. South and west of the mound in that basket-shaped cloud, there is activity. Uh, there is a tail. I've seen it to be dropping down; unknown whether it is hitting the ground or not and then rescinding back up."[92]

"How far southwest is it from the mound?" Hood asked.

"Ten, possibly 12, 15 miles."

Hood, the dispatcher, picked up the phone to call the Weather Bureau. Just then, another line lit up. Not coincidentally, it was Eland at the bureau. Hood relayed Hathaway's report. "Go ahead and sound the sirens," Eland said in a level voice. "We can see it on radar." It was 7:02 p.m.

Hood jumped up from the dispatcher's desk, raced across the hall and quickly unscrewed the wing nuts that held a Plexiglas cover shielding the two siren buttons. Beside the top button was a green label: FOR USE ONLY IN CASE OF NUCLEAR ATTACK ON THE UNITED STATES. Beside the other button, the label read: FOR USE ONLY IN CASE OF TORNADO.[93]

Hood punched the lower button, and in an instant, the 19 Thunderbolt sirens standing like sentinels across the city growled to life. The sirens began low, with a hoarse, rumbling snarl, then steadily ascended in pitch until they reached their desolate, all-pervasive wail. The sirens' rotation added an eerie Doppler effect to the sound, and the roar seemed to advance and retreat with each pass, as if to underscore the danger.

— • —

Meinholdt took a long last look at the twister. It was much closer now, clearly visible against the lighter sky to the west. How far away, he couldn't say for sure. But it was definitely on the ground. It was time to go. He climbed into his Ranchero, radioed that he was leaving the mound, swung the little truck around and headed down the hill.

At the police station, the telephone was ringing off the hook. Dispatcher Marc Hood was being bombarded by sightings. He couldn't tell if there were several tornadoes out there or just one big one that people were seeing from different angles.

"Forty-five, do you see the one at Dover Road and Auburn Road on the ground?"

"No. But this number one we're talking about is still headed in a northeasterly direction, right toward Topeka," Hathaway replied.

"Can you judge its speed?" Hood asked.

"Ah . . . It's about half the distance it was when we first started talking about it, Marc. How long ago has that been?"

"About 10 minutes."

Other officers and several Kansas State Troopers on weather watch weighed in from vantage points nearby.

107: "I'm by the south turnpike entrance, and I can see a funnel-type cloud off there. It is still probably five or eight miles southwest of the mound."

43: "I'm about a mile or so south on Wanamaker Road and it's coming directly toward me. I couldn't tell you how far it is — about five, six, seven miles."

"You watching that *real* big one out there?" Hathaway asked.

107: "Yeah, I'd advise you to get off that mound."

A moment later, Hathaway's voice broke through static.

"Car 45 is getting off the mound, headquarters. This thing is coming in a little faster than, I think, ah, either one of us would anticipate right now."[94]

The radio crackled in concert with a lightning flash.

— • —

Sue Goodin and her friends were just sitting down to dinner when the sirens sounded. A moment later, there was a knock on the door. It was a neighbor from downstairs. "Hey, there's a tornado warning and we've got to get into the shelter. They said on TV that it's heading for southwest Topeka. Everybody needs to get to the shelter right now!"

Goodin and her friends left the apartment and walked along the open balcony to the stairs at the end of the building. Fast, dark clouds that marked the vanguard of the storm were rolling in like thick columns of volcanic ash. The sky's hue had changed from unnatural green-yellow to charcoal black. The sun wouldn't set for a good hour, but cars moving on nearby Gage Boulevard already had their headlights on. The boom of thunder was nearly continuous, intermittently audible above the wail of the sirens. Lightning clawed the sky to the west. From every corner of the apartment complex, people were streaming toward the clubhouse shelter at the center of the Huntington's courtyard. To Goodin, the scene was like a dark, unsettled dream: People were moving like ants in single file. No one spoke. No one hurried or panicked. It was as if everything in life except life itself suddenly had been stripped away and only one objective remained: to survive. The world was now a foreboding place of stillness and doom.

Nearby, 23-year-old Dan Hudkins watched the sky above Burnett's Mound. Hudkins worked at the Huntington Park Texaco, the service station beside the little strip mall off Gage Boulevard, just north of the interstate. He was working that night with another man, Johnny House. They had cars up on racks, changing oil and doing brakes. Hudkins was a country boy. He grew up in the farming community of Silver Lake. He'd seen a lot of storms. But he'd never seen anything like this. How to describe it? Above the mound, the clouds looked like boiling, gray lava as they tumbled toward the Earth.

It was cold-sweat scary.

"Johnny, we need to get out of here!" Hudkins yelled from the front of the station. The men locked up. Hudkins thought for a moment about which vehicle to take. He had a '46 Dodge pickup that he was restoring. The thing was, it had an old flat-head, six-cylinder motor. If water got onto the engine block, it tended to pool around the cylinder heads and the spark plug wires would short out. The old motors were notorious for that. "Let's take the wrecker," he said. They jumped into the red Chevy one-ton tow truck with Hudkins behind the wheel. He wound it up, jammed the gears and swung north onto Gage Boulevard.

Goodin's apartment building, the Huntington, was the northernmost of the three buildings that made up the Embassy complex. Next to it was the Embassy building proper, and furthest south, toward the interstate, was the El Dorado. Behind the Huntington, there were parking lots, a short stretch of open ground and finally, a small creek. This nameless tributary of the Shunganunga flowed north and south. Beyond the creek, the homes of the new Prairie Vista subdivision ascended the long, low ridge. The homes were a little bigger than those in County Fair Estates, the subdivision closest to the mound. Most were split-levels and tri-levels and many had basements. Nearly every yard had been landscaped with fast-growing pin oaks. But the trees were still young and small.

Paul Marmet, the union meat cutter, and his wife, Peg, the physical education teacher who'd recently left her job at Topeka West High School, lived in Prairie Vista in a split-level ranch. The Marmets' house was on the southwest corner of 30<sup>th</sup> Terrace and Atwood, at the base of the ridge, a couple of blocks south of 29<sup>th</sup> Street. Twenty-ninth was the main east–west drag that climbed the ridge from its intersection with Gage Boulevard.

For the Marmets, it had been a red-letter day of sorts. Almost 10 months earlier, they'd moved into the home on Atwood. They'd come from a furnished apartment and consequently had zero furniture, except for a hi-fi. But they'd chipped away and saved and looked for bargains, and eventually they were able to furnish the entire house, one room at a time. Wednesday was Paul's day off, so they'd gone shopping in the afternoon. With the purchase of a single light fixture for the front hallway — one of those big, white, frosted globes that hung on a single cord from the ceiling — the house was officially done. The style was contemporary. The furniture was modern. The place looked beautiful.

Peg celebrated with another purchase: a Herb Alpert and the Tijuana Brass album called *Going Places*. The album featured the hit "Tijuana Taxi," a brassy, camp instrumental that had been released in December. Peg loved the song, and she'd slapped the album on the turntable as soon as they got home, collapsing on the couch as Paul installed the new fixture. Then Peg went upstairs to get ready for a friend's wedding shower. Peg had lived in Kansas for more than a decade, but she wasn't one to give the weather a second thought. She was still a California girl at heart.

But Paul was a Kansan. A tornado had wrecked some outbuildings on the family farm north of Sabetha when he was a kid, and he'd seen more than one since then. So he never let his guard down if there was the potential for severe weather. He'd been following the situation since the tornado watch had been issued in late morning. He'd even stuck a flashlight and transistor radio in his pocket, just in case.

When the sky began turning black, he flipped on the radio and heard that a tornado was heading for the mound.

"Peg, you need to get down here!" he shouted up the stairs. "There's a tornado warning. The sirens are going off. Come on! Right now!"

Earlier, Jim Ward, the assistant U.S. attorney, his wife, Carolyn; one-and-a-half-year-old daughter, Sally; and seven-year-old son, Greg, had climbed into the family's '62 Nash Ambassador to head for Greg's Little League game. Jim brought along his Brownie Kodak 8-millimeter home movie camera to film some of the action. But with all the rain the night before, the game was scrubbed. So the family headed back to their home on Burnett Road in County Fair Estates. On the way, though, Jim decided to make a quick detour through Prairie Vista to check out the new homes going up along the southern end of the ridge. No doubt about it: The family needed a bigger place. The little house was cramped. But moving right now was more or less out of the question financially. Still, wouldn't one of these big, new places be nice?

The Wards were near 33rd Street and Atwood, a couple of blocks south of the Marmets', when the sirens sounded. Jim had a decision to make. His home was a half mile away as the crow flies, but probably a mile by road. And it didn't have a basement. But these new split-levels all had basements, and one of them under construction was more or less finished, except for the installation of windows and doors. It would work. He wheeled his Nash into the open garage. Carolyn got out, gathered Sally, took Greg by the hand and headed for the basement. Jim was about to slam the car door when he noticed the movie camera lying on the backseat. He grabbed it.

— • —

Officer Hathaway reached Gage Boulevard at the base of the mound, turned left and in a moment pulled to the shoulder beneath the I-470 underpass. The supercell that had been loping toward the city finally pounced. The black clouds opened up and the rain came down in blinding, sideways sheets. Lightning bolts slammed the Earth like mortar rounds. Hathaway sat tight.

Further up Gage Boulevard, disc jockey Rick Douglass could hardly see the road through the deluge. Then hail began to pound the WREN-mobile. He turned on the roof emergency light and radioed that he was passing through a traffic jam at the intersection of 29th and Gage. He could see the 470 overpass just ahead. At the bridge, Douglass noticed the police car. There was a flash of recognition as he caught sight of the officer inside. Hathaway? What was he doing here? Douglass had met Hathaway a few years earlier at the all-night Fluffy Fresh donut shop on California Avenue. Cops and newsmen liked to grab a cup of coffee there in the late-night hours. He'd talked with Hathaway quite a bit. He seemed like a good cop, from back East somewhere. Douglass subsequently had run into Hathaway a number of other times, usually at breaking news events: car wrecks or shootings or robbery scenes. Now here they both were in the middle of a tornado warning at the foot of Burnett's Mound. Douglass thought about it. It was funny. Whenever there was trouble, Hathaway seemed to be there.

Fellow disc jockey Steve Southerland was manning the board at WREN and periodically patching Douglass through to provide listeners with live reports as he headed toward the mound. Douglass's radio handle was 33. He turned right and radioed that he was climbing the mound. It was about 7:05 p.m.

Hathaway knew he had to act. He switched on the emergency lights, put on his light-blue riot helmet, pulled on his yellow rain slicker, grabbed some safety flares from the back of the car and stepped out onto Gage to begin flagging down southbound traffic. Cars pulled to a stop and Hathaway would run to the driver's side. "There's a tornado coming on the other side of the mound! You need to turn around or get under cover! You can't go south. Go!"

Several miles to the west, Washburn geology professor Al Stallard stood outside his house and watched transfixed as the tornado moved diagonally away from him and in toward the city. He called to his wife and children in the basement. "Come look at this!" The tornado was enormous, perhaps 4,000 or 5,000 feet from the ground to the base of the clouds. It wasn't shaped like a funnel — more like a barrel or giant wedge. Stallard figured it had to be at least a half mile wide at the base. From his perspective — with the dark thunderstorm in the background to the east — the twister wasn't white but black, almost blue. He could see it churning and spitting like a great engine. Moving across open country, the tornado behaved as though equipped with some kind of advanced guidance system. Climbing over low hills, the vortex seemed to retract and telescope back into itself at the base, even as the upper portion remained stationary. Then, as it dropped into shallow valleys, the base would extend back down to maintain unbroken contact with the Earth. Clouds of debris periodically exploded upward as the tornado smashed and scattered the occasional home or barn in its path.

Thousands of people by now had learned of the twister's approach as it spun toward Topeka with that strangely clear, sunlit sky behind it. Many, like Stallard, were tracking its progress. And yet, during those agonizing, elastic minutes, there was nothing anyone in the world could have done to thwart the danger. You couldn't bomb it with every B-52 in the Strategic Air Command. You couldn't shoot it with a high-powered rifle. You couldn't call the police or file a lawsuit or form a committee or register a complaint. This thing was coming in. That was it. And all people could do now was to try to save themselves.

And pray.

— • —

"John. *John! Wake up!* There's a tornado coming! We gotta do something!" Sherry Griebat was shaking her 23-year-old husband from the fitful, exhausted sleep of a night-shift worker. John Griebat was the younger brother of gym teacher Peg Marmet. He lived with his wife and 18-month-old daughter, Julie, in a two-bedroom atomic rancher with no basement on Eveningside Drive. The little place was one of hundreds of nearly identical houses that crowded a subdivision less than a mile north of Peg and Paul's place, on the far side of the Shunganunga Creek and west of Gage Boulevard. The Griebats' house was very close to the original site of Chief Burnett's cabin, gone now these many decades and long erased from memory.

Griebat was built like an iron worker, six foot four inches and maybe 215. He looked like Tom Selleck, the television actor from the 1980s. He liked to fish and hunt. And he was flat sick of his job. He worked the graveyard shift, 11:00 p.m.–7:00 a.m., at the Goodyear plant north of the river. He ran the sprayer that coated the tires inside and out to keep the rubber from sticking to the presses. He'd hang a tire, spray it and toss it onto the conveyor, then grab the next one. It was back-breaking, soul-killing work. But the money was good. During one period in '66, Griebat put in 58 days straight without a day off, knocking down double time on Sundays. A monkey could have done his job, though. That's what he thought. Once, his foreman had called him in to see if John was interested in working his way up to a supervisory position. But Griebat declined. He didn't want a better job at Goodyear. He didn't want to get comfortable. He wanted the toughest, most-mind-numbing task on the line, because it would remind him that he couldn't stay, that he had to go back to college to get his degree. He'd keep it up until Sherry finished her degree in education at Washburn. And until he'd paid off his new '65 Chevy Impala Super Sport. But not a minute more.

Griebat mumbled through the haze of half-sleep. "It's okay. We'll be fine."

"NO! We need to get out of here right now. *Get up*!"

Griebat slowly lifted himself out of bed. He pulled on a T-shirt, stepped into some shorts and found his house slippers on the floor. Then he cleared his head and thought for a moment. There was a community center with a gymnasium a few blocks from the house. Surely they could find shelter there. The family went out the front door and climbed into the shiny, black Impala. Sherry held the baby in her arms. The 327 roared to life and Griebat backed onto Eveningside. Then he jumped on it up the deserted street.

⌒ • ⌒

White's Pony Farm filled the wide valley directly below Burnett's Mound on the southwest side of the hill at the end of Fairlawn Road. Ray White had been a contractor before getting into dairy farming and later, beef cattle. He'd done well in all his pursuits, and in retirement, he'd taken an interest in Shetland ponies. He showed them, bred them, bought them and sold them. More than 250 Shetlands grazed across the 420 acres of the old dairy farm. White even built a half-mile oval track to run the ponies on near the farmhouse and barn. The 20-foot-wide racetrack was enclosed by two rings of white fencing. White no longer lived at the farm; the big frame house was occupied by Clarence Irish, a lanky, aging cowboy who looked after the place. Irish lived in the house with his wife and son. White's son, Dean, a builder like his father, had constructed a fine, new home for his wife and four children across Fairlawn Road, at the base of Burnett's Mound.

Irish and his wife stepped onto the back porch when the sirens went off and watched the tornado approach. As it drew closer, they could see it shredding stands of timber and flicking trees into the air like matchsticks. The couple watched a moment more and then headed for the basement.

Across the road, 18-year-old Jim was the only one home at Dean White's place. His father called him not long after the sirens went off.

"What do you see, Jim?"

"It looks like a wide scoop on the ground," Jim said.

"You need to go to the basement right now, son. Go."

"Oh, crap! Here it comes!"

The line clicked.

Jim ran.

The pony herd undoubtedly tried to flee as the tornado swept into White's pastures, the animals scattering before this strange and terrible new force. But they may as well have been insects at the feet of a sadistic child, for the tornado no longer showed the deference it had exhibited with the Nicelys' horses. Dozens of ponies were lifted and slammed back to Earth or carried off. Others were struck — disemboweled, decapitated, crushed or impaled — by tree branches, fence posts, barbed wire and other debris packed in the spinning winds. The tornado then moved on to White's farmstead. In an instant, the house, barn and silo were obliterated. Across the road a moment later, Jim White huddled alone in the basement as the home above him vaporized.

On the other side of the mound, Rick Douglass swung the WREN-mobile onto the winding road and radioed to WREN listeners that he was making the final climb to the top of the ridge. The windshield wipers were slapping double time. The quarter-size hail that had been pelting the car like handfuls of gravel suddenly grew larger. Douglass leaned into the windshield to follow the road. BANG! BANG! BANG! Now the hail was the size of grapefruits. It crashed into the hood and Douglass heard the emergency light on the roof shatter as he reached the open parking area at the top of the ridge. He assumed he'd find other public safety personnel up there — fire, police or civilian spotters. But there was no one.

He couldn't see much through the rain and hail except a gray-brown mass of cloud that looked like dirty ground fog coming in. The wind was howling. The radio popped and crackled: "33, 33, come in, come in!" Douglass bent down near the speaker to hear above the din. It was Vernon, WREN's news director.

"33, this is 22. Is that you up there?"

"Up where?" Douglass said.

"Up on the mound!"

"Yeah, it's me. It's crazy. Got grapefruit-size hail."

"I'm down here in the valley to the west. I can see you. The tornado's coming straight at you, Rick! You need to get out of there!"

"Roger . . ."

The hail began to ease and the rain abated. Douglass looked up. Directly in front of him, a long, white fence rail from White's pony track was swirling in the air. The board was probably a one-by-eight, 10 or 12 feet long, and it still had a thick post attached at one end. The board danced and circled vertically in front of the car like some kind of crazy performance art.

*Oh, boy,* Douglass thought. He slammed the wagon into reverse. The gravel flew as he swung around and started back down the winding road. He grabbed the microphone.

"This is 33. Give it to me right now, Steve. This is hot!"

"Okay, GO!"

Douglass was broadcasting live.

"Ladies and gentlemen, this is Rick Douglass, and I'm driving like mad down Burnett's Mound." He was yelling. "Tornadic winds are right behind me. It's coming over the mound right now. If you're anywhere in the southwest part of the city, you need to take cover immediately. This thing is gigantic!"

In a thousand homes, people listened, and the cold, prickly sensation of imminent mortality raced across Topeka at the speed of light.

Douglass pushed the WREN-mobile hard into the switchback corners, cranking the wheel like a dirt-track driver, first one way and then the other, as he skillfully broadslided through the gravel curves. But then he felt something odd. The rear end of the car was being pulled, restrained, almost as if someone had thrown a logging chain over the bumper and hooked it to a truck that was braking hard. The rear of the car felt light, too, as though it was being lifted.

The winds were reaching out to him.

"I've got to drop the mike to steer," he yelled. "It's catching me!"

Douglass rounded the last corner and made the turn onto Skyline Drive. The area was set to be developed, and already a new home stood alone halfway up the east side of the mound at the corner of Skyline and 33rd Street. The one-story house was robin's-egg blue and owned by a minister. As Douglass passed it, he could see the house literally starting to shake and siding beginning to peel off in long, irregular shards. Gage Boulevard was straight downhill from the turn on 33rd. Douglass put the pedal down. He glanced at the speedometer: He was pushing 90 before he started to brake. Then he swung north on Gage and in a moment, skidded to a halt on the shoulder near the underpass. The rain had stopped. The sky was bright.

Officer Hathaway was nearby, standing half in his vehicle and watching the ridge with microphone in hand. Then Hathaway heard a rumbling buzz that sounded like "a freight train full of angry bees." He called dispatcher Hood. The tornado was on the mound, he said.

From the front seat of the WREN-mobile, Douglass turned and looked back toward the hill.

"Here it comes!" Hathaway shouted.

Like the leering devil himself, the towering funnel was making its grand entrance at last, shambling up the back side of the mound like a derelict king reclaiming his earthen throne. The funnel's wobbly black crown rose and spread like a mushroom cloud against the curdled-milk sky in the west. Seconds later, Douglass and Hathaway watched the robin's-egg-blue house on the side of the mound suddenly detach from its foundation and shoot 200 feet straight up in the air, *Wizard of Oz*–style, as if it were riding a geyser. Then it dipped and spun and, in an instant, exploded in a blizzard of brightly colored confetti. Hathaway was yelling into the mike. Dispatcher Marc Hood and patrolmen across the city leaned into their speakers, trying to pull words out of the static and the roar.

"The house! (*unintelligible*) The house! Got the house! . . . Gettin' the hell out of here."

At that point, transmissions from Car 45 ceased.

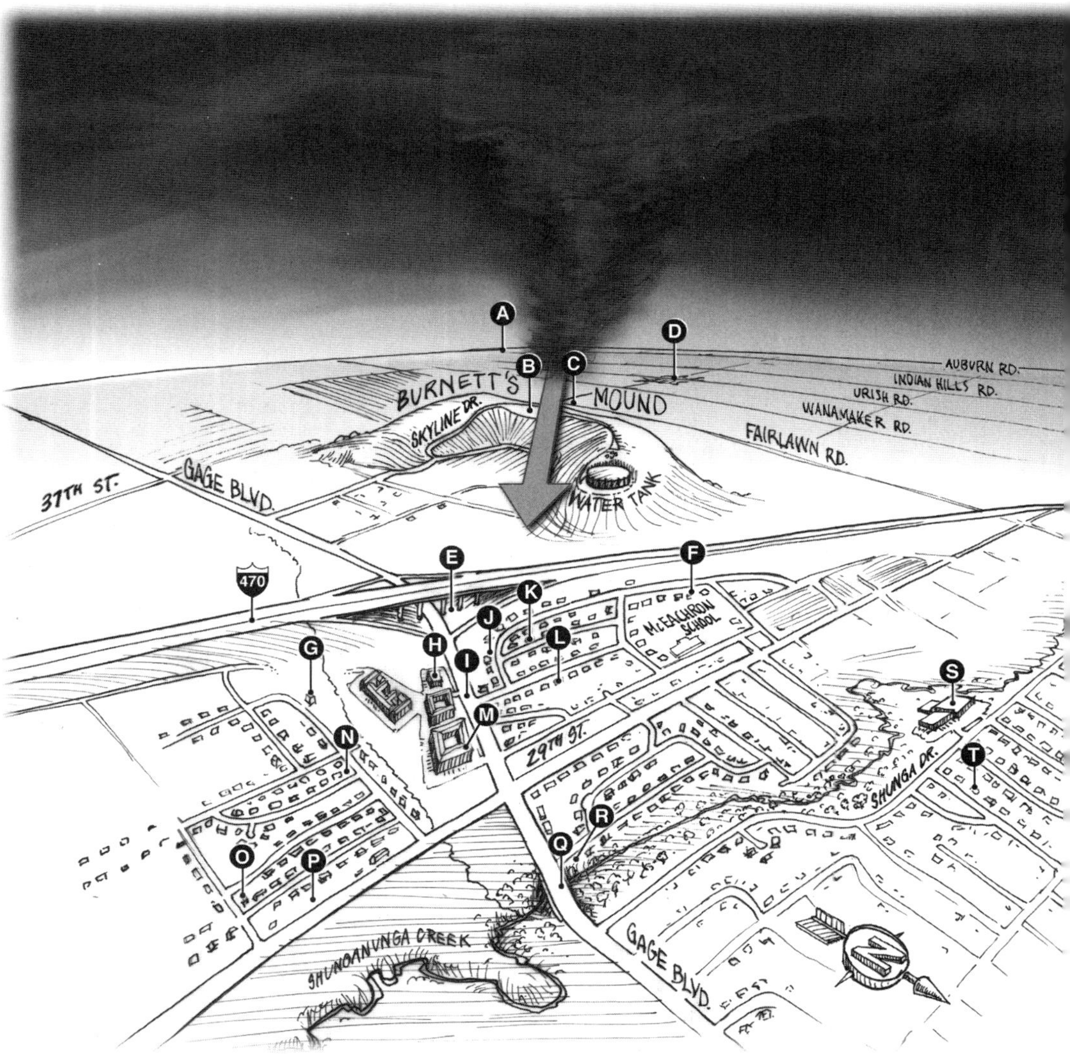


## 1   Burnett's Mound / 29th & Gage

A – Nicely, *Auburn Rd.*

B – Meinholdt, Hathaway, Douglass; Spotters' vantage point *Burnett's Mound*

C – White's Pony Farm

D – Lake Sherwood Estates

E – I-470 / Gage Blvd. overpass

F – Noack, *SW Twilight Dr.*

G – Ward, *SW 33rd St. & Atwood*

H – Hudkins, *Huntington Park Texaco*

I – Lollar car stalls

J – Beymer, *SW Twilight Dr.*

K – Lollar, *SW 30th Terr.*

L – Huffman, *SW 30th St.*

M – Goodin, *Huntington Apartments*

N – Marmet, *SW 30th Terr.*

O – Olson, *SW 30th St.*

P – Steuri, *29th St.*

Q – Griebat, *Shunganunga Creek Bridge*

R – Tuttle, *SW 28th St.*

S – Crestview Recreation Center

T – Griebat, *SW Eveningside Dr.*

# CHAPTER SEVEN

# "For God's Sake, Take Cover!"

Greg Ward stood with his father, the assistant U.S. attorney, and watched the sky above Burnett's Mound from the driveway of the partially completed house where the Wards had sought shelter after the sirens went off.

"There it is!" the boy cried.

The tornado was nearing the ridge a quarter mile away. "Get in the basement with your mother right now!" Jim Ward commanded. He watched his son dash back through the open garage. Then he turned toward the hill, lifted the movie camera to his eye, opened the aperture and started to shoot.

The tornado seemed to pause for a moment after ascending the ridge, as if gathering itself to decide which way to go. Then it swung slightly to the north and made a straight line for the squat, now-aqua-green water tank set into the far side of the mound. The funnel's rotation was clearly visible through Jim's viewfinder. The column spun furiously as ragged eddies of cloud curled and looped along its edges like oily smoke from an enormous blaze.

Jim was hypnotized. He couldn't stop watching. The tornado drew closer and began to engulf the water tank. The distant roar grew louder. He kept shooting.

Then his wife, Carolyn, was at his side, screaming.

"C'mon! C'mon! C'mon! Get in the basement!"

"In a minute . . . Just a little bit more."

"No! *Now*!" She was pulling on him with both hands. But Carolyn was five feet two inches, and Jim was six foot. He caught his balance and turned toward her. Carolyn was terrified by the tornado's approach. But what she saw in Jim's eyes scared her almost as much. They had a glazed, faraway look, fixed and peaceful, as though he'd been sedated. Jim slowly turned back toward the tornado.

"Goddamn it, Jim! We've got to get back to the children! Let's go!"

The words hit like bullets and shattered the trance. Jim was momentarily stunned. *I don't believe I've ever heard Carolyn use language like that before in all the years I've known her. I didn't know she even knew how to swear . . .*

They turned and ran for the basement.

⌒ • ⌒

A few blocks north of Burnett's Mound, at the Huffman home on Southwest 30th Street, 10-year-old Teri and 12-year-old Tami had finally accepted their mother's strange decision to bring them in early from playtime. Dinner was over and they'd settled down to watch *Batman* on Channel 9 out of Kansas City. But soon after the program began, the broadcast was interrupted and the words "Tornado Warning" were pasted across the screen. The girls assumed the danger was in Kansas City.

In any case, Teri was watching her mother, Joanna, a lean, pretty woman with auburn hair. All afternoon, Joanna had been weighted down by an enormous feeling of dread. Now she was pacing like a cat from one end of the small house to the other: first to the family room to check on the girls, then to the back bedroom to peer out the window closest to the mound. Then back to the family room. Then back to the window.

"Mom, what are you doing?" Teri asked. But Joanna didn't answer. Instead, she went into the bathroom where her husband, Harold, was taking a shower. A minute later, Harold burst out dripping and naked. He grabbed his glasses and dashed for the back window, then returned 30 seconds later.

"C'mon girls!" he said. "C'mon!" There wasn't panic in his voice. But there was an urgency there that Teri had never heard before.

"What's happening, Daddy? What's going on?" Harold didn't answer as he hustled the girls down the hall. Now they were crying as he lifted the queen-size bed — frame, box spring, mattress and all.

"Climb under there right now! Go!"

"What's going to happen?" Teri was petrified. She started shrieking. Her mother lay down first, then Tami. Teri, the youngest and smallest, was out on the end. Harold gently lowered the bed and then lay down beside it, bracing himself along the frame on the side closest to the mound.

"It's gonna be all right. It's gonna be all right," Joanna said.

— • —

Harold and Virginia Tuttle lived in a three-bedroom home with an attached double garage on 28th Street, just west of Gage, along the banks of the Shunga Creek. Harold was a Kansas Highway patrolman. He was also a Pearl Harbor survivor. He'd been an infantryman stationed at Schofield Barracks on Oahu on December 7, 1941. His building was strafed. Harold went on to fight the Japanese all the way across the Pacific. On June 8, 1966, he'd worked the 7:00 a.m.–4:00 p.m. shift. He was napping on the couch in his T-shirt when Virginia's father called from north of Topeka to warn of the approaching tornado. A few minutes later, Virginia's dad called again, more insistent this time.

"You need to get under cover!"

Finally, Virginia told Harold, "We'd better go." Virginia was a tall, dignified woman. She was not the nervous kind.

The Tuttles had their grandchildren in from Kansas City that day: five-year-old Dena and two-year-old Adam. Everyone piled into the '65 Ford Fairlane, including Gypsy, the Tuttles' Boston terrier. Virginia was behind the wheel. Head for the interstate, Harold told her. We'll outrun it. He held Adam in his lap. But as the car approached the I-470 overpass, the Tuttles saw a police officer in the road.

"That's Hathaway," Harold said. And then: "It's too late. There it is. We've got to take cover. Pull over right here." Everyone got out except Gypsy, the terrier. Virginia held Dena's hand and Harold carried the toddler.

Several others had gathered under the bridge for safety and someone yelled, "Run for it!" The Tuttles started up the steep embankment toward the small shelf where the bottom of the bridge deck met the abutment. Hathaway was climbing beside them. So were two other young men, Jim Russell and Tom Lux. Hathaway had flagged them down moments before. The tornado was close.

"Oh, God, we're going to be killed," Lux yelled.

Everyone pushed up tightly against the abutment. Harold Tuttle lay over his grandson, Adam, his feet hanging down toward the street. Virginia lay on top of Dena. She was facing south. The wind began to blow in earnest.

Disc jockey Rick Douglass had radioed WREN immediately after he'd seen the blue house explode. "I can give a report that I just saw a house blow up on the mound!"

"Roger. Stand by . . ."

But there would be no standing by. Debris was beginning to pelt the WREN-mobile. The tornado was moving diagonally along the ridge an eighth of a mile west and was nearly to the water tower. Douglass tossed the mike to the passenger seat and opened the door. The roar from the twister engulfed him as he dashed across Gage for the bridge. He could see Hathaway standing at the top, bracing himself against the bottom of the deck. Pieces of wood and metal were flying past as Douglass started up the embankment. But he was heavy and the slope was steep and muddy and slick. Halfway up, his feet went out from under him and he tumbled back to the bottom.

The wind hissed and howled.

Douglass groped for one of the massive, concrete bridge pillars and tried to get his muddy arms around it. The wind was screaming now and it tore the back of his jacket right down the middle. Then it ripped off each sleeve — *zip, zip* — just like that. He could hear metallic banging as the cars parked under the bridge were gathered and rearranged by the wind. Up on the abutment, sand and gravel peppered Virginia Tuttle's face like blasts of birdshot. She closed her eyes. The tornado was sucking all the air. It was hard to breathe.

"God save us," Virginia cried into the desolate roar. Then she felt herself begin to slip away. Slowly she was being pulled out the north side of the overpass. Now she was airborne amid the whirling debris. She shut her eyes tighter. Something struck her hard across the midsection. She clawed toward Earth but the wind was too strong.

At about the same time, Douglass lost his grip on the big concrete pillar and fell. He tried to get up. But his feet weren't touching the ground. Next, he was horizontal, flailing in the gale as though trying to swim upstream against a raging river. His body was facing south but he was moving north. He hit the ground and reached out to grab the earth. But it slipped through his fingers as the wind's crushing grip tightened again and yanked him back into the air. He bounced and flew and tumbled north.

*I must look ridiculous* was the only thought in his mind.

⌒ • ⌒

Tom Noack, the electrician who lived just across the interstate from Burnett's Mound — the one who'd watched the water tank go up six years before — knew the tornado was close. He'd heard Douglass's warning on WREN. Now Noack stood on his back porch and watched the hill. Connie and the kids — seven-year-old Tom Jr., five-year-old Chris and one-year-old Leslie — already had gone to the basement. But Tom lingered. Connie kept yelling for him to come down.

"I gotta see this!" he shouted back.

Pretty quickly, the clearing sky was turning black again as the mighty column began to rise over the hill. "My God, it's here!" Noack raced to the basement. It was 7:14 p.m.

At this point, as the tornado stood at the edge of the city, the funnel was a half mile wide, at least 4,000 or 5,000 feet tall, spinning in excess of 200 miles an hour and traveling northeast at about 32 miles an hour.

Then it slipped down the north side of the mound, loped across the interstate and plunged into the pastel houses of County Fair Estates.

Noack just made it down the stairs. He could see the house starting to shake as he dove under a mattress with his family. *Oh, Lord, it's all gone! We're losing our house* is pretty much what he was thinking. The pressure of the air was like a vise and the volume of the sound was impossible to describe. For a moment, amid the chaos and tumult, the Noacks and the mattress were weightless, floating a few inches above the basement floor.

A few blocks away, under the bed at the Huffman home, Teri's sobs were soon drowned out by a steadily building wall of sound. The last memories she had, along with the rumble and roar, were the sudden darkness as the approaching tornado blotted out the sunlight that had filled the bedroom and a crushing pressure that made it hard to breathe.

Teri's mother, Joanna, felt the ground violently shaking beneath her. Then the bed lifted and flipped away and a wall flew past. The house was coming apart. Joanna reached over and tried to keep a grip on Teri. But the wind was determined to take the child. She couldn't hold her. The little girl was slowly rising when Harold reached up with a powerful right hand and grabbed Teri and held her just like a ragged flag in the wind.

⚬ • ⚬

A mile away, spotter John Meinholdt pulled off the interstate and turned to look back. He watched in astonishment as the tornado slid off the mound and crashed into the homes of the subdivision, blasting them off their foundations and scattering a million objects into the air. Dark shards of debris circled the funnel like a flock of angry birds.

*This can't be real. Burnett's Mound was supposed to protect Topeka. A tornado can't do this.*

But it was just getting started.

— • —

Albert Lollar had ushered his family to the basement after the sirens went off. Then he stood in the backyard of his home on Southwest 30th Terrace, a block from the Huffmans', and watched the mound. The black clouds above the hill were cataclysmic, as dire as anything he'd ever seen. So ominous was the sky that Lollar began to second-guess himself and think that perhaps his family wasn't safe after all, even in the basement. A few minutes more and he was sure of it. So he ran inside and yelled to everyone. They had to go, they had to get in the car and get away. It was a full house: Lollar's wife, Darlene, a nine-year-old-son, seven-year-old daughter, six-month-old girl, a niece and her five-month-old baby — seven people in all, plus the family dog. Juggling babies, young and old ran upstairs and jumped into the Lollars' new Pontiac. They backed out the driveway, raced down the short street and turned south on Gage, heading for the interstate.

But the time for getting away had passed. The family watched the house on the side of the mound explode. They saw the tornado churn down the north side of the hill and cross the interstate. Now it was chewing through the homes along Twilight Drive, the curving, winding street closest to the highway. The homes were lifting in front of the tornado like leaves before a blower.

Lollar sped up, but the Pontiac sputtered and died. He tried to start it again but could not. The tornado was sucking air for thousands of feet in every direction. The carburetor was starved for oxygen. Lollar glanced to the shoulder, but there was no ditch to speak of. Nowhere to run. The tornado was heading straight for them.

"Everybody duck down!" he yelled as debris began to pummel the car.

*We're going to be killed.*

Then the car was airborne, spinning like a Frisbee, first one direction, then the other. The windows exploded outward. But there was a strange stillness inside the car. Darlene opened her eyes at one point to check on the baby. Large objects were flying and whirling by out-side. Everything was suspended in a cloud of fine, brown dust.

How long did it last? A minute? A year? The car slammed into something solid.

—  •  —

With 40 or 50 others, Sue Goodin, the schoolteacher, huddled on the floor in the basement shelter of the clubhouse at the Hunting-ton Apartments. The shelter doubled as the laundry room. She heard the approaching roar just before the lights flickered and went out. A moment later, there was pounding on the door at the top of the stairs. Several men ran up. Goodin followed. The men fought to open the door against the fury of the wind. A woman was standing there. She was middle-aged and holding a laundry basket. She was covered with mud. Her eyes were wide and her face contorted in fear, as if she'd seen a ghost. Her hair stood out in every direction. Goodin took the laun-dry basket and the men reeled the woman in the way you'd haul some-one over the side of a ship in a raging sea. They yanked the door shut.

"I didn't know there was a warning! I was just going to do some laundry!" the woman said. She was sobbing and in shock.

Goodin made it back down to the basement. The roar grew louder. No one spoke. Then someone shouted: "Cover your head!" The com-ment struck Goodin as ridiculous, for she was certain that they all were just moments from death. The floor above them would collapse, she was sure of it. Then it began: The buffalo were returning, rid-ing the wind. Ten thousand hoofbeats pounded the ceiling above in a thundering, clattering stampede. Goodin felt her ears exploding from the change in air pressure. Time became rubbery as she waited for death.

—  •  —

Two miles away, a 29-year-old photographer with the *Topeka Daily Capital* named Perry Riddle was tracking the tornado as it entered the city, composing and shooting and making pictures. He'd heard the warning and gathered his family, and because they had no basement, he'd driven four blocks to the Countryside Methodist Church on Burlingame Road. He put his family off at the door, parked the car, then opened the trunk and grabbed his Nikon 35-millimeter. Riddle started shooting a few minutes before the tornado crested the mound.

It was still raining, so to keep his lens dry, Riddle periodically would pull up the front of his jockey shorts and use the soft cotton to wipe his lens clean. Then he'd start shooting again, advancing and retreating across the church parking lot as the tornado drew closer or seemed to move off. He wasn't thinking much, just reacting in the moment, like all good photographers, and focusing on the shot. But he remembers being struck by the enormity of the funnel. From his vantage point, its full height and width were evident against the white sky in the west. And it was a colossus, completely off the scale when compared to anything in the human world.

Riddle shot 20 to 30 pictures in all. The church parking lot and cars rushing to the shelter fill the foreground; the houses and wet streets of a nearby subdivision are visible in the middle distance. The tornado dominates the horizon, moving in from behind the ridge alongside Burnett's Mound in the early frames, then climbing the hill and topping it. The brutish, wedge-like funnel morphs through the sequence, leaning forward like an animal springing to attack, and finally, in latter shots — after it had dropped into the subdivision below the mound — it seems to explode into a black, angry mass. All the pictures are exceptional for their clarity and drama, particularly those that captured fleeting figures running for the building.

But one shot stands out. In the foreground, a family is sprinting for cover, nearly silhouetted in the strange light of that afternoon. A man is bent low and determined, like a soldier charging the enemy. A boy runs in front of him and a small girl is scampering out ahead. A woman, with a small child wrapped awkwardly but firmly under her left arm, is keeping pace to the man's right. In the shadowy background stands a tall, slender cross attached to a church building. On the horizon, the tornado dominates the center of the picture. It is a desperate, earnest photograph and — given where it was and what it was — as iconic as any ever taken.

— • —

Attorney Jim Ward and his family huddled as one in the corner of the unfinished basement. Jim had spotted a roll of insulation on the floor and pulled it close to their heads, paper-side down. Now the roar was upon them and crashing and ripping started as the house began to go. The pressure was crushing. The tornado's snarling growl grew louder and louder and wood was flying around the basement. And then, as the sound finally began to abate, Ward heard his wife's voice clearly beside him:

". . . and forgive us our trespasses as we forgive those that trespass against us. And lead us not into temptation but deliver us from evil. For thine is the kingdom and the power and the glory. For ever and ever. Amen."

Ward took a deep breath.

Forty years later, Carolyn Ward's hands would start shaking when she talked about the sound the tornado made.

— • —

"It doesn't look like there's anyone here, John."

Goodyear night-shift worker John Griebat and his wife, Sherry, pulled up in front of the Crestview Recreation Center on Shunga Drive, looking for shelter.

"I'll check the doors."

Griebat jumped out and ran in his slippers to the main double doors of the center. Locked. He jogged around and rattled a side door to the gymnasium. Buttoned up. So he turned and ran back to the car. The air was dead still.

"We'll go to Peg's," he said as he slid back into the idling, black muscle car and dropped it into gear.

Shunga Drive ran east and west and paralleled the Shunganunga. A thick belt of trees along both banks of the creek blocked the Griebats' view to the south as they sped down the deserted street toward Gage. At the stop sign, Griebat looked both ways and then rolled right through, cranking the wheel hard as he turned south on the main thoroughfare.

And there it was, big as life. The tornado was straight up Gage, less than a quarter mile ahead. It looked like a huge gray, spinning wall, firing debris in every direction.

"Hang on!"

Griebat punched the Impala and the car leapt toward a small bridge that spanned the creek.

*You dumb ass. You're driving right toward it.*

Then . . .

*The bridge.*

"We'll get under the bridge!"

Griebat bounced the Chevy up over the curb and onto the shoulder on the far side of the short, low concrete span. He hit the brakes and the car slid to a stop in the wet grass. The front bumper just kissed a light pole.

"Let's go!"

Griebat wrapped his right arm tightly around his daughter, Julie, and opened the car door. Sherry jumped out on the other side. And the noise just swept through them: a deep, percussive, thunderous roar. It sounded to Griebat like the continuous explosions of a carpet bombing, *boom-boom-boom-boom*, all the way up Gage. So scary was the sound that he thought they were about to die. It was the kind of fear that makes the limbs grow heavy and the flesh crawl, the kind where you can easily lose control of your bodily functions and your mind reverts to ancient mechanisms designed to quickly choose between life and death. The Griebats half-slid, half-fell down the steep embankment to the creek, John breaking a trail through the thick nettles with his body, balancing Julie in one arm and grabbing fistfuls of earth and vine with the other to slow his descent and keep his feet. When he reached the bottom, he saw two other people, a man and a woman, standing in the cool, black shadows beneath the bridge.

"Thank God, you're here," the man shouted to Griebat.

*What? What did he mean? Were they expected? Did he know this man?* It was an eerie, surreal moment.

But there was no time to reflect, for the roar kept getting louder and very quickly a torrent of sticks and leaves was swirling under the bridge. Griebat covered the baby, pulled Sherry close to him and buried his face in the dirt.

—  •  —

Five blocks away, John's sister, Peg, the gym teacher, and her husband, Paul, the meat cutter, were peering out a shoulder-high basement window toward Burnett's Mound. They watched the tornado cross Gage and slam into the Embassy Apartments. The building complex exploded upward in a thick cloud of red bricks, dust and lumber.

To Paul, the tornado sounded like a hammer mill, an extremely loud piece of farm machinery used to mill grain into coarse flour to feed livestock. The sound had a high-speed, mechanical whirl to it.

"That thing's coming straight for us," he said.

Peg watched the apartment complex disintegrate, then saw the tornado march into the open, undeveloped ground between the Embassy and their street. The twister was whitish-gray and engorged with debris. It was less than a quarter mile away. Peg turned to Paul and said, more in surprised, bitter disappointment than in fear, "We're gonna die."

And Paul was in no position to argue, for he was likewise certain that they were about to be killed. He wasn't scared by the thought. Just shocked and taken aback. At this point, the noise grew so loud that the couple was convinced the sound alone would kill them, that it would literally split their skulls like some kind of sonic ax. Nothing could survive such an onslaught.

But then, suddenly, the base of the tornado bounced as it approached the tree line along the small creek that ran behind the houses across the street. The massive column was beginning to lift. The swirling base was almost even with the roofs of the homes that backed up to the creek across Atwood Street.

"Get up! Get up!" Paul and Peg yelled frantically. They were motioning their outstretched palms upward like football fans trying to coax a long field goal through the uprights. But the moment didn't last. The massive funnel slowly began to settle back toward Earth. They ran from the window and ducked under a heavy coffee table in the corner of the basement. Then all the savage sounds converged into one. A cacophony of breaking glass, snapping lumber, ripping shingles and collapsing walls engulfed them.

*This is it*, Peg thought.

—  •  —

Bill Kurtis was rooted in front of the camera at the WIBW-TV studios, passing along what information he could about the tornado's whereabouts and apparent path. Citizens and police observers were feeding reports to the station in near real time, and the audio portion of the broadcast was being simulcast on WIBW 580 radio. From off-camera, someone handed Kurtis a note that read: "The Embassy and Huntington apartments have been destroyed."

A flood of thoughts and emotions swept through him. Kurtis immediately thought of his family. He could draw a line mentally between Auburn Road, Burnett's Mound and the Embassy Apartments and deduce that the twister was heading straight into the city and moving toward the Washburn campus. That's where he lived, in student housing, in a small, one-story duplex with no basement. That's where his wife and daughter were right now. Kurtis always told Helen not to worry, that if the weather became especially bad, he'd give her a call and she'd have plenty of warning. But now he was stuck in front of the camera, broadcasting live. He couldn't get away. His mind kept running. If the tornado had wrecked the sprawling Embassy complex, that meant it was big and wide and not just a slender little funnel. And if it was big, it probably would stay on the ground.

Panic bordering on hysteria began to rise inside him as the gravity of the moment sunk in. What could he do? What could he say? So powerful was the tangle of emotions that swept over him that he thought for a moment he might burst into tears. But he caught himself. His responsibility was great. What he said next could mean life or death for hundreds, if not thousands of people, including his own wife and child. He understood that. So should he shout? Should he swear? This all was happening in a matter of seconds. He had to act now; there was no time to waste. So he conveyed the information about the apartments' destruction and the tornado's apparent path.

And then he just blurted it out: "For God's sake, take cover!"

The words, in and of themselves, were relatively mild, considering what was going through Kurtis's mind at the moment. But in the era before broadcasters became "personalities," before happy chatter choked the six o'clock news, back when anchors were newsmen who never showed emotion, the warning had a galvanizing effect. With those five words, Kurtis had crossed a line between the objective and the personal. His delivery was rock-steady, serious and precise. Pure Walter Cronkite. Yet in its effect, he might as well have been reaching through the TV and grabbing viewers by the lapels. People heard him. Anyone who was inclined to doubt how serious the situation had become could doubt no longer. Those who weren't yet under cover got there fast. And those who were hunkered down a little lower.

—  •  —

Ron Olson was listening. Olson lived in a tri-level on 30th Street, at the top of the ridge that paralleled Gage, just up the hill from the Marmets' house. Olson was a bookish 30-year-old who'd just completed his master's thesis in education. He was a social studies teacher at Jardine Junior High School and had started teaching summer school that Monday at Topeka High School. His wife, Linda, was a phys ed teacher. She was good friends with Peg Marmet. The couple had a six-week-old baby girl named Tawnia.

They had company that day. Linda's cousin from California was in town with her two children. It was their first trip to Kansas. They'd come up from Burlington, 30 miles south, with Linda's Aunt Ruth and Ron's mother, India Olson. The whole group, eight people in all, had gone out to dinner in two cars. It began to pour on the drive home and hadn't yet let up when they pulled into the driveway. So everyone but Olson stayed in the cars to avoid getting soaked. Olson didn't hear the sirens. But he was worried about the weather and went inside to turn on the television. He caught Kurtis's first warning about a tornado heading for the city, so he ran back out and told everyone they needed to get inside. The rain had stopped.

The group sought cover in the den on the lowest of the home's three levels. The room essentially was a partial basement. The cousin from California got under a big walnut table with her children. The rest of the women and the baby got behind a divan. In those days, conventional wisdom held that opening windows would equalize the air pressure if a tornado was approaching. Theoretically, this would help keep the house from exploding. So Olson dashed through the house, pushing up windows. Then he went back outside. He could see the tornado coming toward the mound from the southwest and he watched it climb over the ridge a little over a mile away. The funnel was so large that Olson initially had a hard time distinguishing it as a tornado. It looked like a giant stepping off the mound. He quickly snapped a couple of photographs and ran back to the basement. The TV was still on. A few moments later, he heard Kurtis's warning, "For God's sake, take cover!" He got down behind the divan with the women and pulled a blanket over the top.

The power failed. The sounds from that point were distinct and progressive. First came a high-frequency whine that rose in pitch, like a jet aircraft starting its takeoff roll. Then Olson heard houses being crushed on the lower slope of the ridge. The noise reminded him of the crunching and snapping that he'd heard as a child when he'd smash the little wooden baskets that strawberries were sold in. It sounded just like that. Then pieces of debris started thudding against the side of the house. First a few, then more, then many more until the barrage became unrelenting. Amid the din, a few very large, boulder-size pieces of debris slammed into the house, and the building shuddered from the blows. Finally, the windows shattered and crashed. And then the tornado was upon them, a deafening growl that to Olson sounded mechanical, like a wood chipper. The group felt weightless, hanging onto the blanket, swimming in air over the floor. It was surreal and slow, like a dream. Everyone had their eyes shut tightly. Then it got quiet and Olson said, "Everyone wait here. I'll go upstairs."

He crawled out and went up a small flight of stairs to the first floor and saw blue sky where the house used to be.

—  •  —

A block away, at the crest of the hill on 29th Street, John and Grace Steuri braced for the worst. The Steuris lived on the second story of a fourplex. They were in their mid-20s, just two years married. John sold mainframes for IBM. Grace taught fourth grade. With school out for the summer, Grace had worked hard all day cleaning and getting the apartment organized. She'd also cooked a fine meatloaf and made a big cherry pie for dessert. At about six o'clock, John ran to a nearby grocery store for milk. He was struck by the yellowish tint of the sky and the stillness of the evening.

"It's really strange out," he remarked when he got back. "Not a bird is singing. Everything is just dead still."

The couple was enjoying dinner when the sirens went off. John flipped on the TV. Then he ran outside, under the porch, and looked toward the mound and kept watching until the rain let up. He saw the tornado climbing the hill.

"It's coming! Go to the basement!"

Grace ran next door to help their elderly neighbors down the stairs. John stayed outside, still watching the mound. The others went to the apartment below. Another older couple lived there and they let everyone in. The building was set into the hill. The first-floor apartment had a pantry closet. Although not a basement per se, the room was largely underground. The group piled in. A few minutes passed and Grace began to worry. Where was John? Why didn't he come down?

Like Jim Ward, John Steuri couldn't take his eyes off the twister. The size was breathtaking, not just the height of it but also the width.

Its sides and top were gray and the base was coal black. It seemed to move ponderously and convulse like a great snake as it came down the mound. Then John watched the bricks cascading upward from the Embassy Apartments, and he could hear the roar. He ran for the first-floor apartment.

In the heat of the moment, the old, frail woman who lived there somehow had managed, by herself, to muscle a mattress into the pantry. Everyone ducked beneath it and pulled it down. In her mind, Grace was praying the tornado would veer off and perhaps they wouldn't take a direct hit. She was very worried that the apartment building would come down on top of them. Then came the machine gun–like volley of debris striking the building. The roar engulfed them. Grace felt a stabbing pain in her ears. Timbers twisted and glass shattered. And all the stored energy of materials, time and human labor that went into constructing the building was released in seconds.

$$\sim \bullet \sim$$

Disc jockey Rick Douglass was spinning like a top on his backside. When the wind finally let him go, he was lying in the muddy gravel and sand on the 470 westbound entrance ramp, a good 100 yards from the overpass. His leg was bleeding badly. He looked back toward the bridge and saw bodies somersaulting and tumbling down the embankment. To the northeast, the tornado was moving away in a dirty, hazy cloud of debris. Then he looked up and saw a maroon-and-white '59 Pontiac Bonneville — a long, heavy piece of Detroit steel — floating 100 feet up in the air, drifting toward the Embassy Apartments.

Its doors and trunk flapped like the wings of a gull.

# CHAPTER EIGHT

# A Blasted Plain

Clarence Irish looked up from the basement of the demolished frame house at White's Pony Farm and saw nothing but blue sky. One of the Shetlands stood at the edge of the foundation and stared down at him with sad, brown eyes. The pony's intestines were exposed. Irish climbed out and could see dead and struggling animals stacked up two and three deep on the road. He started digging through the wreckage for his rifle.

On the other side of the mound, a Kansas State Trooper helped Rick Douglass to his feet. The officer wore a Smokey the Bear hat, and a silver badge hung from his belt. But he must have been off duty, because he had on brightly colored Bermuda shorts and a Stanley Kowalski T-shirt. It was a bizarre sight to the dazed and battered Douglass.

"You'd better get back under the bridge in case it comes back," the trooper said.

Douglass was soaked and filthy and his arms were cut and scraped. A big chunk of flesh was missing from his left leg near the knee. The wound continued to bleed. But that wasn't the worst of it. The truth was, Douglass didn't really look human anymore. Nearly all of his head was encased in a thick layer of mud, sprayed on like gooey paint by the 200-mile-an-hour-plus winds. Bits of grass, twigs, gravel and sand were embedded in the mud and skin. A sliver of wood four inches long had pierced his upper lip and dangled casually like a cigarette.

He looked like a beast from hell.

Dorothy McKinney saw him. She was among the first to arrive at the underpass after the tornado moved off. The 53-year-old realtor had been showing homes to a couple from out of town. They'd found themselves in the tornado's crosshairs at the intersection of 29th and Gage. The would-be home buyer, a Mr. Ralph Anderson, was behind the wheel. The car nearly stalled for want of oxygen, just as the Lollars' had. But Anderson was able to keep it running and they raced off to the east. Then they double-backed to the interstate and pulled off at the Gage ramp. Anderson parked and ran with McKinney down the hill. They could see bodies under the bridge.

*Everyone's dead,* McKinney thought. People were scattered in curious, rigid, unnatural positions. But as McKinney got closer, she could see movement. Some were heaving, taking deep, gasping breaths, like they'd been trapped underwater. Others were green in the face and coughing and spitting. One by one, they struggled to recover.

Officer Hathaway was among them. He pulled himself unsteadily to his feet. Then he walked out from under the bridge, stared off to the north and slowly shook his head.

"Shit," he said quietly.

A ragged, brown carpet of ruin stretched nearly as far as the eye could see. Jumbled wreckage blanketed virtually the entire County Fair Estates subdivision. More than 60 homes were leveled or badly damaged west of Gage. The wide, dirt-colored band of devastation stretched across where the Embassy Apartments had been and climbed the ridge to the northeast. In the Prairie Vista subdivision, in excess of 100 homes and at least a half a dozen fourplexes and duplexes were destroyed.

Above, the sky was the purest shade of blue. Not a particle of dust hung in the air. The silence was so intense that it seemed like the entire world, even time itself, had suddenly stopped. Only one sound emerged from the shattered landscape: the ominous hiss of natural gas as it escaped shorn gas lines in dozens of homes. The air reeked of mud, gas and wet garbage. Hathaway's patrol wagon was still parked under the bridge. He turned and walked back to it. The hood was off and the front end smashed. But the radio worked.

"Car 45 calling . . ."

"Go ahead, 45 . . ."

There was a long pause. Hathaway was panting, still trying to catch his breath.

"This place is leveled out here," he said. His voice was hollow and spent. "These houses are gone, Marc. Gone."

"10-4, 45. Help is on the way."

Virginia Tuttle, the highway patrolman's wife, picked herself up and slowly walked back to the underpass. Her face was cherry red and abraded, as if she'd been sandblasted. Her ribs and abdomen ached. Her husband, Harold, lay nearby. He, too, had been sucked out from under the bridge. But he hadn't traveled nearly so far as his wife.

"I think my back is broken," he said. A piece of lumber had hit him hard. The grandchildren fared better. Dena's ankle was slightly injured and little Adam had a cut on the head. Then Virginia heard yapping near the bridge. It was little Gypsy, bouncing in the car. The Ford was smashed. A telephone pole evidently had shot straight through the passenger compartment, judging by the symmetry and size of the holes in the front and rear windows. But the dog was fine.

Rick Douglass asked an older man who'd sought shelter under the bridge if he'd seen the flying Bonneville.

"We saw a lot of things flying," the old man said. "We saw *you* flying." They had a good laugh and then Douglass was wandering, looking for the WREN-mobile. He couldn't find it. It wasn't where he left it on the shoulder just south of the underpass. It wasn't anywhere. He lay down in the grass and waited for help.

*They'll fire me if I lost that car.*

Officer Hathaway heard voices coming from the ruins of County Fair Estates. He walked toward them. Time had stretched way out, like a curious dream. Most of the houses on Twilight Drive, the street closest to the interstate, were scraped to the foundation. In the distance, Hathaway could see movement as people began to emerge from the wreckage. There were shouts.

"Are you okay? Is there anyone in there?"

He saw a figure sitting alone amid the ruins. He moved closer and could see that it was a woman. She was muddy and bleeding and her clothes were in tatters. He approached and asked if she was all right. She looked up but didn't say a word. Then Hathaway heard crying: forlorn, unbearable sobs. The sounds seemed to come from under a pile of shattered lumber. He started yanking boards and two-by-fours out of the way and a human shape gradually emerged. It was a little boy, probably a first- or second-grader. Black, dirty blood covered his entire head and body. He had a deep gash above his left eye and a purple, gaping wound in his side. One leg was badly mangled. The bone glistened like wet china through shredded flesh and blood.

"That's my boy," the woman said softly.

Now a man in a dark suit and tie was there, and he and Hathaway found a piece of plywood and laid it close and ever so gently lifted the broken boy onto it. The little fellow never screamed or yelled. He just sobbed quietly. A station wagon stopped on Gage and someone pushed the backseat down, and Hathaway and the man in the suit carefully carried the plywood and its cargo out from the wreckage and eased it into the car. Then they helped the boy's mother crawl in so she could lay by her son and cradle his head in her muddy arms. The car drove off, and Hathaway heard someone say, "You're hurt. You're bleeding from the head." He felt his knees buckle. A couple of men grabbed his elbows as he started to go down.

Hathaway was unconscious when they loaded him into a camper shell for the trip to the hospital. They put Harold Tuttle on a piece of plywood and stuck him in a station wagon. But whoever found the board that served as a stretcher forgot to check it for nails, and Harold's back was perforated on the long and painful ride into town.

An off-duty nurse pulled up in a black sedan and offered to take some of the wounded to the hospital. Virginia Tuttle and the kids climbed in the front. Dorothy McKinney assured Virginia that she'd take care of her dog, Gypsy, until the Tuttles were back on their feet.

Rick Douglass was about to get into the car, but when he saw the interior — red and immaculate — he told the woman he couldn't do it. He didn't want to get the car dirty. She told him not to worry, but Douglass demurred, and they went back and forth that way for a moment. Then Douglass felt a boot in his backside and he tumbled in. It was the state trooper in the Bermuda shorts.

— • —

Tom Noack, the electrician, started up the stairs and a wave of pure joy washed over him when he reached the top. The house was still there.

"Connie! We've got a house yet!" he yelled down.

The home's front windows were blown in and glass littered the carpet. A two-by-four was sticking down through the living room ceiling like a spear. But the place was intact. Noack stepped over the shattered glass and out the front door. The neighborhood he'd lived in for six years, the one he'd helped build, was no more. Looking toward the mound, he could see the interstate for the first time. All the houses that had obscured his view before were gone. Noack's house sat on a cul-de-sac at the top of a small rise. Everything below it — all the way east to Gage and beyond — was leveled or nearly so. He could see the wreckage of the Embassy Apartments and his eyes followed the raw, dirty path that undulated up the distant ridge.

Noack smelled gas and ran to the garage to grab some wrenches. He yelled to Connie and then, with a neighbor boy, Mark Luksa, started at a trot down the ruined block, moving rapidly from meter to meter, shutting down the main gas valve to each home. There were muffled yells coming from the wreckage of a house on the corner. Several people were moving Sheetrock and framing, and Noack and Mark pitched in until they reached a young man who was maybe 14 years old. He'd sought shelter in a bathtub when the tornado approached and he was there still, safe, without a scratch. No one else had been home. It had been a heads-up, lifesaving move by the kid to get into the tub.

Noack kept moving east. Cars were stopping now along the shoulder of I-470 above the neighborhood.

*What the hell?*

Noack watched in disbelief as people began to get out and run down to the yards that backed up to the interstate. They'd grab objects from the debris field and dash back up the embankment. Then they would jump in their cars and speed away. Not just one or two, but maybe a dozen people, alone and in small groups. Looters. The tornado hadn't been gone five minutes. Noack's heart sank and his stomach turned. Anger rose inside him. He shut off as many gas meters as he could. Then he started slowly back up the destroyed street.

A few blocks away, 10-year-old Teri Huffman was coming to. She raised her head and looked around. She was covered with mud and shivering violently, as if an arctic front had blown through. But the air was warm and still and the sky was blue. Her sister lay beneath her. Their bodies were askew in the muddy grass near a concrete slab that a few moments before had been their home. Everything was gone, everything, just vacuumed away. The tornado was thorough: Even the floorboards and wall-to-wall carpet had been ripped up and carried off. Only gray concrete remained. A hot water heater lay on its side in the center of the slab, slowly leaking water.

Teri looked around. She didn't understand why her mother was climbing a pile of rubble in the backyard, digging frantically with her hands. In a moment, Joanna came down with a pair of men's pants and a child's T-shirt. She walked back to the slab where Teri's father was pulling himself to his feet.

"Put these on," she said unsteadily.

Harold was naked and covered with mud. On his back and side was the perfect imprint of a chain-link fence, outlined by a matrix of red welts. Teri's head was pounding. Something had hit her and knocked her cold. She had a goose egg the size of a fist on the back of her skull. But her sister, Tami, seemed to have fared the worst. She had three deep cuts in her back that looked like claw marks and her two front teeth were broken. Her mouth was just blood.

Harold put on the pants, which were much too large, and the shirt, which was much too small, and he helped the girls across the street to a neighbor's house that had not been destroyed. Joanna was following but collapsed coming up the driveway. Some men found a door and put her on it, and another station wagon was pressed into ambulance duty. The rest of the family climbed in.

— • —

The stampede that thundered across the laundry room of the Huntington Apartments seemed to last for all eternity. But the ceiling didn't collapse, much to Sue Goodin's everlasting amazement, gratitude and relief. When silence finally returned, someone went up the stairs and yelled that it was safe to come out. The group slowly made their way from darkness to light. There were murmurs and gasps as people stepped into the day. The square, two-story apartment building that surrounded the courtyard — modern and solid and full of life moments before — was shattered on every side. The apartments were opened like a rabbit warren or simply blown away. In the three-building Embassy complex, all 150 apartments were destroyed or severely damaged. A car was perched in a second-story apartment. Another lay at the bottom of the swimming pool. Everyday objects that correlated to someone's existence were scattered across the fractured landscape: a child's doll, a muddy Bible, a broken highchair, a pink Princess telephone.

The destruction was so stunning that Goodin had a hard time taking it in. She looked up and thanked God she was alive and marveled at the beauty of the sky.

*I need to get a hold of my sister and let her know I'm okay.*

— • —

The Lollars' car had come to a rest, right side up, amid the rubble of the Embassy Apartments. Albert Lollar tried to lift his head but could not. A plank had run through the front window, through the spokes of the steering wheel and out the back window. It was lodged there still. Everyone in the car was coated with mud and tar. A few had cuts, but nothing severe. The group slowly climbed out of the battered Pontiac and made their way to Gage Boulevard. Albert flagged down a passing car and a man gave them a ride to the hospital.

The family eventually made it back to their home and found the house destroyed. A wall had collapsed into the southwest corner of the basement and filled it with debris. Albert's instincts, as it turned out, had been correct: The southwest corner would have been a death trap had the family stayed put. Strangely, though, in the opposite corner of the basement, two vases stood untouched on a stand. And odd curios littered the wreckage — a stereo cabinet containing a packet of lunch meat, a dinner fork stabbed into a board, a sealed soft drink bottle with only an inch or so of fluid left in it.

— • —

Aside from tiny fibers of insulation embedded in their skin, attorney Jim Ward, his wife, Carolyn, and their two children were unhurt. The family walked out of the basement of the unfinished home on Atwood Street. The house was badly damaged. The north wall and roof of the garage were gone. The family's Nash was still parked inside but covered with a thick layer of mud and sand.

Carolyn stared out to the west and north.

"My God, Jim."

Below, the shallow valley between Atwood and Burnett's Mound was impossibly wrecked. It looked to Jim like a scene from World War II. Cars were upside down, scattered and piled in heaps in the parking lots of the Embassy Apartments. Tons of debris lay in long, irregular windrows, recklessly gathered by the great spinning machine. The brown trail of devastation swept up the ridge to the top of the hill, as far as the Wards could see to the north. Silence lay like a thick blanket across the ruin.

*Everyone in Topeka is dead,* Carolyn thought. *Thousands of people are dead.*

What else could you think?

Suddenly, a car roared down the hill and screeched to a halt in front of the house. A teenager — shirtless, his eyes blazing with panic and his face covered with shaving cream — stuck his head out the window and shouted urgently, "What happened? Are you all right?"

—  •  —

Junior high schoolteacher Ron Olson came upstairs to find the roof and most of the second floor of his home gone. A two-by-ten floor joist was sticking through the west wall of an upstairs bedroom like an arrow. He stepped outside and saw that the detached garage was gone. He immediately thought of Beowulf, the family's Doberman. There'd been no time to get the dog to shelter. But just then the dog came trotting up, muddy and dazed but apparently okay. Olson looked down the shattered street. No color was visible. Even the blades of grass were gone. Only black and brown stood out in sharp contrast to the blue sky above. Olson's own front yard bristled with dozens of boards driven like porcupine quills deep into the ground. His wife, Linda, made her way up from the basement and somehow managed to find a clean diaper for six-week-old Tawnia. She gasped when she opened the old one. The wind had infiltrated the diaper and filled it with tiny shards of glass and insulation. Tawnia had a few cuts and scratches, but she wasn't badly hurt. Neither was anyone else in the home. The cars were destroyed. Soon a friend made his way up the wrecked street and Olson loaded the family into the car. They would escape to Burlington. He would stay to stand watch over what was left of their home.

—  •  —

Grace and John Steuri opened the pantry door in the first-floor apartment on 29th Street and saw blue sky. It appeared as if the apartment building had been bombed. They picked their way out through the rubble. Everyone in the closet was okay, although Grace's inner ear evidently had been damaged by the roar or the pressure drop because she was having trouble keeping her balance. They looked back toward the mound. Tiny fountains had sprouted from the broken water lines in many of the destroyed homes. The air was pungent with natural gas. Across the street, a Volkswagen Beetle was balled up and lodged in the crotch of a tree.

— • —

John Griebat had waited for death beneath the Shunganunga Creek Bridge. It wasn't until the roar began to fade that he realized he and his family just might get out with their lives. When the ordeal was over, John, Sherry and their daughter, Julie, and the other couple stood around for a moment. No one said anything. Finally the man suggested that the Griebats come to their house nearby.

"You go, Sherry. I've got to check on Peg and Paul."

The group helped one another up the steep, muddy bank. Then John took off running south. It was immediately clear that the area ahead had been entirely wrecked. The adrenaline was pumping as John quickened his pace. He ran out of his slippers somewhere on Gage, and then he was barefoot, dodging the glass, shards of metal and boards bristling with nails. Hot power lines were down at 29th and Gage, and he leapt them without breaking stride.

He had just one thought in his mind: *Get up to that house. See if Peg and Paul are okay.*

He reached Atwood, a block up from the base of the 29th Street hill, and then turned south. The devastation was even more complete there. Everything was flattened. Griebat looked ahead to where his sister's house should have been. But he could see only rubble. He counted back the blocks from 29th to make sure he had the right corner. Then he pulled up panting and slowly walked toward the site. He got closer and stopped, afraid of what he was about to see. He could recognize familiar items in the wrecked basement. But there was not a soul around. In fact, he hadn't seen another human being since he'd left the bridge. It was as if everyone had been killed. The realization began to sink in that Peg and Paul probably were dead, too.

And then . . .

"John? Is that you?"

Griebat looked up. It was his sister, Peg, walking up the street toward him. Paul was with her. She still had on the brightly colored, floral-patterned dress she'd planned to wear to the wedding shower that night. But it was stained and muddy. Her finger had been badly cut, and they'd gone up the street in search of a bandage. Peg's hair was wild and she didn't have any shoes. Paul appeared unhurt but likewise was covered with mud. His crew cut and scalp were oddly speckled with dozens of tiny dots of tar, almost like a tattoo, probably from the many asphalt and gravel roofs in the neighborhood.

A wide grin spread across John's face as he ran toward them. He swept Peg up in one arm and Paul in the other and lifted them straight off the ground. And then he squeezed them both so tightly that Paul thought John liked to nearly kill them.

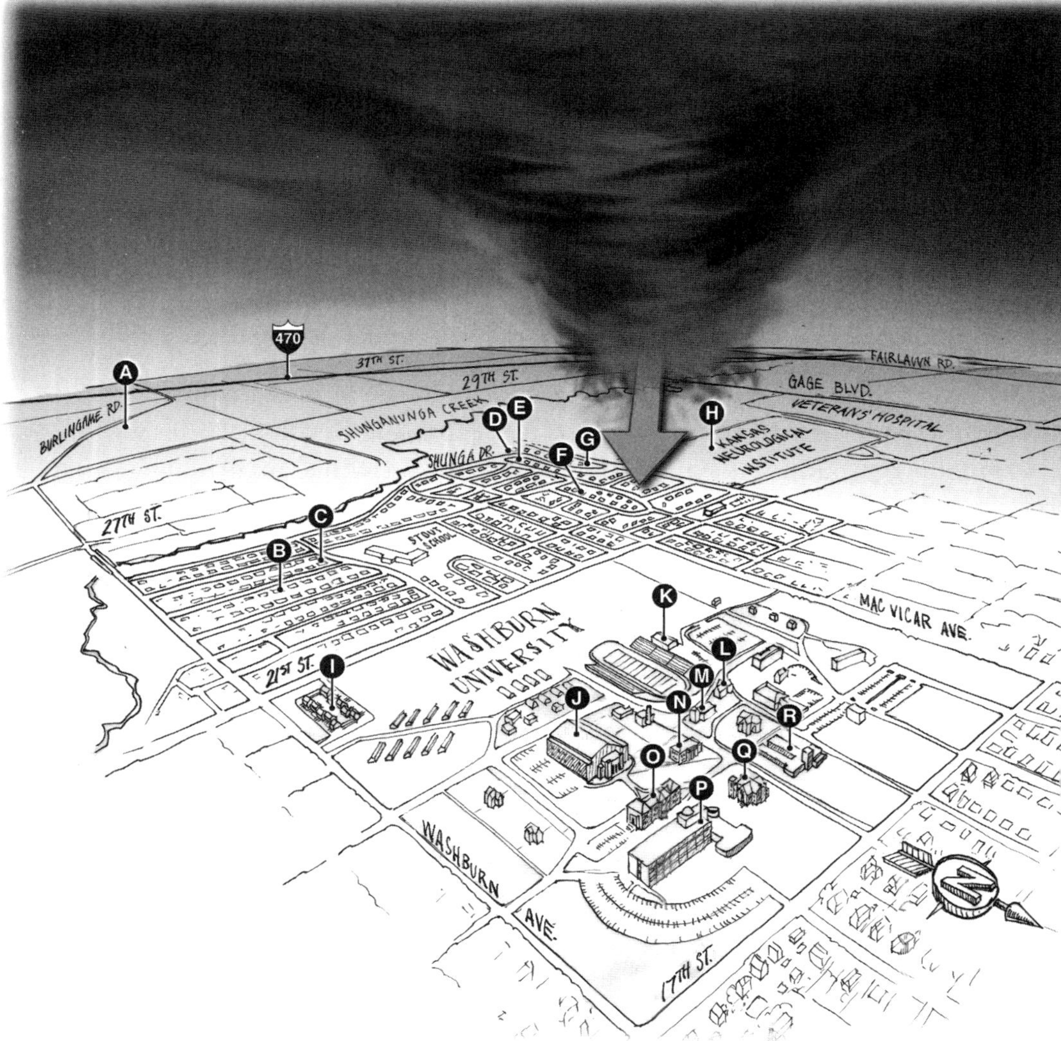



## 2 Shunga Park / Washburn University

A – Riddle, *Countryside Methodist Church*

B – Breuninger, *SW 23rd St. Park*

C – Fernstrom, *College Ave.*

D – Scheibe, *Shunga Dr.*

E – McDiffett, *Shunga Dr.*

F – Warfel, *Wayne Ave.*

G – Martin (Cleve, Hazel & Carol), *Randolph Ave.*

H – Torrence (Mary), *Kansas Neurological Institute*

I – Martin (John & Elaine), *Washburn married student housing*

J – Whiting Fieldhouse

K – ROTC Building

L – Crane Observatory

M – Thomas Women's Gymnasium

N – Fernstrom, Taylor (Leon), Summerville, *Carnegie Hall*

O – Rice Hall

P – Martin (John & Elaine), *Stoffer Science Hall*

Q – Hillebert, Snyder, Tarnower, Drayer, *MacVicar Chapel, Recital*

R – Hutton, *Morgan Hall*

# CHAPTER NINE

# A Recital Interrupted

"My gosh, Ruth! Look at the sky!"

Twenty-nine-year-old John Fernstrom gazed up as he stepped out the door of his home near Washburn University at about 10 minutes before seven o'clock. The sirens had not yet sounded. The sky was mustard-green and swollen with the grotesque bulges of mammatus clouds, hundreds of pendulous sacks that rolled off to the southwest like an enormous field of boulders. The clouds, though harmless, indicate heavy turbulence in the atmosphere and often precede severe thunderstorms. Short of a tornado, mammatus are among the most apocalyptic cloud formations Mother Nature can invoke.

Fernstrom and his wife stared up in silence.

Finally, John said, "I doubt we'll ever see another sky like this," and Ruth agreed. "I just hope it doesn't mean something bad is going to happen."

The couple climbed into their white '65 Buick Skylark and drove several blocks to the Washburn campus. John was a Washburn grad, a hail-fellow-well-met type and a rising star at the Kaw Valley State Bank in North Topeka. Tonight was the final exam in a continuing education course he'd been taking on the emerging role of computers in banking. Ruth was a social worker for Shawnee County. Conscientious and practical, she'd been swamped at work and decided to go back into the office to catch up.

The Skylark swung wide into a parking lot on the east side of the Washburn campus. John grabbed his raincoat, gave his wife a hurried kiss good-bye and strode briskly toward an imposing stone structure known as Carnegie Hall. The building housed Washburn's law school.

In 1966, Washburn University encompassed 13 major buildings and several dozen smaller ones on a 160-acre campus a quarter-mile square. The newer structures — Stoffer Science Hall, the Student Union and Morgan Hall (the library and administrative building) — all evoked the dreary, austere functionality of the Cold War era. But they didn't dominate the campus. Rather, it was a group of six older limestone buildings that gave Washburn its character and charm. The two- and three-story structures had gone up between 1874 and World War I, and each reflected the style and budget of its time. Some were plain and stern like the people who built them; others incorporated Romanesque and Classical Revival features, such as arches and columns. The buildings were not laid out on a quad or grid but instead were scattered around the north side of campus like huts in an ancient village.

The result could have been an aesthetic mishmash, given the architectural disparities and the absence of a master plan. But consistent use of the yellow limestone native to Kansas — hewed in large, rough blocks — unified the buildings and imbued the campus with a warm and graceful dignity. A pleasant network of walkways shaded by abundant pine, elm and pin oak completed the effect.

To 13-year-old Irma Hillebert, the university appeared almost enchanted that night. She'd arrived with her parents a little before 7:00 p.m. at MacVicar Chapel, the music building adjacent to Carnegie Hall. She was to play in a preparatory flute recital. Irma had been taking lessons through the spring from a Washburn music professor, Robert Snyder, and all of Snyder's students from across the city would be there tonight. Snyder's wife, Jackie, taught clarinet and bassoon, and her students would play in the recital as well. It was a major event. Irma wore a fine, blue organza dress, and her long, blond hair was done up in looping braids. She would perform a flute solo titled

"Sioux Serenade." The piece was not easy, and though she'd practiced for weeks, Irma had butterflies as the appointed hour drew near.

Still, she couldn't help but marvel at how incredibly vivid the campus appeared under the queer, ominous light of that fading day. It was almost as if she were seeing the world for the first time. The grass never looked greener or the trees more vibrant and alive or the old stone buildings more majestic. MacVicar Chapel, built in 1880, featured a solemn stone archway on one end and a tall bell tower on the other. So handsome did the chapel and the other buildings appear that a person might just have thought — if given to such turns of mind — that the old, stone giants were taking a bow.

And it wasn't just the strange light that burned the moment into Irma's memory. Curious electricity seemed to hover in the air, so palpable you could almost touch it. Even the birds seemed affected. They were singing their hearts out — singing for all they were worth in the unnatural stillness of the dying afternoon.

"Look how beautiful the campus looks!" Irma exclaimed to her mother. "I've never seen it like this!"

Thunder growled in the distance.

—  •  —

Elaine Martin baked two chickens, one for dinner and one to cut up for lunch for the rest of the week. The 23-year-old was six months' pregnant and living with her husband, John, in a nondescript, one-story duplex in the student housing area on the southeast corner of campus. Elaine worked part-time as an administrative assistant. John worked full-time as a manufacturer's sales rep. But he had still managed to knock down 12 credit hours at Washburn through the spring semester. The Martins were outgoing and optimistic people. And Elaine was so beautiful, she might have been a movie star. She had long, dark hair and a smile that would nearly blind you.

The couple was finishing dinner when the sirens wailed. Almost immediately, fat, solitary raindrops began hitting the driveway like water balloons. The mustard sky grew dark. The young woman with a newborn who lived next door, whose husband worked nights, came over and asked the Martins if they could give her a lift to Stoffer Science Hall, the designated storm shelter for residents of student housing. Absolutely, the Martins said. The group piled into John's sand-colored '66 VW Beetle and drove across campus in the pelting rain.

— • —

On the second floor of Carnegie Hall, John Fernstrom and about 20 others were just putting pencil to paper to begin the computer banking test when the sirens cranked to life. People looked up from their tests and glanced at each other. The teacher, a local banker, took measure of the moment and said: "Well, do you want to go to the basement or finish the test? It's up to you." There was a brief discussion and a consensus emerged. They'd finish the test.

In nearby MacVicar Chapel, 40 family members and friends quietly filed into the chapel's plain wooden pews for the music recital. Snyder handed out programs, and the 13 performers, aged 10 to 17, took their seats near the front. The room grew hushed as the first clarinet soloist, Jean Tarnower, screwed up her courage and stepped onto the broad stage. She was about to begin her selection, a tune titled "Dorothy's Dance" (to piano accompaniment), when the sirens started.

Snyder didn't hesitate. He quickly stood up and addressed the group.

"I think we should all move to the basement," he said. "We can wait for the all clear or maybe continue the recital down there."

Snyder was in his 40s, of average build, with thinning, black hair and the fine, well-groomed hands of a musician. He wore thick-framed glasses, a white dress shirt and a narrow tie. He was a fair but demanding teacher and well known in Topeka. If you hadn't practiced, he knew, and he'd let you know he knew. His sometimes abrupt manner could be intimidating to younger people. But like his wife, a willowy, soft-spoken woman, he cared deeply for his students. Both Snyder and his wife were gifted musicians.

Conventional wisdom in 1966 held that the southwest corner of any building was the safest spot to ride out a tornado. The notion seemed somewhat counterintuitive, given that most tornadoes approach from that direction. But the thinking was that if a building was hit, the wind would blow the debris up and away from the corner of impact and deposit it on the far side of the structure. Snyder and nearly everyone else who had spent any time in Kansas knew this, thanks to the Weather Bureau's Richard Garrett and the preparedness mantra he'd so relentlessly drilled into the population.

Snyder led the way down to a classroom in the basement's southwest corner. But as people filed in, Snyder played a quick scale on the classroom's piano and realized that it was badly out of tune. This simply would not do. He apologized and led the group to a second classroom across the hall. Unfortunately, the piano there also was out of tune. Snyder then suggested that perhaps they could move chairs into his practice studio and continue the recital there. The studio was in the southeast corner of the basement and was smaller than the classrooms. But Snyder's piano was serviceable and the surroundings were familiar to the student performers. Fathers and brothers made quick work of scooting enough wood-and-metal desk chairs into the room to accommodate the group. It was a tight fit, so some of the men and boys stood near the back.

The chapel's basement was actually a half-basement, and above the waist-high foundation, tall windows extended nearly to the ceiling. The group settled in and only the steady drum of rain could be heard as Jean Tarnower stepped up to play the first notes of "Dorothy's Dance."

—  •  —

Chris Hutton was restless, marking time in the backseat of his dad's Corvair. His father was behind the wheel, and Craig, his older brother, was in the passenger seat. The little compact was parked in front of Morgan Hall, Washburn's administrative building, which was across the street from MacVicar Chapel. They'd come to fetch Craig's car. Craig had been at Washburn earlier in the day to enroll in summer school. But his old '55 had a bad battery and wouldn't start when the time came to leave. So he'd caught a ride home, and after dinner, Bill and the boys had come back to retrieve the Chevy. Right now, though, it was raining so hard, you couldn't see 10 feet. So they sat tight.

Bill Hutton was a piece of work. A lean, muscular man with light brown hair and green eyes, he ran Hutton Monuments with his brother, Clint. They'd taken over the business after the war from their father, a stonecutter who had started the gravestone company around the turn of the century. Clint had fought as an infantryman in the Pacific, Bill as an artilleryman in Europe. Bill nearly froze in the Battle of the Bulge and he'd fought his way across Germany. He never talked about the war but instead seemed to channel all his energy into work. He was relentless: chain-smoking Camels, drinking black coffee all day and seemingly doing the work of five men. If there was one clue that perhaps revealed the toll the war had taken, it was his language, for Bill just cussed all the time, with everyone, matter-of-factly and in ordinary conversation, as in, "Pass the goddamn mashed potatoes, please." Or "What in the name of Christ are those kids doin'?" He was not a wicked man and there was seldom malice in his words. That's just the way he'd talked during the war and that's how he talked when he got home. Naturally, his wife was horrified, and eventually she was able to get Bill to clean it up a bit. But foul language or not, Bill Hutton was an uncommonly dedicated and loving father.

Chris, his youngest son, was an extrovert, a class cutup popular with the girls. He'd graduated from Seaman High School in North Topeka a week or so earlier. In high school, he lived for sports, rolling through the seasons from baseball to football to basketball to track. He was a big kid and a budding entrepreneur: He had opened a coin shop in high school and was making money buying and selling rare coins. He planned to attend Washburn in the fall. But as far as what he wanted to do with his life, he had no clue.

His older brother, on the other hand, knew exactly where he was going and what it would take to get there. The more studious of the two, Craig had just graduated from Baker University in Baldwin, Kansas, and intended to enroll in law school in the fall.

Driving in from North Topeka, the Huttons didn't hear the sirens. In fact, they were unaware that a tornado watch had been issued earlier in the day. As far as they knew, this was just another Kansas thunderstorm. A good one, but it would soon pass.

And sure enough, the rain began to let up.

— • —

Leon Taylor, on campus for a law review class, was standing with a group of others outside Carnegie Hall. The bar exam was a couple of weeks away and Taylor, 27, was determined to nail it the first time. But the review session was quickly proving to be something of a bust. So when a student came in and said a tornado had been spotted southwest of town, Taylor and a few others slipped outside to take a look.

It was just sprinkling now. The clouds were beginning to break.

And he could see it.

Taylor watched as the tornado pushed in from the southwest, heading for Burnett's Mound and then rising to climb the hill. From a distance of several miles, the broad, dark wedge seemed to move ponderously but relentlessly forward. He was mesmerized.

*This is appalling. This cannot be real.*

But it was, and very soon, the tornado had crossed the mound and was smashing the subdivisions north and east of the hill. At one point, something combustible — perhaps a propane or gasoline tank — ripped loose and was ignited in the twister. For a brief instant, a dazzling, orange fireball lit up the funnel's gray-black core. Taylor heard a muffled explosion.

The tornado slipped down a steep, wooded bluff from the top of the 29th Street hill after wrecking the neighborhoods on the ridge northeast of Burnett's Mound. Then it crossed the meandering Shunganunga Creek 400 yards east of the bridge where John Griebat had sought shelter with his family. From there, it moved into the vast, open park grounds south of veterans administration hospital.

A half mile ahead lay the Kansas Neurological Institute. KNI was home to more than 200 severely retarded children and young adults from across Kansas. Many of the patients, aged seven to 20, barely functioned at an infant level. They were warehoused — there was no other word for it — in dozens of barrack-like buildings lined up across the sprawling campus. The compound originally had been built as a temporary military hospital during the war but was later acquired by the state to house the infirm. None of the flimsy, wooden wards had basements.

Mary Torrence, an 18-year-old aide, scrambled with a co-worker when the sirens went off to move the 25 kids on her ward — all of them boys, all of them developmentally disabled, all of them blind — into the building's central laundry room. This was institute policy. The aides were then supposed to drag mattresses in and cover the children. But Mary's co-worker was pregnant, and Mary, just three days on the job, wasn't big enough to move the mattresses alone. So the two women began yanking blankets, pillows and sheets off the laundry room shelves and piling them atop the frightened, bellowing boys.

It was all they could do.

Fortunately, the tornado had narrowed slightly by the time it crossed the Shunganunga Creek and was closer to one-third of a mile wide as it moved in toward KNI. Call it luck, fate or divine intervention, but the result was that the monster just winged the institution, wrecking portions of the physical plant and several storage buildings on the compound's southeast corner but missing entirely the wards and their vulnerable inhabitants therein.

The people living directly east of KNI were not so fortunate. Carol Martin — the 16-year-old who'd just gotten her driver's license, the one who so loved the Beatles and who was heading for the choir contest in Hutchinson, Kansas, the next day — lived with her parents on Randolph Avenue. The Martins' house was on the edge of a subdivision of small, basement-less homes that had gone up after the Korean War. Across the street to the west were the rolling fields of Big Shunga Park.

Carol had left at around 6:30 p.m. for singing group practice downtown. Her parents, Cleve and Hazel, were at home, and Cleve had a clear view of the tornado as it rumbled straight for them across open ground. He called to his wife. But Hazel was haunted by schizophrenia. She didn't fully grasp what was happening and at first refused to get into the crawl space.

And then she demanded to know: "What on Earth is that train doing so close to our house?!"

Cleve pulled Hazel into the blackness and held her tightly as the roar grew louder. He braced for impact.

—  •  —

A friend of Carol's, Patti McDiffett, lived one street over. After the sirens went off, the 15-year-old was glued to the TV with her mother, Norma, tracking the storm. Her father, Pat, went outside to watch the sky. But he came back in pretty quick. "I can hear it coming," Mr. McDiffett said. The family debated for a moment, then decided to get into the crawl space. Patti grabbed Mitzi, her Chihuahua. Then the group went down through a trapdoor and crawled beneath the floor joists in the darkness across the dirt, to the home's southwest corner. A vent on the west side of the foundation offered a parcel of light, and Mr. McDiffett was able to peer through the small opening to the west. He watched and waited. A few minutes passed. Then he said, "My God, I can see it. It's coming."

Patti started to scream. She and her parents embraced and pushed up hard against the foundation. The distant rumble grew steadily louder and then it was on them. It was thunderous. Patti's ears and head were exploding as mud, sand and debris blasted across the shadowy cave.

*Oh, God, we're about to die!*

Patti heard glass and wood shatter and crack and then huge ripping sounds as the house detached from the foundation and lifted off.

—  •  —

Nineteen-year-old Johnny Scheibe lived across the street with his mom and dad and little brother. He was a big, personable kid with brown hair: six feet four inches and 210 pounds. He had a learning disability but got through school and even set a school record for shot put at Boswell Junior High. He was good with his hands and loved to work with wood. For now, he was employed as a delivery driver for Westboro Cleaners.

This afternoon his mom and brother were at White Lakes Mall. Johnny was supposed to go out that night to shoot pool with a friend. But he'd called his buddy at the last minute to say he was too tired. He must have lain down to take a nap.

As it happened, John's father, Glen — a city building inspector — was working part-time as a bartender at the nearby Gage Tavern. From outside the bar, he could see the tornado come over the mound, and he knew right away that it was heading for the family's home. He went inside and frantically tried to call his son. But Johnny didn't pick up. Evidently, he didn't hear the phone.

Or the tornado, either, probably.

Until it was too late.

—  •  —

A few blocks to the north, 46-year-old Ruth Warfel, her husband, two daughters and a family friend had just finished dinner. The Warfels didn't put much stock in tornado warnings. You had them all the time in Kansas and they never seemed to amount to much. So they'd ignored the sirens. But Ruth just happened to glance out the window as she was putting dirty dishes in the sink.

Hell was coming, just a block away. To Ruth, the tornado looked like a giant, black, tumbling ball, spewing cars and trees and buckets and chairs. She screamed but the roar was around them and then the windows came crashing in. The wind grabbed a dining room chair and flung it like a boomerang, striking Mr. Warfel hard in the back. Everyone dove under the table as the roof pulled off.

John Fernstrom was trying to concentrate on his banking test. But he couldn't stay focused. Instead, he was straining to pick out an odd noise in the distance. It was a low, laboring mechanical sound, almost a grinding growl, seemingly far off. *What in the world could that be? A truck? A turbine at the power plant? A plane flying too low?* He couldn't place it. But the noise grew steadily louder as the minutes slipped past. Then Fernstrom began to hear other sounds beneath the rumble: hard, violent, crunching noises, like wood breaking and snapping. Still distant, but closer now.

When John was a boy, his father had never been one to take tornadoes lightly. In fact, he'd been something of a fanatic about getting the family to the basement when severe weather threatened. But family members were considerably less concerned about the danger, and frequently they'd ignore his pleas to come to the cellar. Afterward, John's father would fume. More than once, he'd say: "I know what's going to happen! Someday the paper is going to have a big headline that reads: 'Father Survives; Family Wiped Out!'"

Maybe it was his father's vigilance smoldering in John's memory. Or the awful beauty of the sky that evening. Or the cavalier decision to ignore the sirens. But all of a sudden, Fernstrom knew exactly what he was hearing.

He jumped up and yelled out across the quiet classroom.

"Something terrible is coming! We need to get out of here! We've got to get to the basement right now!"

There was no debate this time. It was as if people were waiting for someone, anyone to act. The students leapt from their desks as one, and 20 or so people raced for the hallway and bolted down the wide stairs two and three abreast, feet flying, catching the steps in swift, tumbling strides. There were screams and piercing shrieks. A couple of people were moving so fast when they reached the bottom that they lost their footing and flew headlong into the girls' restroom. The scene might have been comical under different circumstances. But no one was laughing now.

—  •  —

Ward Summerville, a 27-year-old part-time librarian in the law library, briefly stepped outside after the sirens wailed and, with Leon Taylor and a handful of others, saw the tornado coming over the mound. He raced back inside and told his wife (who'd been keeping him company) to head for the basement. He made sure the library was cleared out and then headed upstairs. One classroom was still occupied, full of undergraduate students taking a test. Taylor burst into the room.

"There's a tornado coming!" he said. "Everybody needs to get out of here!"

The instructor demurred.

"We have a test to finish here," he said.

"There isn't any time!" Summerville said. He turned and spoke directly to the students. "Get out of here right now! Go to the basement as fast as you can!"

The students complied.

—  •  —

Leon Taylor, the law review student who had been standing outside Carnegie Hall — the one who'd seen the explosion inside the twister — had continued watching with a half a dozen others as the tornado moved diagonally into the city. There was some conversation. The observers were convinced that the twister's course would take it west of Washburn. It would miss them. Taylor was spellbound. He could see roofs and trees swirling in the funnel. The roar, punctuated by loud crashing bangs, moved ahead of the twister like an enormous wave. Soon Taylor noticed leaves and papers fluttering gently above him in a stirring wind. The outer bands of circulation were approaching.

And then, suddenly, there were cries and oaths. The tornado appeared to be turning.

Someone shouted, "It's heading right for us!"

Still Taylor stood his ground, locked in rapt, frozen amazement. Now bigger pieces of debris were floating overhead and the swirling winds grew thicker and darker. He looked around but there was no one else. All others had fled. He turned and ran for the building as the sky seemed to collapse around him.

*This is really stupid of me. I've probably gone and gotten myself killed.*

—  •  —

The rumbling was growing more intense as John Fernstrom and some others in the basement of Carnegie Hall ran to a classroom in the building's southwest corner and looked out. Thomas Women's Gymnasium, one of the old stone giants, built in 1911, was just across the street. Fernstrom watched as the building's massive, red tile roof lifted off — more or less intact — and wavered for a moment like a magic carpet before atomizing in the howling gale. A car flew past seconds later, tumbling and bouncing like an errant football.

There were guttural screams and the prickly, draining sensation of imminent death filled the room. People instinctively retreated toward the building's interior hallway and went to the ground.

—  •  —

The rain had slowed to a light sprinkle as Bill Hutton and his sons — still unaware of the approaching tornado — prepared to get out of their car to jump-start Craig's '55 Chevy. But then they saw something odd to the southwest. Three hundred yards away, beyond the football stadium, an explosion ripped the single-story, wood-frame ROTC building literally off its foundation. Pieces of the building shot upward in an enormous plume of debris. The wooden structure was gone.

"Damn, the ROTC building just blew up!" Craig said. He was sitting in the passenger seat beside his father. He had the best view of it.

"Jesus Christ! It did!" Bill said. For a moment, all three thought that perhaps there'd been a gas explosion. But Craig quickly realized what they were seeing.

"Dad! That's a tornado!"

A long pause followed as the words sunk in.

Then Craig said, "We need to get out of here!"

But his father wasn't so sure. "Maybe we ought to just stay in the car."

Objects were beginning to fly past and a few thumped into the Corvair.

"No, Dad! We need to get out of this car right now. Let's get out. We'll head up to Morgan Hall. We can get inside."

Bill didn't argue.

"Okay. Let's go!"

The doors flew open. The youngest son, Chris, pushed the passenger seat forward and pulled himself out of the cramped backseat. He stood up, and for a moment, the 17-year-old stared straight into the heart of the abyss, not 200 yards away and closing fast. It didn't look like a tornado: just a towering black wall, a tidal wave, so wide Chris couldn't see the edges, and so tall that he couldn't see the top. It was filled with cars and trees and lumber and roofs.

It was death.

The three men sprinted for the main entrance of Morgan Hall and were leaping up the building's wide concrete steps when the double-glass doors blew out in a hail of glass. The blast knocked them backward and hard to the ground. Miraculously, the shards didn't cause serious injury. But other objects were striking the men now and after just 30 seconds in the wind, already they were covered with mud from head to toe. The noise had become a crushing, crackling roar, like a jet fighter with full afterburners on.

Bill tried to scream above the din. He motioned toward the concrete landing in front of the door.

"Get down beside the door! BY THE LANDING!"

The group ran low to the corner where the three-foot-high landing met the building and crouched down in a tight huddle, bracing and interlocking their arms in an attempt to cover their heads.

"HOLD ON! HOLD ON AS TIGHT AS YOU CAN!"

Missiles were flying into them: boards, shingles, sticks, everything. From the huddle, Chris could see his brother's back beneath his own arm and he watched a brick slam into Craig like a slug from a .44 Magnum. Craig convulsed from the impact but didn't let go.

If he screamed, Chris never heard it.

In the basement of MacVicar Chapel, Jean Tarnower had finished "Dorothy's Dance," and the second recital performer, Ralph Drayer, was halfway through his bassoon solo when Irma Hillebert turned to the window. She could see dozens of small, pink puffs drifting by like cherry blossoms floating on a gentle breeze. Except they weren't flowers. They were pieces of insulation. Irma's father, Roy Hillebert, was standing at the back of the room near a window. He saw nearby Carnegie Hall begin to come apart as giant stones were ripped loose and lifted like feathers into the wind.

"Here it comes! Everybody get down!"

The power failed and darkness descended. Outside the windows, all was inky, black-green like the bottom of the sea, as swirling dirt and gravel sprayed and hissed against the glass. Objects of unknown origin were speeding past. Kids and parents dove under the small desks. A group that included Irma, the music instructor and his wife crawled under the nine-foot grand piano. Irma's father was still near the window and Irma's mother and another woman grabbed Roy's legs, as much for support as to keep him from being sucked away. The glass crashed and the wind hurtled desk chairs furiously against the interior wall. The roaring force was all-powerful now, spraying plaster dust, pebbles, mud and sand through the room and sandblasting any exposed skin. Seventy-five-pound chunks of limestone were tumbling three stories down to the window wells and bouncing randomly into the room or out into the grass. A couple dashed out of the studio just before the ceiling in the hallway collapsed. At that point, the howling winds suddenly reversed direction, and, according to Snyder, "blew straight west in a crescendo of torments beyond comprehension or narration."

Snyder felt as though his head was exploding.

— • —

Leon Taylor, the one who'd lingered too long outside, just made it to the basement of the law building, Carnegie Hall, when the tornado struck. The main corridor was lined with people, maybe 50 or more, huddled on the tile floor with their backs to the wall, heads covered, some praying, some crying. Taylor was late. There was no room for him.

Outside, the ravenous wind burrowed and clawed and ripped at the old building like a wolf hungry for the prize inside. Glass panes were exploding all over the building and enormous bangs were coming from above. Taylor sprinted past a soft drink vending machine just before the heavy box fell to the floor behind him. He saw a coatrack attached to the wall and reached out to grab it. Then he lowered his head and closed his eyes.

To Ward Summerville, the law librarian, the roar of the twister sounded like thrust reversers deployed on a jet aircraft. It became very, very hot as the tornado drew near.

John Fernstrom hunched on the floor. The noise was overwhelming: He was drowning at the bottom of a sea of sound and the pain was excruciating. People screamed silently and covered their ears. Finally, the wind gained the entry it had so relentlessly sought and the full fury of the storm was upon them, blasting through the corridor in a blizzard of debris. Strangers hugged one another to keep from being carried off. Fernstrom glanced up and saw huge limbs from an Osage orange tree, rocketing horizontally down the hall like guided missiles, just overhead.

*This building is coming down. I'm going to die and a lot of others are going to die. Right now. At Washburn University. Over a silly computer test. I could have never imagined this . . . Not in a million years.*

*I should have done a better job of saying good-bye to Ruth.*

— • —

John and Elaine Martin scrambled with their neighbor and her baby into a small custodian's room in the basement of Stoffer Science Hall. The room was packed. Pretty quickly, two young men who had been standing watch at the front door dashed down the stairs, shouting, "Here it comes!" John and Elaine hugged each other tightly, sitting on the floor, hunched over, their backs to the wall. Next they heard an enormous whooshing sound that rose steadily in pitch and intensity. Then came huge concussive crashes and bangs, like a foundry or factory at full production. Except these were not the sounds of things being built.

— • —

Four blocks south of the Washburn campus, in a small, cracker-box ranch house with no basement, Sue Breuninger waited and listened. Earlier in the day, after the sun had finally burned through, the 26-year-old housewife had taken her two children to the pool. They had enjoyed the water and didn't mind coming home when the clouds rolled in. But Sue didn't know about the tornado watch. And she never heard the sirens. Her husband was playing golf. She was making dinner in her small kitchen as six-year-old Larry Jr. and three-year-old Jill watched TV. The telephone rang.

It was her mother-in-law. Her voice was agitated and insistent.

"You need to get those children to safety right now! This tornado is coming and it's real. Get them out of there right now!"

Sue glanced at her kids, still watching TV. Bill Kurtis was on the screen, urging viewers to take cover. She looked out the sliding-glass porch door. A piece of lawn furniture shot past.

*It's too dangerous to take them out in this wind . . . Too late to go to the neighbor's basement.*

Fear began to rise in her.

"Okay, kids, we're going to play a game. We're going to sit in the closet and eat our dinner. Doesn't that sound like fun?"

Sue sat the kids down in a narrow bedroom closet behind a flimsy sliding door and brought them their plates. She recalled that you're supposed to open windows to equalize the pressure if a tornado is approaching. So she cranked open the bedroom window and then went to the kitchen and opened the window there before returning to sit outside the closet with the door partially open. There wasn't enough room inside for her.

All the while, her mind was ravished by guilt.

*How could I have been so stupid and not paid more attention to the weather? What was I thinking? Now look what I've done . . . My children's lives are in danger.*

Time inched ahead. Then Sue heard something.

*A train? Why am I hearing a train when there aren't any tracks around here? It must be a plane flying low. But who would be crazy enough to fly in this weather?*

She got up and went to the kitchen window. The wind was howling outside, and the screen was bowed out from the suction as far as it could go. The curtain was plastered tight against it. Sue peeled the curtain back and looked north into a chaotic, gray-black miasma filled with flying debris. It was the ugliest sight she'd ever seen. The world had become monochromatic: The only color visible was the red-and-white playhouse Sue's father had built for the kids in the corner of the backyard. It stood out incongruously against the hideous, churning atmosphere. Trees were twisting sideways in the wind.

A toxic mix of terror and guilt rose like bile inside her. She fought to contain the emotions, but she was losing ground and could barely resist the urge to simply start screaming. When Sue returned to the closet, three-year-old Jill stared up at her. The child was silent. But the abject fear in her wide, blue eyes betrayed her own grim take on the situation.

Sue was fighting tears as she knelt by the door.

*I can't lose it. I've got to be strong for these kids.*

And so, although not a particularly religious person, she began to pray:

*Take me if you want, Lord. But please don't hurt these children.*

And just like that, she felt a warm hand on her shoulder. She startled and turned. Who was there? Had her husband slipped in unnoticed? But there was no one. And then — immediately and completely — all the fear and anguish that had roiled her fell away, and in their place, a sense of peace and certainty emerged, the likes of which she hadn't known before — nor since. The beauty of the moment was indescribable and she instantly knew they would be all right.

Sue leaned forward and spoke gently but directly to the children. "It's okay, kids. You're going to feel the house shake a little and the ground is going to rumble, and then you'll feel it move away to the neighbor's house. But we're going to be okay. We'll be just fine."

And sure enough, the house shook and the ground rumbled.

And then it was over.

# CHAPTER TEN

# "It Looks Like Berlin"

The thunderous roar that left such an indelible mark on so many Topekans on June 8, 1966, was shaped by many forces. Tornadic sound emanates from the swirling, high-speed updraft, from the violent expansion and contraction, or bursting, of the funnel's core and from the wind's interaction with fixed objects it encounters. High-speed eddies and mini-vortices curl around wires and spin off the edges of buildings to create howling, musical sounds known as aeolian tones. The friction of the wind against the Earth at the base of the funnel contributes a deep, vacuumlike growl. Throw in the sound of breaking glass, power lines shorting out, transformers exploding, buildings being ripped from their foundations, and automobiles, air conditioners and other large objects being hurled to the ground at terminal velocity, and you have a cacophony that defies description. What's more, because a tornado is hollow, it essentially functions like a giant amplifying device, akin to a massive speaker or pipe organ. Like an organ, the bigger the pipe, the deeper and louder the sound.

Given the array of forces at work, it is not surprising that the sounds generated by a tornado moving through a residential area are considerably worse than those made by a twister spinning across open country.

"A tornado is louder, more terrifying and more thunderous when it's going through a neighborhood, unfortunately," said Tim

Samaras, a veteran storm chaser, engineer and pioneering builder of probes designed to measure atmospheric conditions within a tornado. "You've got a whole lot more things happening in an urban environment. They're happening simultaneously and they're all producing sound. The result is that every second it's going to sound like an incredible, thunderous, rolling roar."

Just how loud tornadoes can get isn't entirely clear. One of the few attempts to analyze tornadic sound was done by a team of acoustical experts in the Department of Physics at the University of Mississippi in the mid-1970s. Scientists Roy Arnold, Henry Bass and Lee Bolen obtained a recording of an EF-5 that struck Guin, Alabama, during the tornadic super-outbreak of April 3–4, 1974. A quick-thinking Guin resident, Richard Allen Lindley, had placed a Panasonic cassette recorder on a table and a microphone in the metal frame of an open, second-floor window as the EF-5 approached. Lindley's tape lasts 10 minutes. The tornado comes to within 300 yards of the microphone before gradually moving away.

From the tape, the scientists speculated that the rising and falling amplitude of the sound (i.e., the laboring, mechanical lope that John Fernstrom and others heard so clearly on June 8) may be caused by the movement of smaller tornadoes, or suction vortices, as they circle within and around the base of the main funnel.

The physicists estimated the peak volume of the Guin tornado at 103 decibels. That's roughly equivalent to a chain saw running at full throttle. But Dr. Henry Bass, one of the Mississippi scientists, acknowledged that the measurement was merely an educated guess. Because the cassette recorder was equipped with automatic volume control, it was impossible to accurately calibrate and quantify the sound from the recording. The 103-decibel peak consequently was extrapolated primarily from the recollections of Lindley and his family about the difficulty they had communicating verbally, even by screaming, as the tornado reached its closest point.

A tornado's maximum volume, according to Bass, could be as high as 140 decibels, or the equivalent of a jet engine at full power. At this level, physical damage to the eardrums begins. The excruciating pain and hearing problems experienced by many Topekans during and after the tornado likely were due to a combination of the sound's intensity and the enormous atmospheric pressure drop associated with the vortex.

Regardless of a tornado's precise volume level, there's little doubt that tornadic storms are among the loudest naturally occurring phenomena on the planet. An especially close and violent clap of thunder or a meteor cracking the atmosphere may be louder for a brief instant. But only a volcanic eruption and perhaps an avalanche can rival a tornado as a sustained noise event.

For all a tornado's sonic fury, perhaps the most intriguing aspect of tornadic sound is the noises funnels make that cannot be heard. Tornadoes are enormous generators of infrasound, or vibrations that occur beneath the threshold of human hearing. Human ears can detect sound waves, or oscillating changes in pressure, at frequencies ranging from 20 hertz to 20,000 hertz. Everything below 20 hertz (a hertz being one cycle per second) is considered infrasound and escapes us entirely, although infrasound can be felt at certain frequencies: The thumping chest pressure produced by a powerful subwoofer is an example.

While the study of infrasound is relatively new and much remains to be learned about its origins and characteristics, one fact is well established: Infrasound is capable of traveling enormous distances. Unlike higher-frequency sounds, which decay rapidly in the molasses-like viscosity of the atmosphere, infrasound vibrations remain intact far longer due to the larger size of the wave. As a result, it is not unusual for infrasound to travel hundreds and even thousands of miles from its source with very little attenuation, hurtling outward like a silent tsunami at the speed of sound, 758 miles per hour.

Dr. Alfred J. Bedard Jr., Infrasonics Group Leader at the National Oceanic and Atmospheric Administration's Earth System Research Laboratory in Boulder, Colorado, has studied tornadic infrasound since the mid-1980s. According to Bedard, tornadoes have a distinct infrasonic signature located between zero and five hertz on the sonic spectrum. To put that into perspective, one hertz is eight octaves below middle C, while A, the lowest audible frequency on a piano, is at about 27.5 hertz. Bedard has detected tornadic infrasound from up to 600 miles away and believes the vibrations have their origins in the tornado's macro-dynamics: The wobbling, toplike oscillation and continual compression and expansion of the funnel likely are responsible for producing the most significant bursts of infrasonic radiation.

Advances in the understanding of tornadic sound, both audible and inaudible, have had a practical impact on tornado safety. Bass and his colleagues at the University of Mississippi built on their pioneering work from the 1970s to eventually develop and commercialize a home warning system that alerts residents if the audible signature of a tornado is detected. Called the HomeSafe Tornado Detector, it was finally mass produced in the late 1990s, with the availability of powerful and inexpensive microprocessors. The HomeSafe detector uses an external sound sensor and an interior control unit to pick up the distinct signal (typically under 350 hertz) and rising volume of an approaching tornado. According to Bass, the device can reliably provide a 30-to-90-second warning of an imminent tornado impact.

On a broader scale, the unique characteristics of infrasound, particularly the ability to detect it from great distances, have opened up new possibilities for improving the accuracy of tornado warnings. According to Bedard, infrasound can help detect smaller tornadoes that may not appear on radar. It also can be used in tandem with radar to deliver greater precision in projecting tornado paths. And because infrasound generation sometimes precedes the formation of a funnel by up to 30 minutes, sensors can help improve warning lead times. In 2001, Bedard and his associates launched an infrasound pilot project that incorporated three tornado-detecting sensors deployed on the plains of eastern Colorado and western Kansas. Bedard said the results have been encouraging, and it is possible that infrasound eventually will play a key role in improving tornado warning systems nationwide.

Chris Hutton couldn't hear a thing. He was deaf from the roar. He was still hunkered down with his father and brother alongside the concrete landing in front of Washburn University's Morgan Hall. But the fury of the wind was dying and the barrage of debris had stopped. The 17-year-old cautiously lifted his head and looked back over his shoulder to the northeast. The tornado was moving away now, departing the campus and crossing the intersection of 17th Street and Washburn Avenue, 300 yards away. From behind, the twister looked much as it had from the front: not a funnel as such, but more like a massive, dirty, rolling waterfall, choked with debris. It moved sluggishly, almost as if in slow motion. And it was — at least to Chris — entirely silent.

Fortunately, his hearing quickly returned, and Chris was next aware of an enormous silence that had settled across campus. Then, suddenly, a large section of Carnegie Hall collapsed and the stones rumbled to Earth with a thundering crash. A cloud of fine, white dust boiled up from inside the wrecked shell of the building.

Bill Hutton stood up.

"My God . . . I can't believe we're not dead!" he said as he reached out and hugged his sons tightly. The three stood for a long moment. Bill knew about death, how unexpectedly and randomly it could arrive. He'd seen men killed in the war. He was sobbing.

*Dad is crying . . .* Chris was stunned by all that had taken place. Now there was this. He had never seen his father cry before.

The men looked around. Washburn was destroyed. The devastation could not have been more complete had the campus been shelled by artillery or bombed by waves of B-17s. In fact, it looked very much like something from the war, like some battered crossroads town where the Germans had tried to make a stand. Every one of the old stone buildings — Carnegie Hall, MacVicar Chapel, Rice Hall, Thomas Women's Gymnasium, Crane Observatory, Boswell Hall — all were gutted and shattered. Roofs were gone, walls collapsed, window and door frames wrecked. The old giants had put up a fight, though, and had given way only grudgingly before the wind. MacVicar Chapel's tower still stood, but the roof was gone and much of the second floor was caved into the basement. Likewise, most of the second floors of Carnegie Hall and Thomas Gymnasium were gone. Rice Hall, Washburn's oldest building, looked like a pile of pulverized quarry rock. Everywhere power lines, phone lines and trees were down. The trees that still stood were entirely denuded of leaves and all but the largest branches. Their skeletal silhouettes clawed toward the sky with bony fingers as if imploring the heavens for mercy.

The Huttons were cut and bleeding and covered with mud. Their hair was black and greasy and stood out ridiculously from the wind. They looked like cartoon characters, looked as though they'd been electrocuted. Bits of glass and wood and other shards of debris were embedded in both scalp and skin. Blood was flowing steadily from the wound in Craig's back. The three stepped through the shattered doors of Morgan Hall and into the women's restroom. Bill grabbed some paper towels and packed them tightly into the hole in his son's shoulder. Then they walked outside. A clean-cut young man approached from the ruins of Carnegie Hall. He anxiously asked if they were all right.

"No, not really," Bill said.

The student told them to walk toward 17th Street; he'd get his car and take them to the hospital. Moments later, the throaty rumble of a V-8 broke the silence as a burgundy-colored '64 GTO accelerated up the street and then screeched to a halt in front of the Huttons. The young man leaned over and popped open the passenger door.

"Get in."

Bill Hutton hesitated. The GTO was the first of Detroit's muscle cars, and the interior of this one was dazzling and immaculate: customized, rolled-and-pleated white vinyl. The Huttons, on the other hand, looked like survivors of the Bataan Death March.

"We can't. We're really going to mess up your interior," Bill said.

"Fuck the interior!" the kid shouted. "Fuck it! Come on, get in!"

So they did.

— • —

Patti McDiffett opened her eyes in the crawl space of her parents' home near the Shunga Creek. She was alive. Her parents were alive. Her dog was alive. The floor above her was gone. The house was gone. Blue sky and sunshine were all she could see. Everything was so still. She heard a bird sing. The McDiffetts climbed up and out and into the yard. They were covered with mud and tar. Their house had blown into some trees at the edge of the backyard and was wedged there still, semi-intact. Patti looked down at where the family had sought shelter. A silhouette of their huddled, human forms stood out in sharp relief against the whitish-gray concrete. Mud had been sprayed everywhere except where they'd been. It was a ghostly image, like something from Hiroshima or Pompeii.

Across the street, the Scheibe house was leveled, too. A 20-foot I beam had been lifted up, twisted like a corkscrew and then bent into the shape of a horseshoe before being dropped back down on the foundation. No sign of Johnny, the 19-year-old delivery driver for Westboro Cleaners. His father showed up a few minutes later and started ripping through the rubble in search of his son. He found him, alive but unconscious and badly cut up. Together with Mr. McDiffett and a couple of other men, Glen Scheibe managed to get Johnny onto a door. They carried him to a station wagon.

— • —

Banker John Fernstrom listened as the dreadful grinding grew more distant and finally ceased altogether. Utter and complete silence ensued. He was still hunched on the floor of the hallway in the basement of Carnegie Hall. He was covered with mud. He had splinters in his arms and face. He was cut and scraped. But he was alive. He looked up and was amazed to see, straight above him through what had been two floors of building, the bluest sky he'd ever seen. People were beginning to stir and stand. Several women were badly cut by broken glass, and they were in a near panic, screaming and sobbing and frantic to get out. Leon Taylor made his way up the stairs to the door with a crowd behind him. But power lines were down outside.

"Get back! Everybody get back! There are live wires all over the place out there!" Taylor said.

The group retreated back down the stairs as Fernstrom and some others picked their way toward a window on the east side of the basement. Someone took a chair and smashed out the remaining pieces of glass from one of the frames. Outside, they heard a crackling buzz. Fernstrom poked his head out and saw a live wire arcing and bouncing above the window.

"For God's sake, you guys, we just came through this all right. Let's don't go outside and get electrocuted!" he said. With jittery caution, one by one, the survivors climbed out of the ruined building, carefully avoiding the dancing wire. Fernstrom was appalled. He'd attended Washburn and knew its every nook and cranny. But as he looked around, he couldn't even recognize the place. The tall, brick smokestack at the nearby power plant was sheared off halfway up. Every building, as far as he could see, was either damaged or destroyed. The accoutrements of a once-vibrant university — books, papers, desks, chairs, typewriters — were scattered across open ground like the wreckage of a sunken ship. The sun was shining brightly.

*It looks like Berlin . . .*

What struck Fernstrom most, though, aside from the enormity of the destruction, were the smells: raw and pungent odors from trees splintered and stripped of their bark, like freshly cut lumber in a sawmill; the sweet, earthy stench of mud, pulverized bushes and leaves; and the must of long-hidden corners and dry wood from buildings many years enclosed. All asserted themselves with each panting breath.

Fernstrom rallied a dozen or so of the refugees from the banking test and slowly the group began to make their way through the wreckage. They would head for Fernstrom's home a few blocks south of campus. When they reached Washburn Avenue, they flagged down a passing car. But the man behind the wheel took one look at the group and shook his head. They were too dirty. He drove off.

So they trudged on.

—  •  —

Ward Summerville, the law librarian, came out a different window with his wife and some others. Eventually the couple made their way to their car, a Corvair parked near the football stadium. All the glass was blown out of the vehicle. As they contemplated whether to try to drive it, the Summervilles felt a deep rumble and watched in amazement as a two-story wall of nearby Crane Observatory collapsed with a roar and a cloud of dust. It had been a good 10 minutes since the tornado had passed.

—  •  —

Silence engulfed the recital group in the basement studio of MacVicar Chapel. Slowly, people began to stir and pull themselves to their feet. The room was smoky with plaster dust. Everyone was covered with what looked like fine, white flour. Irma Hillebert looked around for her mother and father and finally spotted them near a window. She couldn't hear a thing. She was deaf from the tornado, just like Chris Hutton. Her mind was blank.

Marjorie Cofran, mother of Tom Cofran, one of the would-be recital performers, saw a man pull himself up in the middle of the room. The man broke the silence by asking, in a high, plaintive voice: "Has anyone notified the authorities?" Cofran laughed then and laughs now at the absurdity of the moment. Of course no authorities had been notified; the tornado had just departed and no one had yet managed to get out of the room. And it wasn't like they had a telephone or two-way radio.

Parents began checking children for injuries. A physician, John Grimshaw, was attending the two individuals who appeared to be hurt the worst. Doris Tarnower, Jean's mom, had numerous shards of glass embedded in her legs and a cut on her forehead from the explosion of the transom over the door. And Ralph Drayer, the boy whose bassoon solo was cut short by the tornado's arrival, had a nasty slice above his ear and a bad cut on his arm. He was bleeding profusely. A quick-thinking Marjorie Cofran removed her slip and pressed it tightly against Ralph's scalp to staunch the blood. Laurie Grimshaw, the 12-year-old daughter of Dr. Grimshaw, would-be clarinet soloist and an inveterate tomboy, was staring down at the dress her parents had bought her especially for the recital. It was red and navy and had big brass buttons and, from what Laurie could determine, it had been enormously expensive. Now it was covered with dust, mud and the blood of Ralph Drayer.

*I've ruined my special dress* was all she could think.

There was water streaming down onto the floor from broken pipes above. The door to the room was packed tight with rubble, like a tunnel cave-in. In a fit of adrenaline-fueled strength, Irma's father managed to pop open one of the tall window frames long since painted shut. And one by one, the men helped the children and women climb from the building. The couple that had bolted from the room just before the hallway collapsed had made it to an interior doorway and survived. They were European and evidently had learned from experience that a door header provided reliable shelter when the bombs started falling. As families stepped into the dazzling sunshine, someone exclaimed, "Look!" The southwest-corner basement room, where by all rights the recital should have taken place but for the out-of-tune piano, was buried under tons of stone and timbers.

After all the sounds finally stopped, John and Elaine Martin remained huddled in the dark basement of Stoffer Science Hall with several dozen others. The reek of gasoline permeated the room.

"Don't anyone light a cigarette!" someone yelled.

"We need to get out of here!"

People raced up the stairs and into the daylight. The Martins would later learn that the gasoline fumes had come from an automobile thrown into air-conditioning vents on the side of the building. Stoffer was a relatively new structure: a long, rectangular, three-story box housing laboratories and classrooms. It wasn't the prettiest thing to look at, but thanks to its sturdy steel construction, it had come through the tornado relatively intact. An adjacent, wood-framed lecture hall was crushed, the observatory dome on the roof housing a powerful telescope was ripped away and nearly every window was broken.

In a nearby parking lot, the wind had built an enormous pyramid of cars, perhaps 25 feet high. Horns were stuck and blared incessantly and the acrid smell of battery acid and gasoline filled the air. The Martins briefly searched for their VW, but it was impossible to tell where it might have ended up. So they joined a group of people moving south and, with their neighbor, began walking back to student housing. Elaine, six months pregnant, was carrying the neighbor's newborn child. As they neared their apartment, who should appear but Elaine's parents, coming up the drive on foot to check on their daughter.

"Good Lord!" Elaine's father cried in amazement and dismay. "Elaine's given birth to the baby!"

Three days later, the police called and told the Martins they'd found their VW: The tan-colored car was flattened to less than a foot high and camouflaged under 20 feet of limestone blocks amid the ruins of Rice Hall.

—— • ——

Nadine Gilbert listened intently as a female voice came across the public address system at Stormont-Vail, the city-owned hospital a half mile north of Washburn University. "Attention all staff: Code 99, repeat, Code 99." The code meant that a community emergency had occurred. The hospital's disaster plan was being implemented and the staff should prepare for multiple casualties.

Gilbert was 25, tall and slender, with a long, delicate face and Roman nose. She wore a white skirt and had a small nurse's cap bobby-pinned precariously to the back of her wavy blond hair. She was working the 3:00–11:00 p.m. shift as charge nurse on the intensive care unit. When word spread that a tornado was approaching the city, she'd called her husband at their home just north of 29th and Gage and urged him to get their two children to a neighbor's basement. Then the hospital's power failed and the emergency generators kicked in. The lights were dim. With the air conditioners down, it quickly became sticky in the dim corridors.

As it happened, one of Gilbert's patients in the ICU was the hospital's longtime administrator, Carl Lamley. He'd suffered a heart attack over Memorial Day weekend. But now he was awake and alert and doing everything he could from his hospital bed to help the staff prepare for the onslaught. "You go help in the ER, Nadine," he said. "We'll be fine."

The acting administrator, 28-year-old Jerry Jorgensen, soon came panting up the drive. He'd set out from his home south of Washburn immediately after the tornado had passed, catching a ride with a physician neighbor. When debris blocked their progress, Jorgensen had jumped out and continued on foot. Walking and running, he'd threaded his way through the damage path to make the final half-mile push to the hospital.

Gilbert could hear the sirens of approaching ambulances, and out the window she could see cars pulling into the emergency room's circle drive and stopping under the brick portico. The Huttons, the father and two sons caught in the open at Washburn, were among the first to arrive. Nurses brought them in and immediately began cleaning their many cuts. Soon doctors were stitching them up. Disc jockey Rick Douglass, Virginia Tuttle and Mrs. Tuttle's grandkids showed up a few moments later. The journey across the city had been difficult for the survivors from the I-470 underpass, as their path had been repeatedly blocked by the tornado's damage. It was only through considerable back-tracking and circumvention that they'd finally made it in.

Douglass was in a bad way. He'd lost a lot of blood from his leg wound, and strangely, he could no longer see in color but only black and white. He'd become frantic when they passed WREN radio's offices a few blocks from the hospital. "Can we pull over real quick?" he said. "I've got to tell them I can't find the WREN-mobile. I'm going to lose my job over this if I don't."

But the Good Samaritan driving the car, an off-duty nurse, would have none of it.

"You just settle down," the woman said. "You're not going to lose your job. You need to get to the hospital and that's where we're going."

Douglass was helped into the emergency room, a tattered, filthy mummy — two white eyes swimming beneath a straw-packed helmet of mud. He was mumbling incoherently at this point. A nurse assumed that the long sliver of wood hanging from his lip was a cigarette and told him smoking wasn't allowed in the hospital. But she quickly realized her mistake and removed the piece of wood. Gilbert, the nurse from the ICU, arrived and, with the assistance of a young man, helped Douglass toward a nearby gurney. A photographer from the *Daily Capital,* Delmar Schmidt, captured the moment's horror and tension forever.

People were streaming into the hospital now and the emergency room quickly became bedlam. As Douglass lay on a gurney awaiting transport, a nurse walked past and, taking him for dead, pulled the sheet over his face. She jumped back when Douglass struggled to push the cover off.

"Oh, I'm so sorry!" she said.

In the ER's concrete entryway, the cacophony of people yelling and car horns honking was deafening, as more cars pulled up to disgorge the wounded. Inside, Gilbert triaged the casualties as they arrived, separating the minor injuries from the life-threatening ones. She knelt on the floor of the waiting room and started IVs in the semidarkness, holding a flashlight in her mouth. An unconscious Officer Hathaway was rolled past on a stretcher. The little boy he'd helped pull from the rubble at the base of the mound — the one who'd been so badly hurt — arrived on a board in the back of a white station wagon. The child was conscious and crying and clinging to life. Physicians sedated him and with three snips of a pair of scissors, completed the amputation of his right leg.

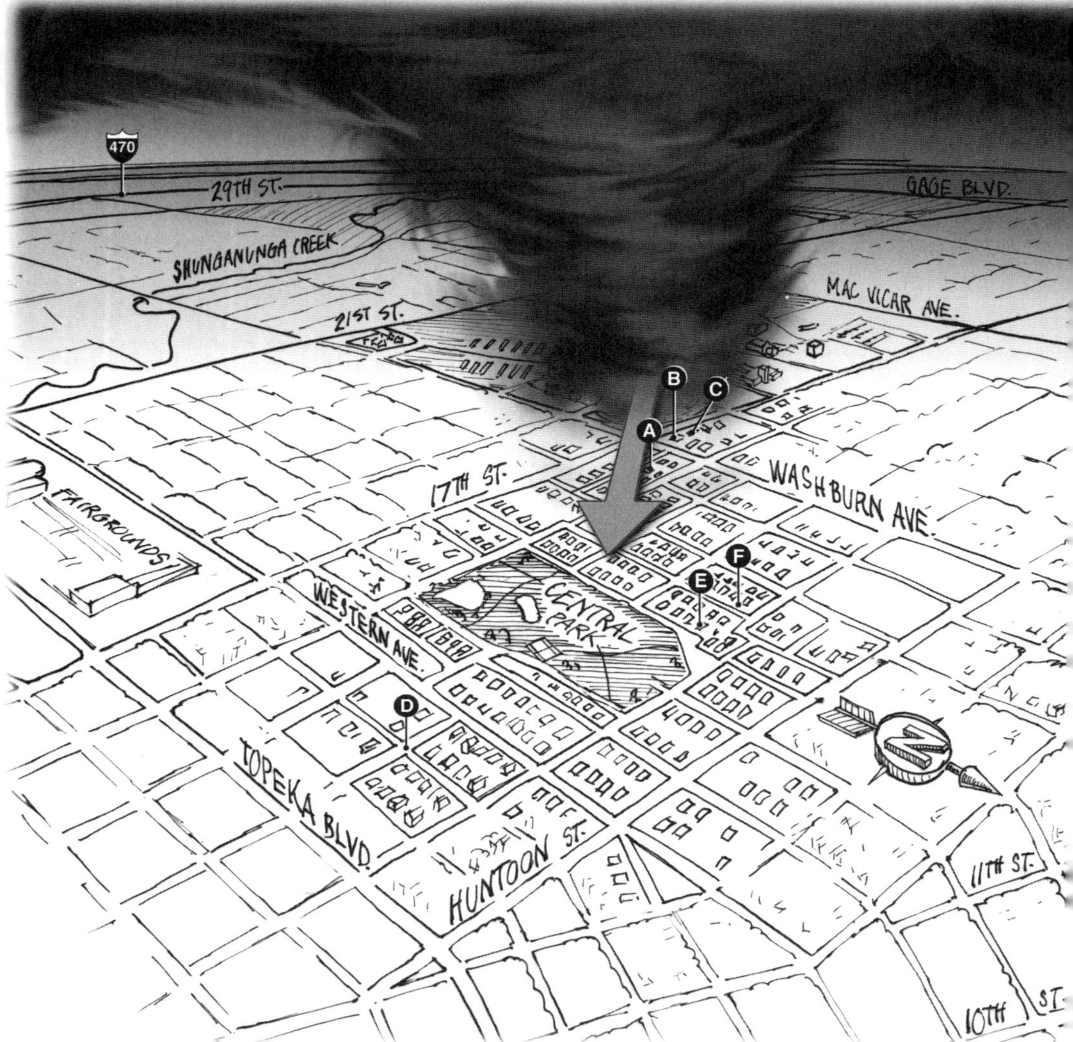


## 3   College Hill / Central Park

A – Stein, *Byron St.*
B – Whitney, *17th St.*
C – Bartley, *17th St.*
D – Maxon, *Polk St.*
E – Hatke, *Clay St.*
F – Johnson, *Buchanan St.*

# CHAPTER ELEVEN

# A Knife to the Heart of the City

The College Hill and Central Park neighborhoods merged into one northeast of Washburn and marched in dense, symmetrical blocks toward downtown. White, two-story clapboard homes built early in the century occupied narrow lots along uneven brick streets shaded by a thick awning of oak and elm. Many of the homes shared old-fashioned driveways, the kind with grassy medians down the middle. Shedlike garages built to house Model Ts slouched along the alleys. Central Park, a few blocks to the east, featured two lagoons, rose and tulip gardens, tennis courts, and groves of pin oak, black oak, blue spruce and ironwood. A row of majestic Craftsman-style homes — two and three stories tall with deep eaves and wide porches — stood along the west side of the park like mighty ships in port.

For 11-year-old Tony Stein, the area was paradise. Stein lived on Byron Street, a quiet dead end a couple of blocks northeast of campus. The street swarmed with kids and Stein and his friends never ran short of things to do. They hunted frogs in the lagoons and played army along the back alleys. They shot baskets in Washburn's field house and periodically harassed the university's parking police, who beetled around campus on motorized three-wheelers.

Stein was the son of a framing carpenter. The tall, quiet, dark-haired boy had just graduated from Central Park Elementary School, an imposing brick building three blocks away. When boys would fight after school, and fight they did, the contests generally took place on a secluded patch of ground behind the old Congregational Church.

On the evening of June 8, a football game was under way on Byron Street. Kids frequently took over the dead-end street to play a rough game of touch between the curbs. But Stein's mother was worried about the tornado watch and she refused to let Tony go outside. He was steamed as he watched the action through the front-room window.

A few blocks away, Mary Hatke eased her T-Bird into the garage and went inside her grand, old home across from the park to prepare dinner. Mary worked with her husband, Roy, at his art supply store downtown. Earlier, she'd been struck by the queer, oppressive nature of the day. Her friend Wilma Gilmore had gone so far as to express apprehension about what the stillness might portend. But Mary had thought no more of it. Her husband arrived home and they sat down to eat. Then the sirens went off.

— • —

Across from the Washburn campus, 22-year-old Neil Bartley stood on the porch, encouraging his father to come to the basement. Bartley's parents lived in an airplane bungalow on busy 17th Street. Neil had just graduated from Washburn. He would begin teaching in the fall and he'd just purchased a home for his wife and two-year-old son. But they wouldn't take possession for a few months, so the family had moved into the empty student apartment in the basement of Neil's parents' home. Now the sirens began to wail and raindrops smacked the pavement. Still, Neil's father, a foreman with the gas service company, wouldn't come in.

"Oh, there's nothing that will come of this," he muttered. Neil kept urging his dad to come to the basement, but Mr. Bartley stayed on the porch to watch the rain. An exasperated Neil finally gave up and joined his wife, Marsha; little Neil Jr.; his mother; and a group of neighbors in the safety of the basement below.

— • —

Bob and Pauline Johnson lived nearby in a large, white house on Buchanan Street, a few doors down from Central Park Elementary School. The couple originally hailed from Kentucky; Bob worked for the Hartford Insurance Company. He'd transferred from Chicago a few years before, and now he sold personal and commercial lines across northeast Kansas. Pauline had her hands full raising six kids. She was only 26.

The big family had finished dinner, and Pauline went upstairs to take a quick bath and get ready for a church meeting. But when she heard the siren on the roof of nearby Central Park Elementary crank up, she hurriedly dressed and came downstairs. Bob and the children were standing around the television, transfixed, as Bill Kurtis warned that a tornado was on the ground and heading for southwest Topeka.

"C'mon, kids. Let's get to the basement," Pauline said.

— • —

The rain was coming down so hard that the wipers on Pete Maxon's '52 Chevy coupe had no chance of keeping up. Maxon, who was 19, was tall and slim, with wavy black hair and black-rimmed glasses. He wore jeans, a T-shirt and tennis shoes. Maxon worked nights on the IBM mainframes at the First National Bank downtown. He'd slept all day, but this was his night off. He was heading over to see his girlfriend, Peggy, at her home near 14th and Polk streets. Peggy wanted to watch the new Charlie Brown special on TV. Maxon didn't care about the show. But he was looking forward to spending some time with his girl. Since he'd slept all day, Maxon was not aware of the tornado watch. Nor did he hear the sirens. Finally, the rain eased up and rays of sunlight began to fracture the turbulent sky.

— • —

Neil Bartley was huddled in the basement of his parents' airplane bungalow with his wife, son, mother and some neighbors when the thought hit him.

"Jesus Christ! The Whitneys!"

He dashed up the stairs and met his father coming down.

"By God, son, it's coming! It's coming!"

"I gotta get the Whitneys . . ."

Neil sprinted out into the backyard and raced next door to the tall frame house that sat on the northwest corner of 17th and Washburn Avenue. The Whitneys were in their 80s. Bartley had known them all his life. They were kind and friendly people. Mr. Whitney was a retired millwright and could fix just about anything. Neil had mowed the Whitneys' lawn and helped them put up storm windows. He'd carried their groceries. Now he leapt up the steps to their side door and rattled the knob, but it was locked. He pounded and yelled: "Mr. and Mrs. Whitney! It's Neil! There's a tornado coming. You need to get to the basement!" But then, from the southwest, a hissing noise came that sounded like grain spilling onto a metal building. Neil looked back toward Washburn and saw debris circling in a low, black cloud. No more time. He ran for his parents' house, made it inside and leapt down the stairs. He lost his footing and tumbled to the bottom. Quickly he regained his feet and grabbed a blanket as he raced to the corner, then crouched low and pulled the blanket over the group. In seconds, his two-year-old son was shrieking and the pressure and pain and din became so great that Neil never heard the house fly apart above him.

⌐ • ⌐

Tony Stein forgot about the street football game when the sirens went off. Now he was standing with his father in the shadows of the family's dark stone cellar. The two peered out a small, high window to the west. There wasn't much to see. A shrub partially blocked the view. The rain had stopped and the sun was coming out, although that strange, yellow cast still washed the sky. The air was dead calm.

Tony's mother, sister, two younger brothers and infant cousin sat in the basement's southwest corner with a transistor radio. Newscaster Bill Kurtis was reporting that the tornado was moving into the city. A few minutes later, Tony noticed the leaves on the bush outside begin to flutter oddly, like a flock of captive butterflies. And then Tony's dad, a towering, powerfully built man, shouted, "Here it comes!" What he saw or heard, Tony never knew, but the young man didn't ask questions. He dashed for the southwest corner to join his siblings and mother. His father grabbed an old mattress and threw it over the group. Then Mr. Stein lay spread-eagled across the top to hold it down. Tony's mother was praying. The younger children were crying. Beneath the mattress, Tony felt an enormous pressure building against his eardrums. What he heard next was an explosion, not a sustained roar but a singular, terrifying blast. To him, it sounded as if dozens of men armed with shotguns had surrounded the house and simultaneously discharged their weapons into every door, window and wall.

A few blocks away at the Johnson household, the big family had made their way to the basement and crowded under an old kitchen table. One of the children held on tightly to Kelly, the beloved family mutt. Bob Johnson went back upstairs and stepped outside. He was having a hard time getting his head around the fact that a very large tornado was moving into the city and apparently heading straight for his family and home. But he could see it now, just beyond Washburn, furious and dark. In the middle distance, trees that looked electric green in the strange light were corkscrewing in the wind, bending and twisting in outlandish, inconceivable ways. Johnson felt an earthquake-like rumble that seemed to roll through his very bones. He raced back to the basement.

"Get up under there as tightly as you can, kids! Cover your heads! The tornado is coming!"

A few moments later, his wife heard the roar. Then she heard the sound of wood being pried loose, nails squealing out, boards popping and snapping, glass shattering. It was as if a large wrecking crew was upstairs taking the house apart.

Amid the bedlam, Pauline noticed dust falling from the ceiling like snow.

*This house is going to come down on top of us . . .*

—  •  —

Mary and Roy Hatke, the couple who owned the art supply store downtown, abandoned the table with dinner half-eaten when the sirens wailed. Mary grabbed the transistor and they retreated to the tall basement of their old home near the park. Listening to WIBW radio, she heard Bill Kurtis warn, "For God's sake, take cover!" *He sounds scared,* she thought. She was scared, too. A few minutes later, the couple heard a low, grinding rumble. It was a terrible, remorseless sound.

"Hold my hand, Mary," Roy said.

Quickly the roar became overwhelming, all-pervasive, and the wind smashed into the house and shoved the couple to their knees, like the pressing hand of a giant.

—  •  —

Pete Maxon pulled up in his '52 Chevy in front of his girlfriend's two-story house on Polk Street. The sky was clearing and the sunlight glared brightly on the wet pavement. He dashed up the steps and rang the doorbell. But there was no answer. Then he heard the rumble. He rang the bell again and tried the knob, but the door was locked and the house was dark. Glancing over his shoulder to the west, Maxon could see pieces of roofing circling in the now-gray-black sky. The rumble was getting louder.

He knew what it was.

*What do I do? Should I get in the car?*

He soon thought better of that, though, knowing that a tornado could fling a car hundreds of feet. So he sprinted for the side of the house. The wind was rising and he could see all manner of material floating just to the west. Maxon ducked down along the south side of the house just as the wind kicked into overdrive. Tree limbs were crashing down all around and mud and sticks pelted him. The sound was omnidirectional, and Maxon was certain the tornado was nearly on top of him.

*Oh, God, I'm going to be carried away . . . If it's my time, Lord, please take care of me, but I really don't want to die.*

He gripped the edge of the siding tighter and lowered his head as the howling winds tried to yank him free. The sound was akin to lying beneath railroad tracks with a diesel locomotive pounding right over the top. Finally, the great roar began to subside, and Maxon stood up and peaked around the corner and watched as the churning, gray-black wall moved toward downtown.

—  •  —

Several miles to the southeast, 26-year-old Patricia Galbraith stood on high ground in her front yard and watched the tornado chew through the city. The funnel was wide and black and brilliantly backlit by the slanting rays of the dying afternoon sun. Pieces of metal and glass suspended in the twister caught the light and the shards glittered like a thousand diamonds against the swirling, dark band.

Never had Galbraith beheld a more breathtaking sight.

*It looks like an angry god . . .*

"For God's sake, Pat! You've got to come inside!" It was her husband, Jim. He stood near the house, gesturing wildly with one arm, holding their one-year-old daughter in the other, frantic with worry. The couple's three other children already were in the basement. But Pat did not come. She could not. She was mesmerized by the tornado's terrible majesty. It was as if the funnel was casting a spell that hypnotized all who dared look upon it. Fortunately, the twister continued on a path perpendicular to Galbraith and the danger subsided.

"There was something extremely seductive about it," Galbraith said 40 years later. "If the tornado would have called my name, I would have gone to it."

When the silence finally came, Tony Stein's father pulled himself up and gently lifted the mattress. The family beneath looked around, bewildered and quiet but for the gasping, broken sobs of one of the children.

"It's okay, it's okay, it's okay."

Tony stood up. Everyone checked for wounds. No one was hurt. A few minutes passed. They heard muffled voices outside.

"Everyone okay in there? Everyone all right?" Two men were moving by the window, bending down to peer inside.

"We're fine," Mr. Stein called back. "Thanks." The family started up the cellar stairs. The door at the top had been ripped away. In the kitchen, china, cereal, canned goods, furniture and plaster lay scattered, smashed and broken. A wall was gone. The roof above and most of the second floor were gone. Mrs. Stein took a long, silent look at the devastation. Then she sank to her knees and sobbed.

Tony helped his mother up and soon she regained her composure. He stepped outside and looked up Byron Street. In both directions, every house was wrecked. Every one of the beautiful old trees was shattered or debarked, ripped white like bone. Every car was smashed. A giant limb had fallen in front of the house and crushed the passenger side of his father's turquoise-and-white '57 Chevy.

It was as if an atomic bomb had detonated high above Byron Street.

*No one will be able to get to us. The destruction is too much.*

Then, a small miracle: Pumpkin, the family's rat terrier, trotted out from behind the house. She'd been in the garage, which had vanished. But somehow the little dog survived.

"We gotta get out of here," Tony's father said. "I'll go to Aunt Judy and Uncle Bob's and get a car and come back. You come with me, Tony." There was no emotion in his voice. Mr. Stein checked on his wife. Then father and son started at a fast walk up the bombed-out street. Twilight was laying in as Tony turned to take a last look

Chief Abram Burnett (1812–1870), leader of a band of Potawatomi Indians forcibly removed from Indiana to Kansas in 1838. (Kansas State Historical Society)

Chief Abram Burnett's cabin near the Shunganunga Creek, circa late 1860s. (Kansas State Historical Society)

In 1960, construction of a 5-million-gallon water tank began on the shoulder of Burnett's Mound. The tank forever altered the hill's appearance and, some believed, disturbed the spirits of Indians buried there. Interstate 470 can be seen under construction in the middle distance. The highway opened in October 1960. (Courtesy of the *Topeka Capital-Journal*)

John and Ruth Fernstrom. (Courtesy of John and Ruth Fernstrom)

Dominic Gutierrez (Courtesy of Dominic Gutierrez)

Richard Albert Garrett was meteorologist-in-charge of the U.S. Weather Bureau's Topeka office for more than 20 years. By 1966, Garrett had turned Topeka into a citadel of tornado preparedness. (Courtesy of Pat Fleenor)

Glenn and Inge Nicely, with their daughter, Angela, playing with Mitzi in 1963. (Courtesy of Inge Nicely)

Lisle Grauer, proprietor of the Pla-Land bowling alley. (Courtesy of Ron Grauer)

The Huffman family standing on the slab of their destroyed home after the tornado (left to right): Joanna, Teri, Tami and Harold. (Courtesy of Teri Huffman Colpitts)

Carol Martin with her parents, Hazel and Cleve. (Courtesy of Carol Martin Yoho)

Peg and Paul Marmet with their daughter, Stacy, circa 1968. (Courtesy of Paul and Peg Marmet)

Sterling "Chick" Taylor (Courtesy of Katherine Taylor Boline)

Johnny Scheibe (Courtesy of Kert Scheibe)

WREN disc jockey Rick Douglass, left, and Topeka police officer Dave Hathaway, standing at the spotters' vantage point on the ridge south of Burnett's Mound a year after the tornado. The mound can be seen in the left middle distance, with the buildings of downtown Topeka faintly visible on the horizon. (Courtesy of the *Topeka Capital-Journal*)

John Meinholdt was a member of a volunteer CB radio spotters' group and the first to alert the Weather Bureau of the approaching tornado from his post on Burnett's Mound. (Courtesy of the *Topeka Capital-Journal*)

*Capital-Journal* photographer Perry Riddle shot more than 20 photos as the tornado approached Topeka from the southwest. The tornado is probably 7 to 10 miles away in this picture. (Courtesy of the *Topeka Capital-Journal*)

As the sirens wail, area residents race for cover in the basement of the Countryside Methodist Church on Burlingame Road. The rain is still falling. Note the illuminated brake lights on the car that's just pulled into the church parking lot. (Courtesy of the *Topeka Capital-Journal*)

This shot probably is the most famous of the Perry Riddle series. (Courtesy of the *Topeka Capital-Journal*)

The tornado is much closer now but still southwest of Burnett's Mound. The sun is shining in the west. (Courtesy of the *Topeka Capital-Journal*)

The enormity of the funnel is apparent in this shot. (Courtesy of the *Topeka Capital-Journal*)

Climbing the ridge south of Burnett's Mound. (Courtesy of the *Topeka Capital-Journal*)

The tornado crosses Burnett's Mound and explodes into the homes of the County Fair Estates subdivision. The outline of the water tank is barely visible on the right shoulder of the mound. Perry Riddle, the photographer, was positioned two miles east of the mound. (Courtesy of the *Topeka Capital-Journal*)

Firing debris in every direction, the tornado hammers the neighborhoods north of I-470.
(Courtesy of the *Topeka Capital-Journal*)

Its path of destruction complete, the now-white tornado begins to weaken and lift after crossing the Kansas River at the northeastern edge of the city. This photo was taken from the Highland Park area looking north. (Courtesy of Delmar Schmidt)

The tornado ropes out over Tecumseh, east of the city. (Courtesy of B. T. Bradford)

Survivors emerge to a shattered world. (Courtesy of the *Topeka Capital-Journal*)

One of the approximately 150 Shetland ponies killed at White's Pony Farm, just west of Burnett's Mound. (Courtesy of Dean White)

A family scrambles from their destroyed home as tornadic clouds move off in the background. (Courtesy of the *Topeka Capital-Journal*)

A badly injured Mary Lee Herndon of Fayette, Missouri, is carried from the ruins below Burnett's Mound shortly after the tornado passed. Mrs. Herndon was visiting her daughter, Mary "Betsy" Clark, and the Clark family, in the 4200 block of Twilight Drive on June 8. The Missouri woman and her daughter were caught outside the house when the tornado struck and were unable to get the front door open because of the wind. Both recovered from their injuries. Mrs. Herndon's son-in-law, Charles F. Clark, is the balding, dark-haired man in the white shirt and light-colored pants at the rear of the group.   (Courtesy of the *Topeka Capital-Journal*)

On the move in the aftermath. (Courtesy of the *Topeka Capital-Journal*)

The water tank on Burnett's Mound. (Courtesy of the AT&T Archives and History Center)

Vehicles piled up beneath the I-470 underpass on Gage Boulevard. Officer Dave Hathaway's K9 station wagon can be seen in front of the nearest car. (Courtesy of the *Topeka Capital-Journal*)

Destruction at the Embassy Apartments just northeast of the mound. (Courtesy of Lloyd Zimmer)

The Embassy Apartments (Courtesy of the *Topeka Capital-Journal*)

Home slabs swept clean by the tornado between Twilight Drive and Gage Boulevard, looking northeast. The Embassy Apartment complex is in the middle distance, and the 29th Street hill and Prairie Vista subdivision are in the background. (Courtesy of the *Topeka Capital-Journal*)

The same area from the opposite direction, with 29th Street in the foreground and Burnett's Mound in the distance. The tornado crossed the Shunganunga Creek just beyond the lower, right-hand corner of the picture. (Courtesy of the *Topeka Capital-Journal*)

Bloody, battered and mud-caked, Rick Douglass — carried 100 yards by the tornado — is helped into the Stormont-Vail Hospital emergency room by nurse Nadine Gilbert and an unidentified man. (Courtesy of the *Topeka Capital-Journal*)

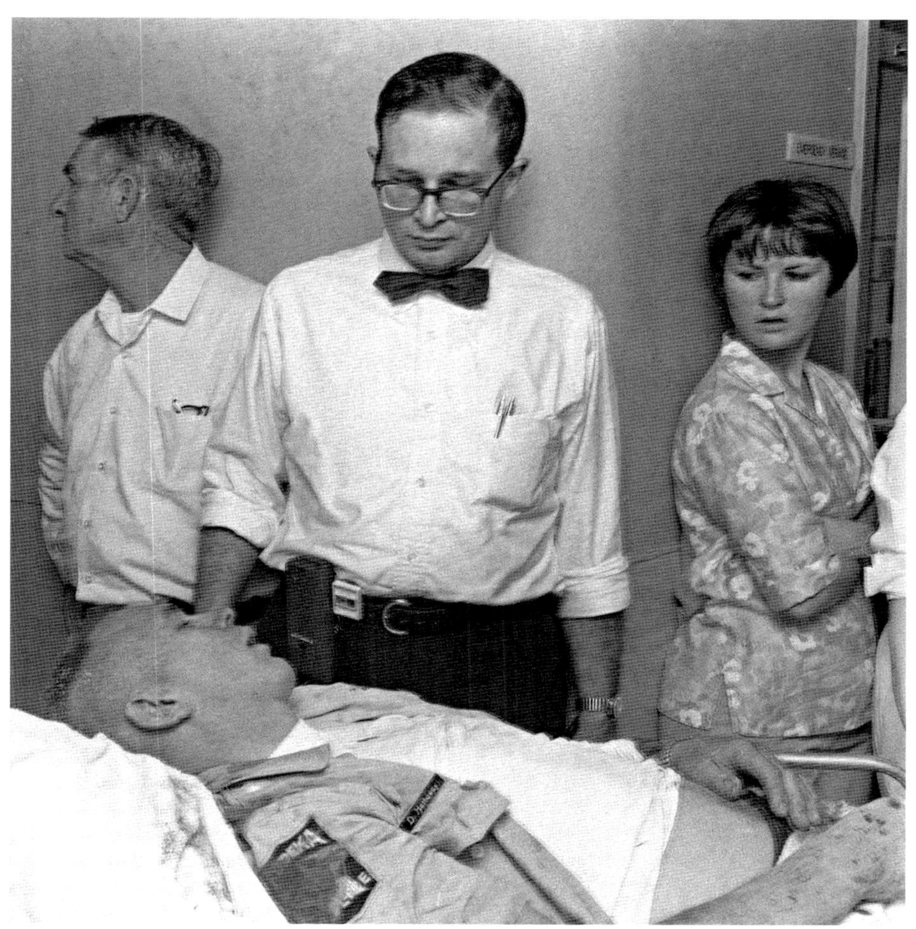

An unconscious Dave Hathaway arrives at the hospital. (Courtesy of the *Topeka Capital-Journal*)

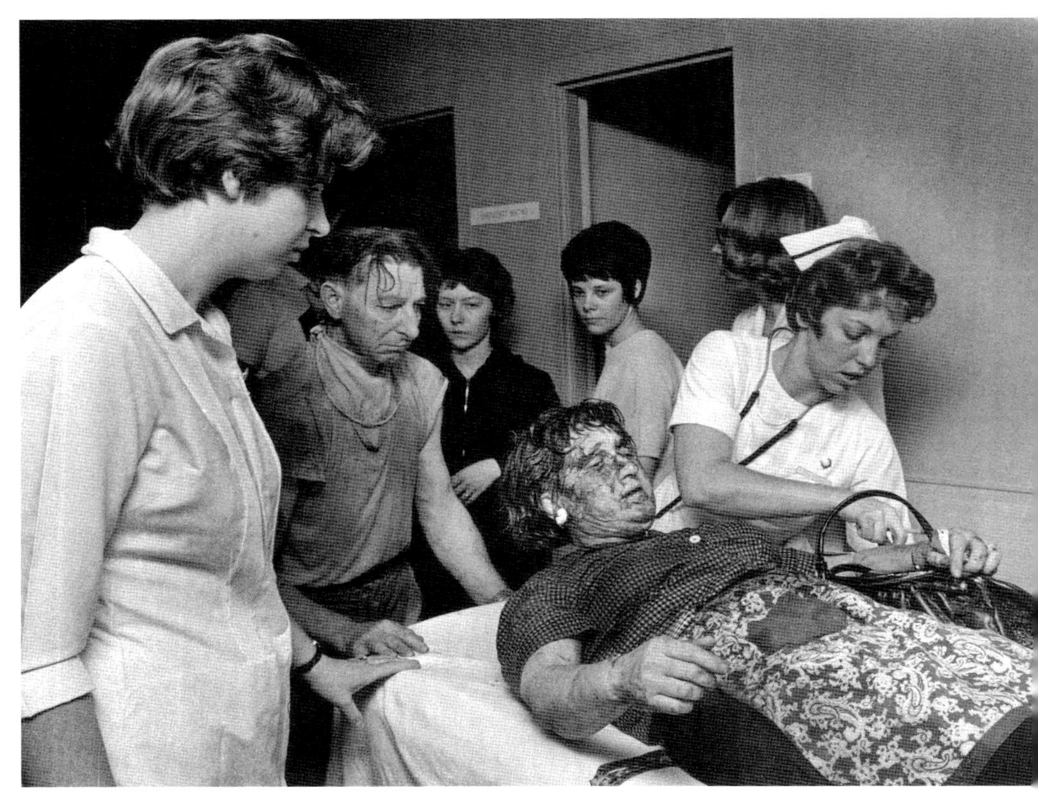

The casualties roll into Stormont-Vail Hospital. (Courtesy of the *Topeka Capital-Journal*)

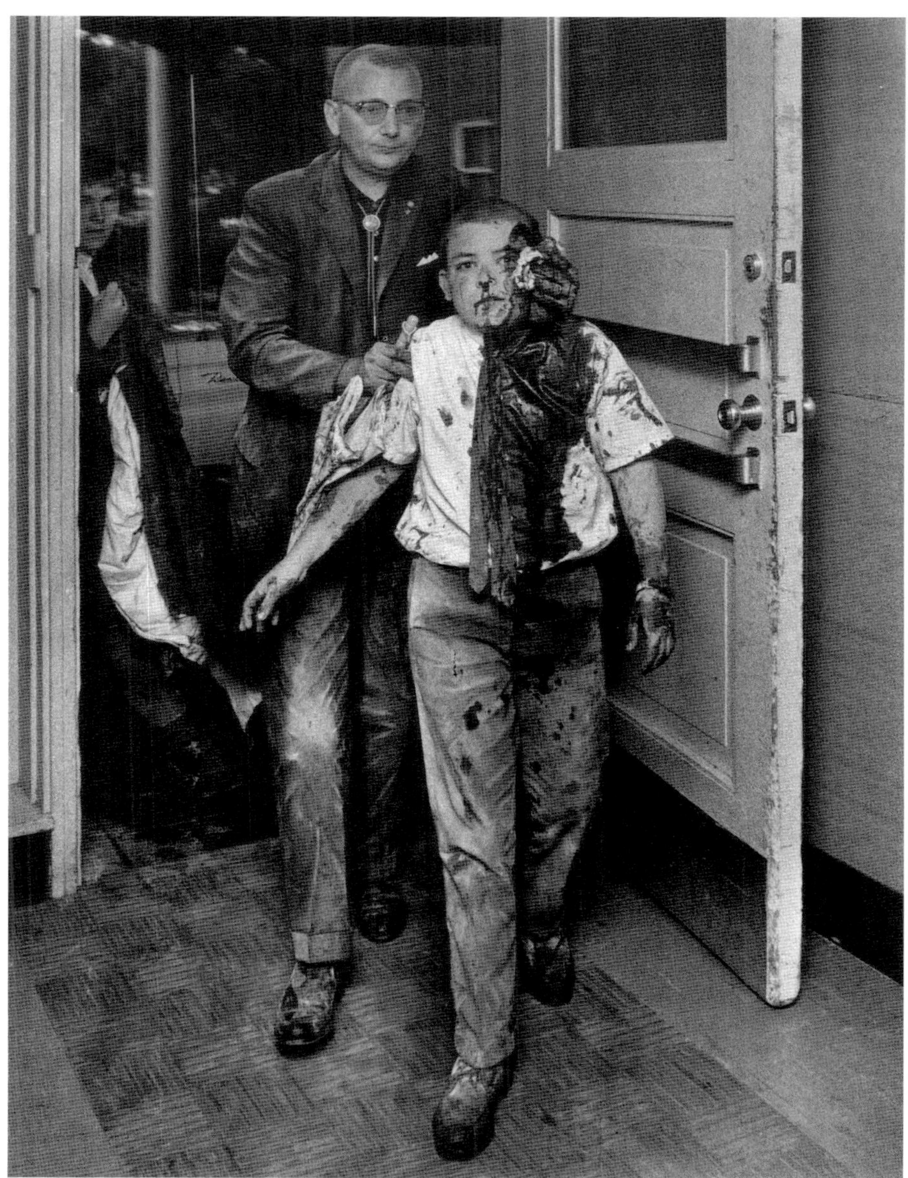

Ralph Drayer was badly cut at the Washburn University music recital but still managed to walk into Stormont-Vail under his own power. (Courtesy of the *Topeka Capital-Journal*)

A night to remember. (Courtesy of the *Topeka Capital-Journal*)

Carnegie Hall on the Washburn University campus. John Fernstrom and 20 or so others were taking a test in the second-floor classroom on the northwest (right) side of the building just before the tornado struck. Carnegie Hall, which was repaired after the tornado, was the only one of the badly damaged, old stone buildings at Washburn that could be saved. (Courtesy of the University Archives, Mabee Library, Washburn University)

Carnegie Hall, viewed from the southwest. (Courtesy of the University Archives, Mabee Library, Washburn University)

MacVicar Chapel, site of the music recital. Recital participants originally gathered in the southwest basement room at the left end of this picture. But because of an out-of-tune piano, they moved to the southeast basement room (on the right side of the picture). This room remained intact during the tornado. Afterward, the group escaped through a window behind the pile of tree limbs and roots. The room where they'd first sought safety was buried under tons of debris from the collapsed second floor. (Courtesy of University Archives, Mabee Library, Washburn University)

MacVicar Chapel, looking northeast. The state capitol dome and smoke from debris burn piles in Central Park are visible in the distance. (Courtesy of the University Archives, Mabee Library, Washburn University)

The stairway area in MacVicar Chapel. (Courtesy of University Archives, Mabee Library, Washburn University)

Rice Hall (Courtesy of University Archives, Mabee Library, Washburn University)

Crane Observatory (Courtesy of the University Archives, Mabee Library, Washburn University)

Wrecked automobiles on the south side of Stoffer Science Hall. (Courtesy of the *Topeka Capital-Journal*)

Thomas Women's Gymnasium. A section of the gym's unusual second-floor track can be seen. In the foreground is the sheared-off smokestack of the university's power plant.
(Courtesy of the University Archives, Mabee Library, Washburn University)

The damage from above. Bill Hutton and his sons, Craig and Chris, rode out the tornado huddled against the east, near side of Morgan Hall, the inverted-F-shaped building in the center of the photo. The tornado moved diagonally from left to right. (Courtesy of the University Archives, Mabee Library, Washburn University)

A ravaged block in the central section of the city. (Courtesy of the *Topeka Capital-Journal*)

In the aftermath, shock and despair. Mrs. James Kaufman. (Courtesy of the *Topeka Capital-Journal*)

Gutted houses. (Kansas State Historical Society)

Shredded roofs near downtown. (Courtesy of the *Topeka Capital-Journal*)

Destruction on the edge of downtown. (Courtesy of the *Topeka Capital-Journal*)

The National Reserve Life building at 10th Street and Kansas Avenue, with its now-ironic advertisement — ". . . a refuge in time of storm" — on the side of the building. One witness who watched from a nearby window said the funnel appeared to coil around the building like a giant, white snake. The ruins of the Pla-Land bowling alley can be seen in the center-right of the picture. (Courtesy of the *Topeka Capital-Journal*)

Kansas Avenue, just south of downtown. (Courtesy of Lloyd Zimmer)

Shortman Dodge on Quincy Street. (Courtesy of Lloyd Zimmer)

Salesman Jerry Estes and others survived a direct hit from the tornado in the basement barbershop of this building next to Joe Smith Motor Company. The men were able to escape the wreckage by crawling up the exterior stairs near where the cardboard sign is located on the left. The '64 Chevy that Estes tried to sell to a Mennonite farmer earlier in the day is the second car from the right. (Courtesy of Lloyd Zimmer)

The destroyed bus barn of the Topeka Transportation Co. (Courtesy of B. T. Bradford)

Battling back. (Courtesy of the *Topeka Capital-Journal*)

Two cold ones to go. (Courtesy of the *Topeka Capital-Journal*)

Hanging on to faith. (Courtesy of the *Topeka Capital-Journal*)

Policemen, firemen and other first responders logged countless, grueling hours in the aftermath of the storm. (Courtesy of the *Topeka Capital-Journal*)

A jagged reflection. (Courtesy of the *Topeka Capital-Journal*)

The damaged copper dome of the capitol building. The west-wing roof also suffered damage. (Courtesy of the *Topeka Capital-Journal*)

An uprooted home. (Courtesy of Rick Schmidt)

The blasted landscape of East Topeka. (Courtesy of the *Topeka Capital-Journal*)

John Hodges, 614 Branner Ave., stares into an uncertain future. (Courtesy of the *Topeka Capital-Journal*)

Ripley Park in East Topeka. (Courtesy of Lloyd Zimmer)

Ravaged by the winds. (Courtesy of Rick Schmidt)

Unbowed: Mrs. Philip Spacek of 410 Lake St. (Courtesy of the *Topeka Capital-Journal*)

Searching for the old neighborhood. (Courtesy of the *Topeka Capital-Journal*)

New obstacles. (Courtesy of the *Topeka Capital-Journal*)

A stove and chairs are all that remain at the home of Tom Coleman, 212 Lime St. (Courtesy of the *Topeka Capital-Journal*)

Destruction at Billard Airport. Wafting smoke from debris burn piles can be seen along the horizon. (Courtesy of B. T. Bradford)

Grounded. (Courtesy of B. T. Bradford)

The work begins. John Zarazua, center, and others search for Zarazua's wallet and other valuables in the ruins of a home he rented on Lake Street. (Courtesy of the *Topeka Capital-Journal*)

A new day, looking northeast from I-470. (Courtesy of the *Topeka Capital-Journal*)

Where to begin? (Courtesy of the *Topeka Capital-Journal*)

Albert Lollar made a last-minute decision to gather his family and escape their home near Burnett's Mound as the tornado drew close, only to be caught up in the funnel in the family car, which was then hurled hundreds of feet. The next day, a pensive Lollar surveys the ruins of his home. (Courtesy of the *Topeka Capital-Journal*)

New heirlooms for Mrs. Bill Reece, Twilight Drive. (Courtesy of the *Topeka Capital-Journal*)

Found the shoes. (Courtesy of the *Topeka Capital-Journal*)

A Corvair on the second floor of the Embassy Apartments. (Courtesy of the *Topeka Capital-Journal*)

The wedding picture! (Courtesy of the *Topeka Capital-Journal*)

Fighting heartache and disbelief. (Courtesy of the *Topeka Capital-Journal*)

Not much left. (Courtesy of the *Topeka Capital-Journal*)

Making the best of it. (Courtesy of the *Topeka Capital-Journal*)

Looking for better days. (Courtesy of the *Topeka Capital-Journal*)

down Byron Street. The only light he could see was the interior dome in his father's smashed '57 Chevy, which had come on when the door sprung open after the tree limb fell. The little light glowed like a forlorn beacon amid the staggering panorama of ruin.

—  •  —

The Bartleys — Neil, his wife, his son and his parents — likewise emerged from their basement to find that the world had changed. The entire front of the airplane bungalow on 17th Street was wrecked and open. Neil's brand-new '66 Fairlane had been in the garage in back; now the garage walls were gone and the roof had dropped. His car and his father's both were smashed down to the doors. Before the storm, Mrs. Bartley had been working on some kitchen cabinets and she'd taken off her wedding ring and set it on a nearby shelf. The shelf and wall were gone. But her ring lay glittering on the floor. In a daze, Neil's dad, the gas company foreman, made his way into the front portion of the house. After work, he'd hung his overalls on the bedroom door. He'd just cashed his paycheck and his wallet was fat. Now the bedroom door and the walls and the overalls had disappeared. Somehow, though, the muddy bed had stayed put. And here was another miracle: Mr. Bartley got down on his knees and found his wallet beneath the bed, cash still in it.

Shouts came from next door. The large, three-story home owned by the Whitneys, the older couple Neil tried to warn, had imploded. Neighbors converged. Old Mr. Whitney was calling for help from somewhere in the jagged pile of rubble. Neil spotted him through shattered boards.

"Where's Mrs. Whitney?" Neil asked.

"I don't know. I think she was on the first floor."

The rescuers heard moaning and began to dig toward the sound, casting aside bricks from the fallen chimney. Finally they reached the elderly woman. She was conscious, although dazed and bloody and covered with mud and plaster dust. Long minutes passed, and then an ambulance finally arrived. Mr. Whitney was pulled out, battered and cut but okay. He took Neil aside as his wife was being loaded onto a gurney.

"Didn't Mrs. Whitney go to the basement?" Neil asked.

"She did. She was coming back up to get me," Mr. Whitney replied. "I've been here a lot of years and been through a lot of these warnings, and nothing ever happens. But I guess it happened today."

The old man's white hair was covered with mud and bits of glass and he had flecks of blood on his face. His face tightened and he looked around.

"Listen, Neil, you got to do me a favor. Keep an eye on the place tonight, will ya? I've got $10,000 hidden in cans in the walls. It's probably still in there somewhere."

— • —

At the Johnson house, the noise and the shaking stopped instantaneously, like the abrupt end of an out-of-control carnival ride. The house didn't come down on top of the big family, as Pauline had feared. Still, they wondered.

*Is it safe? Should we go outside?*

The family took stock. All were covered with dust. But there wasn't a scratch on any of them. Bob and Pauline made their way up the stairs. The first floor suffered little damage. Dinner dishes were still on the table. But when they stepped outside and looked back and up, they could see that the attic, the roof and most of the second floor were gone. All along the block, houses were flattened. Nearby Central Park Elementary School looked as though it had been hit by dive bombers. People were coming out of their shelters and into the street now, stunned, drifting like ghosts amid the ruin. The sun didn't know about tragedy and continued to shine brightly.

— • —

Roy and Mary Hatke emerged from the basement to find their beautiful old house — with its grand staircase and high ceilings, thick crown molding and wide front porch — twisted on its foundation and irrevocably askew. Walls and ceilings had cracked and dropped and the back was ripped open. The couple stepped into the yard. The next home to the south, a duplex, was mauled. A young family lived there: an airman from Forbes Air Force Base and his wife and two children. Roy called and called but got no response. Dread swept over Mary as Roy picked his way into the house to find the stairs to the basement. He tossed rubble aside and made his way down. Finally, amid the patchy sunlight filtering into the cellar, he saw the airman and his family. They were huddled in the corner in a tight human ball, eyes wide, paralyzed with fear. Roy helped them out of the house.

— • —

Pete Maxon, the young man who had ridden out the tornado along-side his girlfriend's house, was immediately struck by the profound silence that enveloped him. It was as though the funnel had sucked every sound from the Earth. He looked around. The house beside him had lost its roof and many others to the north were destroyed. Every car on the street, save his, was smashed by fallen trees. He glanced down at the spot where he'd made his stand. A large nail had been driven into the siding like a dart, just above where his head had been. Then he heard voices as his girlfriend and her family emerged from the house. They were nearly inconsolable when they saw him standing there. He was battered and filthy but unhurt.

"Oh, we didn't know, we didn't know, we didn't know . . ."

— • —

In the short mile between the Washburn campus and Topeka Boulevard, the north-south artery that served as the spine of the city, the tornado smashed, scraped, exploded or badly damaged more than 250 homes. The neighborhoods struck were among the oldest in Topeka and ranged from comfortable middle-class to working poor. Although the twister's footprint had narrowed slightly since it leapt off Burnett's Mound, the main damage path was still at least one-third of a mile wide and the peripheral damage from rocketing debris extended the destruction well beyond that.

—  •  —

Pete Maxon and his girlfriend and her parents started up Polk Street in search of survivors. They found an Air Force sergeant buried in the rubble a few doors down. His arm was broken. Maxon's Chevy was the only car on the street still serviceable, so they helped the airman in to take him to the hospital at Forbes Air Force Base. As they prepared to leave, Maxon noticed something laying in the front yard. It was his baseball glove. It had been on the front seat of the Chevy when he'd pulled up moments before. Now here it was in the wet grass, 30 feet away. Yet the car's windows weren't broken. Nor had the doors been flung open during the storm, as far as he could tell. There was no evidence of it.

The tornado had strange and mighty powers.

## 4   Downtown

A – 10th St. & I-70 overpass

B – Esquivel, *Heumann Dental Laboratory, Monroe St.*

C – Sommers, *Quincy St.*

D – Grauer, Jackson (Pete), *Pla-Land bowling alley S. Kansas Ave.*

E – Estes, Smith, Benge, Steele, *Barbershop basement S. Kansas Ave.*

F – Estes, Smith, *Joe Smith Motor Company, S. Kansas Ave.*

G – National Reserve Life building, *SE corner, 10th St. & Kansas Ave.*

H – Fleenor, *Kansas Ave.*

I – Decker, *picked up by the wind, NW corner, 9th St. & Kansas Ave.*

J – Decker, *dropped by the wind 10th St. & Kansas Ave.*

K – Lyle, Brumme, *Santa Fe Railroad General Office Building, 9th St. & Jackson St.*

L – Dalrymple, *Southwestern Bell Building, 9th St. & Jackson St.*

M – State capitol building

N – Santa Fe Hospital, *6th St. & Madison St.*

O – Eiesland, Laird (David), *Police Garage, 5th St. & Van Buren St.*

# CHAPTER TWELVE

# The Maelstrom

Pete Jackson stood still and straight, carefully sighting his blue-and-white Brunswick Crown Jewel on the triangle of pins 62 feet away. He cocked his shoulder back, took three quick steps and then whirled his arm forward like a propeller blade before releasing the ball at the nadir of its arc. The 16-pound ball jumped to the polished maple and sped down the lane, seeming to accelerate as it drifted in a tight spiral from the edge of the alley toward the center. Impact occurred just to the right of the lead pin. The red-and-white formation exploded in a rattling crash.

Jackson smiled.

Another strike.

The loping rumble of bowling balls, the clatter of pins, the ring of pinball machines, and the smell of popcorn, cigarettes and beer filled the air in Lisle Grauer's Pla-Land bowling alley at 1024 Kansas Avenue just after 7:00 p.m. The best bowlers in the city had gathered for the first night of summer leagues. Twenty-one-year-old Jackson, five foot six and stocky, had been bowling since he was 15. He carried a respectable 186 average. But this was his first time competing with the big boys at Pla-Land. And Grauer's eight lanes were unforgiving, expertly polished and oiled. The young apprentice printer wasn't intimidated, though. Far from it. He'd just bowled three strikes in a row.

Mainly, Jackson was just glad to be off the job. Serving as a printer's apprentice was hard, loud and dirty work. Jackson would run the cutter, stack and box paper as jobs flew off the press, help switch out heavy lead plates, bring up ink, and spend eight hours every two months breaking down the press to clean its every nook and cranny. He'd come home at night with ink stained up to his elbows. And always, there was the oily smell of the ink and the whirring clatter of the colossal machine. But you don't complain. When you're 21 and have a wife and two-year-old son to support, you do what you have to do. Jackson did know this much, though: the wild freedom of youth, of high school?

Those days were gone for good.

—  •  —

Kansas Avenue between 10<sup>th</sup> and 12<sup>th</sup> streets hummed with commerce and life in 1966. There were shops, businesses and walk-up apartments — a café, liquor store, locksmith, printer, bakery, bar, dry cleaner, laundromat, barbershop and a grocery store. And car lots. Superior Lincoln-Mercury was just south of the giant neon bowling pin that adorned Pla-Land. A block east on Quincy was Tom Mix Rambler Ranch and next to it, Shortman Dodge. Joe Smith Motor Company occupied a lot south and west, on the far side of Kansas Avenue.

Joe Smith had been selling cars in Topeka since the early 1930s. He was a big man with a terrific sense of humor and a deep belly laugh to match. He'd been a great pitcher in his younger days and even played a season with the Cincinnati Reds before throwing his arm away. Now the car business was Joe's life. So there he was on that Wednesday evening, working the lot with 32-year-old Jerry Estes. Estes was a good-natured family man. He held fast to the principles espoused by Green Bay Packers coach Vince Lombardi: In life, the most important things were God, country, family and work. In that order.

Workwise, it had been a slow day. Some Mennonites up from Garnett, Kansas, had come in earlier. The man was dressed in black britches, suspenders, a homespun white blouse and a straw hat. The woman wore a bonnet and long dress. The kids dressed the same.

The family looked around for a while before the man finally made an offer on a dark blue '64 Chevy Impala. But Estes and the farmer couldn't get together on price. They were $50 apart and stayed there. So the Mennonites left without the car and Estes missed the sale. Now heavy rain swept in and rattled the little steel building that served as the car lot's office. Estes and Smith were listening to the radio, waiting for the storm to pass, when the sirens went off.

"We'd better go over to the shop," Smith said, motioning toward the small garage at the corner of the lot.

"No, if we get hit, that building will come down right on top of us, Joe," Estes replied. "It's nothing. The barbershop is where we need to be."

"You think so?"

"Yeah, I know. I've checked it out. It's below ground with a concrete reinforced ceiling and a 12-inch I beam running down the center. It's just about the safest place around here.

"You go on over," Estes added. "I'll pull the keys and be right there."

Smith nodded and started for the barbershop a half block away. Estes grabbed the public address microphone used to page employees and locked the talk key down. Then he laid the mike beside the radio. With WREN broadcasting across the PA system, Estes would be able to track the storm as he pulled keys from 58 cars on the lot. It wouldn't do to leave the cars unattended with the keys still in them. Rick Douglass was warning of the approaching storm as Estes dashed to the first car. He carried a big ring fashioned from an old coat hanger to hold the keys.

The rain was letting up.

— • —

The Santa Fe Railroad General Office Building — an ornate, buff-colored skyscraper erected in stages in the early decades of the century — stood two blocks north and west of Joe Smith Motor Company on Jackson Street. The building served as the railroad's operational nerve center and employed more than 1,800 people.

At 7:00 p.m., 28-year-old Tim Lyle and co-worker Dick Brumme, 26, made their way down to the lobby for their dinner break. Both worked the 3:00–11:00 p.m. shift on different floors in the tabulation department. They'd been friends since high school. Each had served in the military. Lyle was single; Brumme, married. Neither was what you might call a man in a gray flannel suit. The two usually went to dinner at one of the restaurants up on Kansas Avenue. But as they walked through the lobby toward the door, the security guard hailed them. A funnel was on the ground southwest of town, the guard said. He'd heard it on the radio.

Lyle and Brumme thanked the man and stepped outside. Across the street, the stark beauty of the state capitol seemed amplified by the strange light of the evening. The statehouse was constructed of cream-colored native limestone and featured four massive wings centered on a towering, limestone- and copper-clad dome gone green from exposure. Like the U.S. Capitol upon which it was modeled, the seat of Kansas government featured broad pediments, classical pillars and wide flights of stone steps that ascended to heavy doors on each wing. The building dominated downtown, sitting squarely on 20 parklike acres like a fortress amid winding sidewalks and towering cottonwood, ash, sycamore and elm. Local legend held that one of the big cottonwoods in fact had sprouted from a wooden stake sunk by capitol construction crews 100 years before.

The rain stopped. Lyle, a tall man with a thin face, marveled at the stillness. Even the highest branches in the tallest trees were entirely devoid of motion. It was as though the air itself was paralyzed with dread.

"Man, is it weird out," Brumme said. "We probably ought to go back inside."

"Yeah, probably should," Lyle replied.

In the lobby, the security guard was busy directing other Santa Fe employees to the basement shelter. "You fellas need to go to the basement," he told Lyle and Brumme. "They're saying the tornado is heading for Burnett's Mound."

The two friends made their way toward the flight of stairs. But as they passed the building's bank of elevators, they paused. Lyle turned to Brumme and spoke quietly.

"You want to go up and check it out?"

The men glanced at the security guard, who was occupied, then quickly stepped into an open elevator. Lyle punched the button for the 10th floor. The doors slid shut and the car started to rise.

— • —

Lois "Dorothy" Decker was 46, brown-haired, short and big-boned, a beloved grandma and nine years into her second marriage in June of 1966. She had just begun making dinner when the telephone rang. It was an aunt calling to wish her a happy anniversary.

"Good Lord, I forgot completely about it!" Dorothy said. "Thanks for reminding me. I think I'll have Earl take me out to eat."

And so it was that Earl Decker, owner of Decker Oil Company, and his wife, Dorothy, found themselves finishing dinner at the Coffee Cup Café in the 900 block of Kansas Avenue, in the heart of downtown, around 7:20 p.m. The couple was sipping coffee when the owner of the restaurant emerged grim-faced from the back. He told customers that a tornado had hit near Burnett's Mound. The man lived out that way and he was determined to get home. The diners could stay if they wanted. Several waitresses and some of the kitchen help were going to wait out the storm in the back. But he was leaving. The Deckers sat for a few minutes until the rain stopped. Then they stepped outside and started walking up Kansas Avenue toward their car. Earl's new Ford Galaxy 500 was angle-parked on the same side of the avenue, halfway along the shadowy canyon of buildings.

"Pick me up on the corner," Dorothy said. "I don't want to get my shoes wet. This gutter is flowing like a river."

— • —

Laura Dalrymple was bewildered. She couldn't figure out what was happening with her switchboard. The 20-year-old telephone operator was working in the windowless third floor of the Southwestern Bell building on Jackson, a half block north of the Santa Fe building. She was one of 60 operators on the shift. The women sat side by side in rows on opposite sides of the room, each manning a separate switchboard.

Dalrymple had come in at six o'clock and was busy connecting person-to-person, station-to-station and collect long-distance calls outbound from Topeka. She wore an ear-set and microphone and used both hands to pull and plug eight sets of jacks attached to cloth-covered cords, to link outbound lines and switching centers across the city.

But here was something she had not seen before. One by one, the lights on her board began to flash. Typically, a white light signified an incoming call and seldom were more than a dozen blinking at once. But now the entire board was beginning to flash, 500 lights representing 500 lines, coming on sequentially from circuits across the city. Even stranger, when Dalrymple would plug in, no one would be on the other end of the line. A dead circuit? But why so many? She looked around. Her co-workers' boards were lighting up in a similar fashion. A nervous rustle swept the room. But no one spoke. You couldn't. Company rules: No speaking to other operators during your shift. No exceptions. If there was a problem, call a supervisor.

Dalrymple suddenly heard a commotion by the door. One of the operators who'd been on break, an older woman, appeared disheveled and frantic. She was running and screaming. She was hysterical.

"It's coming! It's coming! It's coming!" the woman cried.

Two male supervisors quickly appeared and wordlessly intercepted the woman. They grabbed her by the elbows, and, with the woman still shouting and flailing, bodily carried her from the room. The men offered no explanation and didn't return.

—  •  —

The elevator doors opened on the deserted 10th floor of the Santa Fe building. Tim Lyle and Dick Brumme stepped out and made their way toward a window in the southwest corner of the large, open room. The two looked off toward the southwest, across the rooftops of the city. The rise of Burnett's Mound stood four miles away as the crow flies.

"Look, Brumme! There it is!"

The tornado was broad and gray, just beyond the mound. It looked hideous; a malformed wedge and seemed to move like a laboring, wounded animal. They watched it climb the mound and inch down the other side and then explode into the homes along I-470.

"*Look* at that big son of a bitch!"

The funnel quickly became engorged with wreckage and turned coal black, a rolling debris cloud, as it moved into the city. Block by block, Lyle and Brumme could track its progress by the white and green flashes that flickered near its base as power transformers shorted out and exploded. On it snaked, growing steadily larger, until they could begin to discern houses disintegrating and shooting up into the funnel. The band of circling debris grew thicker.

Lyle had no mental reference point, no memory, to help him process what he was seeing. As a result, time seemed to slow way down and the world became thick and surreal, almost as if he and Brumme were occupants of a dream.

"It looks like it's going through Washburn," Brumme said.

They kept watching.

⌒ • ⌒

Pete Jackson had done it again: four strikes in a row. He was on fire. He nodded coolly to his teammates and was just about to take a seat when he heard proprietor Lisle Grauer shout across the din of the bowling alley.

"Hey, everybody! There's a tornado coming! No joke. Come up here and listen to this!"

Grauer stood by the television near the snack bar. More than 30 bowlers quickly gathered around the set. Bill Kurtis was on the screen.

". . . and now we've just received a report that the tornado is approaching the intersection of 12th and Topeka Boulevard," Kurtis said.

The bowlers scattered. The tornado was four blocks away.

Grauer called out: "I don't care where you go, but I'm getting under that pool table!"

Jackson glanced out the window. He could see papers and leaves swirling wildly in the street.

*We're in serious trouble here . . .*

Most of the bowlers dashed for the concrete restrooms. But the rooms were small and Jackson knew not everyone could fit. So he and another bowler, a short, heavyset man named Joe Ramirez (who went by the nickname Dodo) ran the other way. Both men spotted a small pantry behind the snack bar along the south wall. The tiny room housed a stove and refrigerator. They flattened themselves against the floor and wall.

"Padre nuestro que estás en los cielos . . ."

Ramirez was praying as Jackson scrunched into a fetal position and covered his head. And he started praying, too.

—  •  —

Across Kansas Avenue at Joe Smith Motors, Jerry Estes was about to pull the last key from the last car on the lot — a white '61 Saab — when a sudden, violent gust of wind ripped the handle from his hand and swung the door hard against the stops. He looked west. Four blocks away, above Topeka Boulevard, a huge tree cartwheeled 50 feet off the ground. Above it, a large section of roof soared and banked like a kite.

*Shit, it's here . . .*

He turned and sprinted for the barbershop and raced down the outside steps. His boss, Joe Smith; Terry Steele, the barber; and Denny Benge, a friend and concrete finisher, all looked up as Estes burst in.

"What's going on, Jerry?" Smith said.

"It's coming, boys! It's heading straight for us!"

Benge immediately leapt from the barber's chair, ran to the back room and dashed up a flight of stairs to the building's rear door.

The other men fled to the dingy room in the back of the basement. A couple of beds were there.

"What should we do, Jerry?" Smith said.

"Let's grab these mattresses and pull 'em over us in case any shit comes flying in here."

—  •  —

Earlier, while Estes was still pulling keys, Steele had remembered a man who lived alone in a third-floor apartment above the barbershop.

"I bet that old man is still upstairs," Steele said.

Benge volunteered to go get him and dashed out. He ran up and pounded on the apartment door until an elderly, bald-headed man opened it.

"Hey, mister, there's a tornado coming," Benge said. "You need to get down to the basement!"

The old man scowled and shook his head.

"I've been living here for years and I ain't never run from no goddamn storm," he snarled. "Hell no. I'm not coming to the basement!"

He slammed the door shut. Benge turned and ran.

—  •  —

Denny Benge had been in tough spots before. The burly ex-Marine was stationed in Vietnam in '63–'64 and had guarded the air base at Da Nang. Before that, he had been floating off Cuba in a transport ship with hundreds of other battle-ready Marines and was just about to climb down the nets into a waiting landing craft — and God knows what — when word came that the missile crisis had eased and the invasion was off.

But nothing could have prepared him for what he faced now. Benge stood at the barbershop's back door, bracing against the doorjamb with one arm and shielding his eyes with the other against the howling, gale-force winds that whipped sand and gravel around like birdshot. He could see the black, ragged-edged funnel just to the west, crawling toward him across Topeka Boulevard. The tornado reminded him of a broadcast spreader, that ingenious piece of lawn care equipment that flings grass seed in a perfect, 360-degree circle with each turn of the wheel or crank of the handle. Except that here, obviously, the tornado wasn't throwing grass seed. Instead, it was spitting out cars, trees, TV antennas, walls, roofs, air conditioners and power poles in a soaring arc hundreds of feet in diameter.

"Estes! C'mere! Look at this!" he cried.

Estes did not come.

The bus storage barn owned by the Topeka Transportation Company was a block west of the barbershop. The company's warehouse-like shop stretched more than 200 feet down Jackson Street. Fifty green-and-white city buses and 20 or so yellow school buses were parked in the building or on the adjacent lot. Benge watched the wind grab the barn's enormous flat roof, lift it more or less intact, and then flip it off to the northeast like a giant Frisbee. After that, the buses started to move — first sliding into each other like a herd of restless cattle, then tipping over and rolling like hay bales, and finally tumbling end-over-end, into each other and into the building.

*Man, this is not going to be good . . .*

He dashed for the basement.

"Get down! It's here!"

Benge dove for the floor, and the men squeezed against the wall and pulled the mattresses tighter over their heads. Then the power failed and the room went pitch black and the whooshing roar of dozens of aircraft was right overhead. Estes could hear the building collapsing.

*We're dead men.*

He thought of his wife and children.

—  •  —

Unlike so many others across the city, Pete Jackson never heard the tornado coming. No more than two or three minutes had passed since he'd gone to ground in the cubbyhole behind the snack bar at the Pla-Land bowling alley. He was squeezing himself tighter against the wall when darkness descended and the room exploded. The building began to disintegrate. The combination of the tornado's growl and the atmospheric pressure made it feel as though his head was caught in a vise and was about to explode. His ears popped hard several times. His eyes were closed, but he could feel objects swirling around and striking him and he could hear the lumber cracking and ripping. It was as if the entire bowling alley had been thrown into a giant blender.

*I'm going to die and there's nothing I can do about it. What a place to die in. What a way to go. And at my young age.*

—  •  —

Tim Lyle and Dick Brumme were still watching from the 10th floor of the Santa Fe building. But by now, they were immobilized as much by fear as fascination. The tornado had quickly closed the last quarter mile and no longer was distinct. Instead, the sky itself appeared to have merged with the ground, and grayish air swirled and boiled as pieces of wreckage raced and skipped across the green grass of the capitol grounds. A portion of the state printing building, a block south on 10th Street, suddenly seemed to liquefy and shoot upward in a graceful, spiraling arc of paper and bricks. Then the lights in the Santa Fe building flickered and failed. The windows on the south and west sides of the 10th floor exploded outward. Papers from office desks hurtled into the void like a flock of panicky birds. The tornado's roar was crushing.

"Get to the stairwell!"

The men dashed for the stairs and slammed the door behind them, then fell to their knees and braced for impact. But only silence ensued. Cautiously, Lyle stood up and peeked out the door. A huge cottonwood was floating just outside the windows to the west. The tree was fully intact and horizontal, so close you could almost touch its rough bark and leafy branches. Lyle watched as the giant drifted slowly north on a mighty river of air, 100 feet off Jackson Street.

Untethered at last.

—  •  —

Operator Laura Dalrymple didn't have much time to ponder the curious spectacle she'd just witnessed in the Southwestern Bell building.

*What on Earth was that woman talking about? What did she mean, 'It's coming!'?*

Dalrymple put her headphones on and once again was trying to make sense of her malfunctioning switchboard when suddenly the interior, windowless room grew very hot, as though the furnace was blasting right beside her. She heard screams. Then she felt a sensation that went well beyond the realm of normal human experience. The pressure change from the tornado was fully upon her, and her body started to move in an involuntary, swaying S-motion. She instantly perceived the movement at a molecular level, as if some kind of wave was passing directly through her. And in that moment she realized — or was made to understand — that the human body really does consist of 90 percent water.

—  •  —

Four blocks north, two men stood at the corner of 5th and Van Buren streets and watched the monster approach. David Laird was a 19-year-old Washburn student studying criminal justice; Fred Eiesland was a plainclothes officer who managed a work-study program at police headquarters. The two had listened in the police radio room as Officer Hathaway called in the initial tornado sighting from Burnett's Mound. They'd watched dispatcher Marc Hood key the warning sirens. After that, Eiesland had decided it would probably make sense to gas up his cruiser, given the undoubtedly long night ahead.

A deep, ominous rumble was building in the southwest as a jail trustee filled the car at the police pumps a block west of the station. Eiesland and Laird jogged out to Van Buren Street and craned their necks toward the sound. Van Buren offered an unobstructed view of the state capitol grounds three blocks south and the men could see the tornado now, looming beyond the statehouse. The capitol's high green dome appeared naked and fatally exposed against the churning funnel behind it. The roar had become deafening.

Laird had never been so scared.

*This could be the end of the world . . .*

As if to underscore that possibility, the tornado whipped a fully intact, two-car garage from its inventory of circling debris and flung it hard against the southwest corner of the capitol dome, 250 feet above the ground, as a child might throw a dollhouse. The garage exploded. Then the wind gathered the fragments and drew them back into its spinning grasp.

The men shouted a warning to the trustee and dashed for the police station basement.

—  •  —

Dorothy Decker had walked most of the way up the 900 block of Kansas Avenue to meet her husband, Earl, after leaving the Coffee Cup Café. He'd pulled the car around to the corner of 9th and Kansas so Dorothy wouldn't get her shoes wet while climbing in. She was standing at the curb and was just about to open the door when the winds arrived. The torrents grabbed her and threw her sideways into the quarter-inch plate glass window in the front of Karlan's Furniture store. Then everything — broken glass, furniture and Dorothy — was sucked back out onto Kansas Avenue and lifted off to the south. She tried grabbing a parking meter as she flew past. But no human could match the tornado's strength. So down Kansas Avenue Dorothy went, just another piece of debris, slamming into the pavement and bouncing back up and hitting again. And the whole time, every agonizing millisecond, she was awake and aware of each new cut and puncture from the countless shards of glass, metal and wood that stabbed at her in their frantic rush to meet the vortex.

*Make it end, make it end, God, make it end!*

— • —

Twenty-four-year-old Gary Fleenor had just finished going through the buffet line at the Pennant Cafeteria, a popular eatery on the second floor of a building just across Kansas Avenue. He was there with 30 or so other Jaycees for their monthly meeting. Fleenor found a seat near the big, plate glass windows that overlooked the avenue.

Then someone said, "Hey, look at all the birds!"

"Those aren't birds! That's paper!"

Then: "My God, it's a tornado!"

Not 10 seconds later, the tall windows crashed outward and clattering dishes and silverware chased the broken glass into the street. The Jaycees hit the floor. Amid the chaos, Fleenor cautiously lifted his head to the windowsill and peered out. He could see the tornado a block south. It was dirty white and coiling like an enormous snake around the National Reserve Life Insurance building, a 10-story monolith that stood alone on the southeast corner of 10th and Kansas. The building shook violently as the tornado squeezed and seemed to tighten its grip, like an anaconda crushing a large mammal.

Fleenor ducked back to the floor.

— • —

Three blocks southeast on Quincy Street, 46-year-old Catherine Sommers crowded closer to her older sister in the dining room of their mother's home. Mrs. Nell Dale was in her 70s. She was a widow and in failing health. That's why Catherine had come to check on her, leaving her two boys at home. That's why her sister, Frances, was in town from Great Bend. That's also why Nell's bed had been moved down to the first floor of the big, two-story house, and why Catherine knew there would be no way of getting her mother to the basement after the sirens went off.

"What do the sirens mean, Catherine?" Frances asked nervously. "What are we to do?" Evidently, they didn't have tornado sirens in Great Bend.

"It means a tornado is coming and we need to take cover right now. Here, help me."

Catherine cleared a card table, and together the sisters lifted it over their mother's bed to create a partial roof that covered the upper half of Nell's frail body. Then both sisters knelt on the floor on one side of the bed and held tight to two legs of the table. Minutes passed before the first winds came in. The old house creaked and groaned. Then the rumble could be heard, faintly at first but growing steadily as the seconds ticked by. Within moments, the noise became so loud that it was exactly as if a locomotive were bearing down on tracks that ran straight through the front parlor and into the dining room. At that point, the windows blew out and the room became a cauldron of flying missiles and crashing furniture.

Catherine hunkered down lower. Frances fainted dead away.

— • —

Nearby, 17-year-old Ramon Esquivel Jr. and two sisters, Marcia, 13, and Sylvia, 11, were helping their father, Ramon Sr., with his janitorial business. The family was cleaning the last building of the night, the Heumann Dental Laboratory, at 1007 Monroe. Ramon Jr. stepped outside to empty the trash and looked up. A swarm of debris was circling in the milky sky above Kansas Avenue.

He ran back inside and shouted to his father and sisters.

"We'd better get out of here. There's a tornado coming!"

Two dental technicians were working late in the building and Ramon told the men what he'd seen. They decided to stay.

But not the Esquivels. "Come on, kids! We'll get under the bridge!" Ramon Sr. yelled. Out to 10th Street the family fled, with fleet-of-foot Marcia leading the way. Interstate 70 snaked through downtown

Topeka in a deep trough set below the grade of surrounding streets. A five-lane bridge spanned the highway at 10th Street. The family made for it. Marcia could hear the crackling roar closing in behind her. Near the bridge, a chain-link fence blocked the way. Marcia and Ramon scrambled over, then Ramon Sr. lifted little Sylvia over and into the waiting hands of his son. The tornado was nearly on them. Ramon Sr. looked back as he pulled himself over. He could see the two-story, cinder-block dental building begin to come apart. He sprinted for shelter under the bridge deck. A couple of strangers already were there. Ramon could see all his children except Marcia. She was below; her momentum had carried her tumbling all the way to the bottom of the overpass.

The wind was howling now.

"Grab the pillar, honey!" Ramon Sr. yelled. "Hang on!"

Ramon Jr. pulled his little sister closer as the roar became fierce and terrible. Squinting against the flying sand and mud, Ramon Jr. watched a passing semi blow over on the interstate.

—  •  —

The ride from Tennessee to Kansas had been long, hot and windy for nine-year-old Jill Nauman. And still she wasn't halfway home. Jill was returning from two weeks' vacation, heading for her hometown of Battle Ground, Washington. She rode with her uncle, Robert Goodson, and two cousins, Wayne and Roger, in a 1940-something Ford. Jill's mother, father, brother and sister took the lead in a separate car. The little convoy was heading for Jill's grandparents' farm in north-central Kansas for the night.

But here's the funny thing. The group usually didn't stop for attractions. And yet, earlier they'd decided to check out the Truman Presidential Library in Independence, Missouri, and they'd spent the better part of two hours there. Plus, the old car Goodson was driving kept overheating and they'd have to stop and let it cool. This happened a couple of times throughout the day. So that's how the travelers found themselves approaching downtown Topeka on I-70 just before 7:30 p.m. At that point, the rain started pelting so hard that the wipers on the old Ford couldn't keep up and Goodson couldn't see to drive, so he pulled over at an underpass to let the weather go by. Jill's parents and siblings didn't see them stop and drove on.

The rain had eased to a sprinkle when Goodson pulled back onto the highway. He hadn't gone a mile, though, when he saw what seemed to be very large, black birds circling in the queer, low clouds above the buildings of downtown. He quickly pulled to the shoulder.

"Get out!"

Jill didn't understand why. But she and the two boys obeyed.

"Come on!"

Bob herded the children across the westbound lanes and helped them over the concrete median barrier. The wind was blowing hard now. The group dashed to the shoulder and then scrambled up a muddy bank to the shelter of the 10th Street Bridge.

Jill was only nine. She was from Washington State. She didn't even know what a tornado was. But she started getting scared when sticks and mud began to blow and swirl beneath the bridge. A couple of other people appeared and huddled near them. Jill had shorts on, and the sand was stinging her legs as if she were at the beach on a windy day.

"Down, everyone!"

Goodson was a big man and he shielded the children as best he could. But more objects were flying now, bigger objects — many more. To Jill, it felt as though someone was punching her hard in the legs and back. There was no light, just swirling shadows.

*Oh, God, please stop this!*

A rock or brick struck Jill, and her prayer was answered. The blow to the head was the last thing she remembered.

# CHAPTER THIRTEEN

# Under a Cobalt Sky

Pete Jackson could hardly believe he was still alive. He opened his eyes, looked up and saw only blue sky where the bowling alley roof had been. Except for a few white, puffy clouds, the sky was clear and perfectly still. Not even the gentlest breeze stirred. Amazingly, Jackson didn't have a scratch on him. But he did feel something odd on his head. He reached up and cautiously touched his crew cut and found countless shards of glass nestled in his hair. He looked down at his shirt. His breast pocket was overflowing with splinters, glass and other tiny scraps of debris. How the winds managed this as Jackson lay face-down, covering his head, he had no idea. The other bowler he'd sought shelter with, Dodo Ramirez, likewise was peppered with wood and bits of glass. But he too, miraculously, was unhurt.

"Look, Dodo . . ."

Jackson pointed to the pin decks at the far end of the bowling alley. The wall behind the lanes was partially gone — a row of wrecked homes was visible off to the east — and the lanes themselves were covered with debris. But the bowling pins still stood, patiently awaiting the frame that now would never come.

Other bowlers emerged from the restrooms where they'd sought shelter a few minutes before. None appeared seriously injured.

Then someone shouted, "I think the old man's hurt!"

Lisle Grauer always told his son that if a tornado ever came, he would get under the pool table. And that's what he did. And now the table was flattened and partially buried, and Pla-Land's proprietor and another man lay beneath it. The other fellow, Bud Brightfield, yelled that he was okay. But Grauer was silent. The bowlers dug frantically through boards and brick to get to the green felt. Then, six or eight to a side, they gently lifted the heavy table away.

Grauer's body was covered with dust. He wasn't moving or breathing. His face was badly scraped and blood trickled from his ears. The men tried to revive him but could not.

He was gone.

"Goddamn . . . ," someone muttered quietly.

One of the bowlers went for help. Another said he'd stay with Grauer's body, so Jackson wandered back to the lane where he'd been bowling. He found his ball still sitting on the return rack. The finger holes were packed tightly with the same detritus that had infiltrated his pocket. His street shoes, too, were brimming with the stuff, as if pack rats had been working overtime. Jackson shook out his shoes and ball and dropped them into his black vinyl ball bag. Then he climbed over the collapsed front of the building and stepped out onto Kansas Avenue.

*The old man is dead. In a tornado. I'm lucky to be alive.*

He took a deep breath.

Up and down the wide boulevard, buildings were flattened, ripped open or scraped clean. The rotten-egg smell of natural gas hung in the air. Dozens of cars from the nearby lots lay scattered and smashed. A V-8 motor sat alone in the middle of the street, air breather still attached, like an offering to the gods. Jackson looked around for his car, a black 1960 Thunderbird. It was his pride and joy, and his heart sank when he saw it. It appeared as if vandals had taken sledgehammers and methodically worked their way around the vehicle, smashing every panel and bending the short tail fins nearly down to the truck. A missile the size of a softball evidently had shot through the front windshield and out the back. The car was totaled.

Jackson began walking north on Kansas Avenue. The tall National

Reserve Life building — the one the tornado had coiled around like a snake — still stood on the corner of 10ᵗʰ and Kansas, though severely damaged. The south face of the building bore a now-ironic advertisement for the insurance firm. In painted letters 10 feet tall, the sign read ". . . a refuge in time of storm."

To the east, on the lot of Tom Mix Rambler Ranch, the wind had stacked cars in a metallic totem pole. Jackson looked north into the heart of downtown and a panicky, sinking sensation swept through him.

*Look at all the bodies . . . .*

In the distance, a half dozen or more inert human forms could be seen lying on the sidewalk and in the street along the 900 block of Kansas Avenue. Jackson quickened his step. Then a wave of relief: As he drew closer, he realized the bodies were actually mannequins that had been sucked from the big display windows of Pelletier's Department Store. It still made for a surreal, grotesque sight. Several of the dummies had been hurtled through windshields, and now their rigid legs and expressionless faces jutted at odd angles from the row of destroyed cars parked along the avenue.

The incessant clang of a burglar alarm announced itself from across the street. The windows of a jewelry store were blown out but expensive watches and diamonds remained. Just then, a man came running around the corner, frantic and waving his arms.

"Take cover! It's coming back!"

*What the hell?*

Jackson dashed to the next block, where he could gain an unobstructed view to the northeast, the direction the tornado had gone. The sky was azure. The tornado wasn't coming back. The idea itself was far-fetched. Seldom do tornadoes reverse course or backtrack.

*Crazy son of a bitch . . .*

Just then, a souped-up, black '36 Ford coupe rumbled up Kansas Avenue and slowed to a stop near Jackson. A couple of scruffy teenagers looked out.

"You all right, mister?" Jackson was ripped and filthy, and with all the glass in his hair, his head glittered as though encased in diamonds.

He told the teenagers about the destruction of the bowling alley and the death of Lisle Grauer.

"Where are you going?"

"I'm trying to get back to my apartment and my wife and kid over by Washburn," Jackson replied.

"We'll give you a ride."

Jackson climbed in, and the hot rod moved off as the teenagers excitedly described their close encounter with the twister. Evidently, the youths had found themselves driving near the edge of the storm. They'd watched a house shoot straight up into the funnel — spinning like Dorothy's farmhouse in *The Wizard of Oz*, high above the treetops and still intact — before disintegrating in a starburst of shattering lumber.

"What happened to your roof?" Jackson asked. Some of the old Fords had a detachable cloth square on the top, kind of a proto-sunroof. But the canvas on this one, save some ragged, torn edges, was gone.

"Tornado ripped it clean away. We were that close, man. I'm telling ya, it was crazy!"

The kids were jacked on adrenaline.

Since this entire ordeal began, Jackson had assumed that the tornado had touched down just west of downtown and started its march there. But when the group repeatedly found their way blocked by downed trees and other debris, the grim realization sunk in that the funnel actually had been on the ground for many blocks before striking the bowling alley. With each new detour, Jackson's anxiety grew.

*Please let them be alive.*

Finally, by bushwhacking along side streets and driving up through yards and around fallen trees and downed power lines, the kid at the wheel managed to reach the north edge of the Washburn campus. Jackson's soul went black as he stared at the devastated university in the fading light of that eventful day. His apartment was on the far side of campus.

*They're dead. I've lost Trish and Shane.*

He thanked the teenagers, bailed out and started running through the ruins, leaping hot lines and juking around wrecked cars and fallen trees, still carrying his bowling bag. He quickly made it past the heart of the campus, and he could just make out his white apartment complex in the gathering dusk across open ground that served as the school's nine-hole golf course. As he drew closer, he began to take heart: The building appeared to be intact. Then he could see people out front. And then, still running, he spotted Trish holding Shane in the crowd.

Elation. Thirty seconds more and Jackson pulled up panting.

The couple embraced for a long moment.

Finally, Trish asked, "What in the world happened to you?"

Jackson explained.

"Oh my God . . . Everybody here figured the tornado went back up after hitting Washburn," Trish said. "How far east did the damage go?"

"As far as the eye can see," Jackson replied.

— • —

Used car salesman Jerry Estes crawled on his stomach through blackness across the rubble-strewn floor of the basement barbershop on Kansas Avenue. He could hear hissing and he smelled gas. The lines that supplied the many dryers in the laundromat above had sheared off and natural gas was filling the basement.

"Don't anybody light a match!"

Narrow shafts of daylight bore down through the darkness near the front of the shop. Fortunately, several large window frames and doors had fallen across the stairs and formed a rough lattice that prevented the stairwell from filling entirely with debris. Estes yelled to his three companions.

"C'mon guys! Let's get outta here. This place could blow."

The men crawled and slithered through narrow openings, amid brick and broken glass and stabbing nails and shattered wood before finally breaking through to daylight at the top of the stairs. Once all had emerged, the men gazed around in amazement. The stillness of death enveloped the city.

Suddenly, a car horn started blaring from the ruins of Joe Smith's lot.

"What in the . . . ?" Smith said.

"One of your cars is talking to you, Joe," Terry Steele said.

The building above the barbershop was destroyed. There was no sign of the stubborn old man on the second-floor apartment, the one who'd refused to come to the basement. There was no second floor. His prospects couldn't be good.

The group heard cries coming from across the street, from one of the old homes that had been converted to offices along the east side of the avenue. A big tree had fallen in front of the property and the path to the door was nearly blocked. Several women were calling from the porch. They were badly cut. The men made a human chain and carefully passed the survivors over and through the limbs. Then Denny Benge flagged down a Cadillac as it drove slowly past. He opened the back door. But the driver balked.

"Hey, I'm not taking them anywhere. They'll get blood all over my seats!" the driver said.

Benge was in no mood.

"Your seats will be a lot bloodier if you don't get these women to a hospital right now, mister!"

With the women loaded and hospital-bound, Benge bid his companions a hasty good-bye and took off jogging for his home near Burnett's Mound, four miles away. Barber Terry Steele went with him. A mechanic named Johnny Means, another mutual acquaintance, pulled up a few minutes later and offered to take Smith and Estes back to his service station on Topeka Boulevard. They could use his telephone to call their wives. But the phone line was dead. So Smith and Estes started walking: Estes heading for his home north of Washburn to find his wife and children, Smith returning to the car lot to see what he could salvage before night fell. Estes happened to look down as the men parted company and was amazed to see that he still carried the big coat-hanger ring full of keys, the ones he'd pulled from all the cars on the lot before the tornado hit. Through it all, he'd never let go.

— • —

Tim Lyle and Dick Brumme made their way down the stairs in the Santa Fe office building to the eighth floor where Brumme worked. The windows were shattered and IBM punch cards were tossed everywhere. Brumme's supervisor assessed the damage.

"Okay, let's get this cleaned up," he said as the men came in.

"Bullshit! I'm not cleaning anything up," Brumme replied. "I think the tornado might have hit my house, and I'm going to check on my wife and daughter."

The supervisor didn't argue. Brumme and Lyle raced down the stairs to the street. Along 9th Street, IBM punch cards were scattered and drifted in piles like snow. The men found Brumme's car with a large tree limb across it, so they jumped into Lyle's green VW Beetle. It had been parked nearby. Except for some dents and nicks, the little car was in good shape.

They drove south on Jackson, the wrong way down the one-way street. The wrecked state printing building across 10th Street looked like a factory in Stalingrad. A man was sitting alone on the sunlit corner, bleeding from the head. A city bus lay on its side nearby. The man appeared to have superficial cuts from debris. He was conscious.

"Stay right there, mister. Don't try to move. Help will be here shortly."

Then Lyle swung west on 10th Street, swerving to avoid objects in the street. Brumme was becoming increasingly agitated.

"I hope Dizi and Crystal are all right. I swear, it looked like the tornado went right through Central Park. Didn't it to you?"

Lyle didn't say a word. But he flogged the VW.

Brumme had met Dizi (pronounced "Die-zee") when he was

stationed at Arlington Cemetery as part of the Army's Old Guard. Many's the time he'd stood watch over JFK's grave. Dizi had grown up in the Washington, D.C., area; her father was a top civilian director in the Department of Defense. The Brummes had been back in Kansas for a little over a year, and Dizi wasn't exactly thrilled with her new home. She didn't have many friends in Topeka.

Driving southwest, Lyle quickly became entangled in the tornado's broad damage path and, like Pete Jackson and the kids in the hot rod, he was forced to make repeated detours. Finally, the bug was three blocks north of Central Park and Lyle could go no further. The men jumped out and ran, avoiding downed trees and hot power lines that burned like flares in the street. They pulled up panting at the shattered north edge of the park and could immediately see the large, old home where Brumme rented a third-floor apartment. The top of the building was sheared off.

"Oh my God!"

Muffled shouts and cries were coming from the storm cellar on the side of the house when the men reached the yard. The cellar stairs were covered with heavy, wooden doors, and wreckage was piled atop the entryway. Lyle and Brumme made quick work of clearing the debris and flung back the doors. And there, in the sudden light at the bottom of the stairs, was Dizi. Her eyes were as big as saucers and she was holding her baby tightly in her arms. She came up slow and crying.

"Are you okay, Dizi?" a shaken Brumme asked. "Is Crystal all right?"

Dizi turned and looked at him when she reached the top step. Every emotion bottled up through 30 minutes of terror came pouring out.

"Yeah, we're okay," she sobbed. "But you can screw Kansas! I'm going home!"

Brumme turned to Lyle and shook his head. He had tears in his eyes and a wry grin on his face.

"What can I say?"

Sure enough, Dizi departed for the East within a week, and Brumme followed soon after. They never did return.

—  •  —

By the time the tornado let go of Dorothy Decker — the woman dragged off by the winds as she prepared to step into her car in the middle of downtown — she'd traveled almost 200 yards, or the full length of the 900 block of Kansas Avenue. That she wasn't pulled into the vortex and lifted high above the city must have been due to some lucky accident of physics and timing. Evidently she was just far enough from the core of the tornado that it was already moving away and thus losing its grip by the time she reached the main damage path near the intersection of 10th and Kansas.

But that, no doubt, was of small consolation at the time. Dorothy was conscious and alive, but barely so. The tornado had ripped off her shoes, dress, blouse and underwear and left her in only her bra. Her left heel and right ankle were broken. And virtually every inch of her body, except for the skin under her bra, was sliced, punctured or scraped. She had a particularly deep wound in one knee, and she was a mass of blood when her husband, Earl, found her heaped in the middle of the street. Earl had ridden the storm out lying on the front seat of the Ford. He and some others applied a tourniquet to Dorothy's leg, carried her into a nearby building and covered her with a blanket. Within minutes, Earl was able to flag down a policeman, who drove her to St. Francis Hospital. But Dorothy was not expected to survive.

How ferocious was the assault that Dorothy Decker endured? When Earl finally got back to his car, he was stunned to see that the entire north side of the vehicle — the side *farthest* from the tornado — had been sandblasted down to bare metal by the grit-packed winds racing to reach the funnel.

—  •  —

After the roar and chaos stopped, Catherine Sommers could hear water running, like a brook. All else was silent. The water was gurgling down through a gap in the ceiling in her mother's dining room.

Catherine's sister, Frances, lay unconscious on the floor. She'd fainted as the storm pressed in. Their mother, Nell, appeared to be okay. She could talk and was still in her bed under the card table roof that Catherine had fashioned after the sirens went off.

"Frances will come to in a minute," Nell said. "She'll be all right."

And sure enough, Frances quickly recovered. She wasn't injured, just covered with glass and dust. They all were.

Catherine stood up. Broken glass and shattered furniture lay everywhere. A piece of limestone the size of a melon — perhaps from one of the buildings at Washburn University — was sitting squarely atop the card table. But for Catherine's quick thinking in setting the table over her, her mother probably would have been badly injured or killed. The sisters lifted the rock and table clear. Then Catherine went to the front door. But debris was stacked so high outside that there was no way through. So she went to a broken window and hailed a man walking by in the street.

"Say, mister! Do we have limbs on the roof?" she called.

The man looked as if he'd seen a ghost.

"My God, lady, you've got no roof!"

Catherine realized they would need to get Nell out quickly.

"You stay here. I'll go for help," she told her sister. Catherine climbed out the window and into the yard. She saw several policemen standing near the corner of 11$^{th}$ and Quincy. Catherine approached and explained that her mother needed to be transported. The officers were writing down the address when a middle-aged woman suddenly appeared, seemingly out of nowhere.

"Help me," the woman said in an uneven voice.

Her face was badly cut and she was bleeding profusely. But she still had the presence of mind to hold out her apron with both hands so the blood wouldn't drip on her dress. The policemen quickly helped the woman to a cruiser at the end of the block as Catherine returned to the house.

Fortunately, Catherine's brother and nephew arrived soon after to check on Nell. They got her into a chair and then carried the chair to a waiting car. They would take her to the home of another sister, in Rossville, a small town northwest of the city. Frances went with them. At that point, Catherine started on foot for her own house, six blocks to the southwest on Harrison Street. Much to her relief, the house wasn't hit. But her two sons, aged 8 and 16, were nowhere to be found — in the basement or anywhere else. Catherine raced back to her mother's house. When she arrived, she found the boys waiting. They'd come to find her on their own. The youngest rode on his brother, piggyback-style, to avoid the downed power lines.

With her mother and boys safe, her husband stuck on the second shift at Goodyear until 11:00 p.m., night coming on and the power out at the house, Catherine decided to retreat to nearby Assumption Church. The stately, mission-style Catholic church was located directly north of the capitol grounds, on 8th Street. The assistant pastor escorted the family back to the parish house, where the head pastor, Father Moriarty, greeted them warmly.

"Are you all right, Catherine?"

The exhaustion and stress finally caught up with her.

"Father, what I've been through is just this side of hell," she said.

Father Moriarty hurriedly turned to an assistant.

"Quickly, my son, bring the altar wine. Lord knows she needs it!"

— • —

At the 10th Street underpass, Ramon Esquivel Jr. pulled himself to his feet, walked out from under the bridge and looked around. Cotton-white clouds drifted past in a cobalt sky. The silence was as pure as the air. Esquivel's sisters and father followed him into the sunlight; Marcia crawled up the bank from the interstate. All were battered but okay. The family climbed back over the chain-link fence and walked slowly toward the dental lab where they'd been working before the tornado hit. The building had been reduced to a pile of cinder blocks. Ramon Sr.'s work car, a behemoth, two-tone green 1955 DeSoto wagon, was buried under the blocks in the back. The Esquivels heard voices. The two dental technicians who'd stayed behind were battling through the wreckage and eventually made their way out. They'd been huddled in a back room when a wall came down. The wall caught the top of the pop machines and created a pocket, which allowed the men to survive. But they were badly shaken. It had been a very near thing.

"Will your bike start?" Ramon Sr. said, pointing to his son's Honda 305 Scrambler lying nearby. Ramon Jr. picked up the motorcycle. It was battered but appeared to be intact. He gave it a couple of kicks and it fired.

"Go to the house to check on your mother and sister," Ramon Sr. said. "It looks like the tornado went that way. I'll walk with the girls. Be careful, son. There are a lot of downed lines."

— • —

Jill Nauman, the nine-year-old whose journey from Tennessee to Washington State was interrupted by the tornado, regained consciousness about the time the rest of the survivors at the underpass were getting up. She made her way down the embankment to the highway with her cousins, Wayne and Roger, and her uncle, Robert Goodson. All were covered with mud. Wayne started crying.

"You're bleeding, Dad!"

Dirty blood was flowing from an ugly gash in Goodson's hand. He looked at Jill.

"My God, you're bleeding, too . . ."

Jill could see the blood dripping off her chin, falling to her knees and splattering at her muddy feet. A sliver of wood about four inches long, an inch wide and a half inch thick, had been driven like a carpenter's shim between her scalp and skull, just above her forehead. Goodson led the children back to the westbound lane of the interstate. They could see their car a quarter mile up the road, smashed and rolled. A semi slowed down; the driver looked but didn't stop. Then a carload of nuns stopped. But they had no room. Finally a couple of men pulled over and quickly opened the back door and the group climbed in. Evidently, the men were salesmen of some sort. The backseat was covered with stacks of business forms.

"Don't worry about the papers," one of the men said. They must have been local, because they knew to take the exit just a few blocks away. They swung quickly into the hospital operated by the Santa Fe railroad for its employees. Jill and her uncle were triaged and tagged, and then Jill was hanging her head over a sink as a nurse washed out the wound in her scalp. But it would take more than a few stitches to repair it.

Jill's parents, brother and sister — traveling west in a separate car — had not stopped for the heavy rain when Goodson pulled over, so they'd dodged the tornado. But they lost contact with the other car. Further up the road they'd finally stopped and waited and when the Ford never appeared, they turned around. Now, driving back through downtown, the group was horrified to see Goodson's battered Ford lying wrecked by the interstate. They frantically began searching and eventually found a policeman who pointed them to some shelters; they checked several but had no luck. They did, however — amazingly — run into the same nuns who'd stopped on the highway, and at that point, Jill's parents at least knew their daughter was alive. A couple of hours later the family was finally reunited at the hospital.

It was an emotional scene.

## 5 East Topeka / Oakland

A – Stormont-Vail Hospital, *10th St. & Washburn Ave.*

B – St. Francis Hospital, *7th St. & Garfield Ave.*

C – Ellis, Johnson, *Capitol City Pawn Shop, SW corner, 6th St. & Branner St.*

D – Ginter, *Vickers station, NW corner, 6th St. & Branner St.*

E – Guthrie & Sons Grocery, *SW corner, 4th St. & Lake St.*

F – Jackson (Norma), *Lime St.*

G – Gutierrez, *Chandler St.*

H – Robbins, *Santa Fe shops*

I – Esquivel (Steph), *Golden Ave.*

J – Jones (Linda), *Arter St.*

K – Laird (Carol & Edna Mae), *Arter St.*

L – Taylor (Chick), *B Street*

M – Idlet, *Winfield Ave.*

N – National Weather Bureau office, *Billard Airport*

O – Briery, *Strait Ave.*

# CHAPTER FOURTEEN

# Behold the Pale Horse

Dave Perkins stood near technician Gordon Brokaw in the darkened radar room at the Weather Bureau office near Billard Airport. A two-way radio crackled as reports of the tornado's progress and position filtered in. Brokaw was staring intently into the green cathode-ray screen, watching the hook advance with each sweep of the beam. Periodically, he'd mutter, "Damn, it's coming down the line . . ."

Finally, Perkins, a volunteer with the local CB weather spotters group, asked, "What do you mean, 'It's coming down the line'?"

Brokaw paused the sweep and pointed to the screen. The tornado's distinctive echo was following the line of the radar beam like a pencil lead tracking a ruler. The Weather Bureau office, of course, was located at the end of the line.

"It's heading straight for us," Brokaw said.

—  •  —

Eight-year-old Dominic Gutierrez peeled out in the alleyway behind his home on his silver stingray bike. He was pedaling fast for Guthrie & Sons, a small, old-fashioned grocery located on 4th Street, a block south and east of his home on Chandler. Dominic lived with his dad, mom, three sisters and two brothers in a plain, two-story, frame house, east of the rail yards beyond downtown and not far from the sprawling Santa Fe car shops. His dad was working the 4:00–midnight shift, sorting mail at the main post office. Dominic's mother, Rosemary, was home with the children. She was worried. She didn't have batteries for the transistor radio or the flashlight. If the storm knocked out the power, or worse, they'd need both. She had asked Dominic to ride to Guthrie's to pick up some batteries.

"Go, Dougie!" she'd yelled from the back porch. That's what she called him. "Be quick!"

Dominic was a skinny kid. He wore cutoffs and a white T-shirt. He pumped his bike furiously from side to side as the gravel crunched beneath his tires. The sky was burnt orange and the light diffuse, eerie and alien. The wind was flat calm. Never in his life had Dominic seen a day like this. Even the dogs that usually growled and barked at him from worn, fenced-in backyards on either side of the alley were silent. The boy swung wide onto 4th Street and skidded to a stop in the gravel in front of Guthrie's. He leaned his bike against the white, one-story, block building; yanked open the squeaky, metal door; and dashed inside.

A window air conditioner hummed near the back. The store had just three aisles, each piled high with canned goods and other foodstuffs. There was a meat counter in the back and a couple of coolers along the far wall. The light was dim. You could smell the years stacked up in the place.

Cyrus, the oldest of the three Guthrie boys, grinned as he stepped out from behind the meat counter. He was a big man. He wore a white T-shirt and stained butcher's apron. The Guthries had their own nickname for Dominic.

"Hey, Skeeter. What'cha doin' out? Don't you know there's a storm comin'?"

Dominic caught his breath and told Cyrus his mom needed batteries for the radio and flashlight. He asked if he could put them on the bill. Cyrus pulled two packs from the shelf behind the cash register, dropped them into a sack, wrote up a ticket and handed the sack to Dominic.

Just then, the sirens growled to life.

"You'd better get your butt home, boy. The sirens are goin' off. Tornado comin'! Go on, now. Git!" Cyrus hurried to close the store.

The wind was stirring outside, as if awakened by the sirens, and the temperature was starting to drop. The streets were empty; the sky still a poisonous yellow. Dominic's heart raced. He jumped on his stingray and pedaled standing up with the bag gripped tightly beneath his fingers. Turning up the alley, he could just make out his mother's panicked, high-pitched cry coming from the far end of the block. It mingled with the sirens' wail.

"Dougie! Dougie! Where are you?!"

It seemed like the end of the world at that moment. But Dominic was home in a flash. He bailed off his bike and leapt up the porch steps.

"I got the batteries!" he cried. His mother hugged him and they ran for the basement.

—  •  —

Nearby, 19-year-old Norma Jackson sat on her front porch and watched the rain sweep in. Her neighbor, an ancient American Indian woman, sat on her porch next door.

"Guess I won't have to wash the car now!" Jackson called out with a laugh as the rain began to let up.

The old woman nodded and smiled.

Norma had grown up in Nicodemus, a central Kansas town founded by ex-slaves after the Civil War. She'd come to Topeka after high school to stay with an aunt and find her way. She landed a job and met a man, got married, and on May 22 she had her first baby, Paul Frederick. Norma lived in the second-floor apartment of a two-story house near Ripley Park, south of the Santa Fe car shops. Her husband, Paul, worked for the railroad. But he was gone for two weeks' training with the National Guard. Norma's sister-in-law, Tessa Hale, lived in the first-floor apartment. Tessa's husband and daughter were out of town as well, so the two women had dinner together in Tessa's apartment. Then Norma put her son down in a bedroom and Tessa went off to get some sleep. She had to work that night.

Now Norma sat alone on the porch. Some family members came for her neighbor, the Indian woman. The rain stopped and the air became still. The sky was molten, like dawn. And then, out of nowhere, a huge piece of brown wrapping paper suddenly appeared, floating 20 or 30 feet above the street. It was rectangular and large enough to cover a car. It seemed to be burned around the edges. Norma watched the strange talisman drift slowly past like a leaf in a stream.

*Now that's just weird. Where did that thing come from?*

—  •  —

A mile and a half away, in a small house on Winfield Avenue in the Garden Park district of Oakland, near the airport, 14-year-old Wanda Idlet turned on the black-and-white TV to watch *Lost in Space*. Her mother, Velma, was preparing dinner. Wanda was an only child. She was that shy, sensitive girl so terribly afraid of tornadoes — the one whose phobia had been fueled by stories she'd heard from her mother and aunt about unimaginable violence visited from the sky. She'd been on edge all day, and the still, muggy afternoon did nothing to ease her dread. It was as if some terrible, unspoken question literally hung in the air. Now, as the sirens howled, the answer Wanda feared most was at hand.

"Mom!" she yelled toward the kitchen. "We need to go to the neighbor's and get to the basement right now!"

"No," Velma replied matter-of-factly. "I don't believe a tornado could hit Topeka." She continued making supper. "Everyone knows a tornado can't come over Burnett's Mound."

"But, Mom, they said on TV that it's heading for Burnett's Mound right now! Come on! Let's go. We should go."

But Velma was unmoved. She was prideful. She wouldn't ask anyone for anything if she could help it.

"You be still, Wanda. Your father will be home any minute. We'll be just fine."

Wanda didn't believe it. She turned back to the TV, and when she heard Bill Kurtis exclaim, "For God's sake, take cover!" her fear doubled and doubled again. She was nearly beside herself.

"Please, Mom, please!!"

Her mother turned suddenly and fixed Wanda with an angry glare. "Now you just pull yourself together, young lady! We're not going anywhere."

— • —

Sterling Taylor fished for carp all afternoon with his brother Harry at Lake Shawnee. He liked to give the fish to a black man in the neighborhood. Sterling was named for a Confederate general from Missouri, Sterling Price, but everyone called him "Chick" because he was born on Easter Day in 1904. Although he grew up near Rock Creek, Kansas, his people were from Savannah, Missouri, and his grandfather used to hide Frank and Jesse James in his basement. "Jesse was mean as a snake," Grandpa used to say. "He'd have probably shot his own mother for a dollar."

Nothing came easy for Chick. Once, when he'd worked at Swartze Basket Company, he was cleaning a big saw blade. Two co-workers were fooling around. When they hit the blade control, the saw dropped and severed three fingers on Chick's right hand. During the Depression, the only way Chick could feed his wife, Fern, and their three girls was to walk 18 miles up to Rock Creek to hunt rabbit and quail. One time Chick and Harry came home with 20 rabbits. Fern would can rabbit and make roast rabbit and rabbit stew.

Chick eventually got work with the WPA, building the dam at Lake Shawnee for 50 cents a day. But times were still hard. Chick's middle daughter, Katherine Boline, remembered more than once breaking up antiques and burning them in the wood stove to keep from freezing. Uncle Harry lived with the family in a small house near Seward Avenue on B Street, in Oakland.

Life wasn't always bleak, of course. Chick loved to sing old western songs and he played the Jew's harp. Uncle Harry played bones, and Fern would join in on the spoons. When the war came, Harry went off to fight at Guadalcanal. He returned intact, but he was never the same.

The thing about Chick, he was a good man but he drank hard for many years. He would get a paycheck and go on a bender and just disappear for days. The girls would finally track him down at one of the taverns in North Topeka and they'd try to get him to come home but usually could not. Chick finally swore off booze after one particularly brutal binge in the summer of 1949.

"When a man falls asleep walking, it's time to quit," he told Katherine. He had a little ceremony and buried a fifth of Old Crow in the backyard and never drank again.

After Fern's parents died, her retarded brother, Everett, and retarded sister, Stella, moved into the house on B Street. Everett had been what they called an "instrument baby," breeched in the birth canal and removed with forceps. It didn't help that the delivery doctor had been drunk. Stella had polio when she was seven and the fever burned her brain. Everett had a bad temper and he would get violent sometimes. Fern couldn't handle him unless Chick was around.

In June of '66, Chick was 62 years old and two months shy of retirement. He'd put in 20 years at Hill's Packing Company, a dog food factory. He was a cooker, boiling up big vats of horse meat. June 8 was his first day of two weeks' vacation. At about 6:30 p.m., he drove to Tilton's Market on Seward Avenue for a couple of loaves of bread. After that, Fern asked him to take some sweet corn to their granddaughter a few blocks away. When he returned around 7:00 p.m., he told Fern he was going to put the car in the garage because it looked like it could hail. The sirens went off, but Chick didn't hear them. He might have been distracted because there was trouble in the house. Everett was in a rage. He was furious that *Lost in Space* had been interrupted by a special weather bulletin. He started swearing and stomping around.

So Fern just flipped the TV off.

—  •  —

The tornado blew out of downtown and across Interstate 70 at the 10th Street overpass, then hammered into a working-class neighborhood east of the highway along Madison, Jefferson and Adams streets. Row upon row of lap-sided, two-story, 40- and 50-year-old frame houses were scattered before the wind like wheat before a scythe. Fortunately, the tornado had narrowed somewhat from its initial, half-mile footprint, and the damage path was now just three or four blocks wide versus the six or eight it had been when the twister entered the city. But it was still a monster as it spun out of the neighborhood and into an industrial area adjacent to the Santa Fe yards. Then it crossed the tracks and started moving straight down the Shunganunga Creek.

A half mile to the northeast, 6th Street crossed the rail yards and the Shunga on a long, low viaduct that met Branner Avenue at a major intersection. The crossroads served as the gateway to East Topeka and Oakland. A Dairy Queen was on one corner and a Vickers gas station on another. The local Dr. Pepper bottling plant was across the street, and next to it, Capitol City Pawn Shop.

Inside the pawnshop, Lanny Ellis and his half-brother, Darrell Johnson, co-owners of the business, stood transfixed in front of the television with watch repairman Darius Gray. Bill Kurtis was providing a play-by-play of the tornado's progress. When Kurtis reported that the tornado had just struck the National Reserve Life building at 10th and Kansas, Ellis said, "We need to get under cover. It's heading our way."

Ellis and Johnson ran to a back room and knelt down beside the thick stone wall that butted up to the Dr. Pepper plant.

Then they looked around. "Where's Darius?" Johnson asked.

"Good Lord!"

Ellis got up and dashed back to the front of the store. Gray was still watching TV, standing in front of the plate glass windows. Ellis gripped his arm and pulled him to the back room.

But now Johnson was getting jumpy.

"We've got to get out of here!" he said. "We gotta go! We can't stay here." He stood up and was poised to run. But Ellis grabbed his shoulders and pushed him back down.

"We're not going anywhere. You'll get yourself killed out there, Darrell. C'mon now, for Christ's sake, stay down!"

There was a series of loud, concussive bangs, like gunshots, as objects began striking the building. Ellis knelt under a console sewing machine and held tight to the legs. Within seconds, he heard the wrenching, popping, cracking sounds of the roof coming apart. Then all the noises were subsumed in the heavy, bottomless roar of the funnel.

⚊ • ⚊

Across the street, 22-year-old Clarence Ginter was working the 2:00–10:00 p.m. shift at the Vickers gasoline station with a young man from Gallatin, Missouri. Ginter heard the sirens go off but didn't pay them much mind. You heard sirens all the time in the spring. Business would be slow for a while; that was about it. The minutes rolled past as Ginter and his co-worker — a skinny, well-mannered kid with a slow Missouri drawl — waited out the storm in the station's glass office. But then Ginter happened to glance to the south. A geyser of debris had suddenly appeared near 8th and Adams streets. Sheets of plywood and siding and smaller chunks of God knows what were rocketing into the air, like sparks from a Fourth of July fountain. The whole thing seemed to be moving.

"Whoa! Look there. We gotta get out of here!" Ginter told the kid. "Come on, we'll go to the creek."

The two men dashed out of the station, rounded the building and sprinted for the Shunga Creek 100 feet away. They slipped down the muddy bank and crouched against a concrete pier beneath the Branner Avenue Bridge. Not a minute had passed before the winds came in, crashing down the narrow defile like a tsunami. Suddenly, the air was alive with missiles and the wind howled. Almost immediately the men were lifted off the ground. Ginter and his co-worker were about a foot into the air when, in desperation, they reached out and grabbed one another. Their combined weight was enough to break the wind's grip and they tumbled back to Earth. But the tornado wasn't finished with them yet. Like a big cat toying with wounded prey, it began dragging the men up the bank. The two held each other tightly as they were slowly pulled across rocks and mud toward the open, east side of the bridge. At that point, the wind grew so intense that it literally sucked the oxygen from their lungs and they were drowning on land, gasping for air that no longer existed.

— • —

Norma Jackson was still on her porch, still pondering the mysterious brown paper shroud, when she heard the strangest noise. It was like a cross between a plane and a train, and yet it was something different. Norma had no idea that a tornado was on the ground or even that the weather was potentially dangerous. She had watched TV earlier but was tuned to a Kansas City station. And she hadn't heard the sirens. Now there was this ominous, grinding, rumbling sound. She didn't like it at all. So she went inside to her sleeping sister-in-law's bedroom and gently called her several times. When Tessa Hale didn't respond, Norma finally spoke loudly.

"Tessa! Wake up! What *is* that noise?"

Tessa awoke with a start and was up on her knees in the middle of the bed, listening intently. Finally, she said, "I have no idea . . ."

"Well, I don't either," Norma replied.

Whatever it was, it was getting louder.

Norma next went to the bedroom to check on her 16-day-old son. He was sleeping well. She stared at him for a moment and thought about how hard it was to get him down. She didn't want to wake him. But a voice inside her spoke:

*Get your baby. Right now. Get your baby.*

So she did, and in that moment, everything changed. The house started shaking, and there were several enormously loud crashing noises, and then the rumble became deafening as Norma raced back to Tessa's room with Paul Frederick in her arms. The two women got down between the bed and the dresser and yanked the mattress over top of them. Norma pulled her son to her chest. He squirmed a little but remained asleep. At that point, all hell broke loose as the windows were sucked out, walls came down and furniture hurtled into the void. Still and all, Paul Frederick slept.

*Please, God. Don't let him wake up to this.*

Sure enough, the little guy kept sleeping as the world disintegrated around him.

—  •  —

Hiding beneath a miniature pool table, eight-year-old Dominic Gutierrez listened in dry-mouth terror to the grinding sound of the approaching tornado. His brothers and sisters were sobbing beside him. His mother was saying the rosary in Spanish and making the sign of the cross. Shafts of late-afternoon sunlight bore into the cellar through two high, small windows and painted the far wall in liquid bronze. But the color quickly faded as darkness swept over the house, like the shadow of an approaching giant, and the roar arrived.

—  •  —

"Look at the birds!" the old German exclaimed. "Look at them!"

The man, a worker at the Atchison, Topeka and Santa Fe Railway car shops, was standing with 10 or 15 others outside the west end of the massive car barn, a brick structure enclosing nearly a dozen tracks. Inside, scores of freight cars sat in various stages of assembly and repair. The men were staring off to the southwest toward a flock of black objects that swirled and dove in the distance.

"Those aren't birds," another man said quickly. "Those are shingles and debris. That's the tornado!"

Workers on the second shift at Santa Fe had been monitoring transistor radios and were aware that a tornado was in the city. So when the cry went up that it was coming, it didn't take long for the men to seek cover wherever they could. Olen Robbins, a lanky, 27-year-old foreman in the wheel shop, quickly realized that the best places to hide were filling up fast. He shouted to some companions.

"Come on! Let's go to the refinery. There's a basement there."

Five men piled into Robbins' '64 Plymouth Valiant Signet parked nearby. He backed out and raced 100 yards to a small, brick building near the center of the shop complex. The refinery had once been used to reprocess waste oil but was no longer operational. Fortunately, the building wasn't locked. As the Plymouth skidded to a stop and the men jumped out, Robbins glanced to the southwest. He could see the tornado. It was enormous, moving steadily between the shops and the sun and quickly turning day almost literally into night.

The wind was frantic and rising.

The men dashed inside and down some stairs to the open basement and crouched in a trash-filled corner near a bank of empty lockers. At that point, the sound began: To Robbins, it was a mechanical lope, like a huge, laboring motor with rpm's that rhythmically rose and fell. The noise grew louder as the men tried to get lower to the ground.

Then someone shouted, "Olen! Look! There goes your car!"

Robbins turned and glanced up through the tall windows along the first floor to see his Valiant soaring past, 20 feet off the ground. At that point, the wind forced its way into the building and trash was flying and the metal lockers were banging open and shut.

*I hope I get through this without losing my life . . .*

—  •  —

Dolores "Steph" Esquivel was a fiery, rebellious beauty and the oldest daughter of Ramon Esquivel Sr., the janitor who'd sought shelter with his son and two youngest daughters at the 10th Street overpass on the edge of downtown. Steph was 19 and living in the family home on Golden Avenue, east of the shops. The Esquivels' house didn't have a basement, so when the sirens went off, Steph and her mother, Phyllis, ran to the Chavezes' across the street. Maybe 20 people from the neighborhood were there: the Torrez, Muñoz, Valdivia and Rangel families and others. Steph was nine months pregnant, with her due date just two weeks away. She wasn't married and the father was gone for Texas. But the women in the neighborhood had held a baby shower for her anyway the week before and now, in the basement — as the rumbling sound drew closer — they surrounded Steph and formed a human shield. Ten or more women nearly covered her.

It was a noble and courageous act. But Steph was still petrified. She was certain she was about to die. Worse, she fully expected immediate and eternal damnation.

*God will punish me for getting pregnant.*

The tornado was blasting now, deafening. At the apex of the sound, Steph looked straight up to see the floorboards ripping loose between the joists above her head, just like someone was popping them up with an enormous pry bar.

*Oh, God, we're going to die!*

— • —

Armco Steel manufactured culverts, spillways and other corrugated steel products at a large plant east of the Santa Fe car shops. After smashing Santa Fe, the tornado plowed into Armco's storage yard and lifted hundreds of heavy culverts into its turbulent, slippery grasp.

A few blocks away, at the Taylor house on B Street, Chick and Fern had finally managed to get Everett calmed down. Chick went into his bedroom to get some cigarettes and Everett tagged along. Fern was already there, hanging up some clothes she'd ironed.

She heard aircraft overhead.

"I wonder why they're flying those airplanes today . . ."

Chick said, "Those aren't planes. It's that damn thing coming . . ."

The words weren't out of his mouth when the cinder-block house exploded. A concrete block struck Fern and knocked her cold. Stella, Fern and Everett's sister, was blown out into the front yard. Everett was badly cut on the head and likewise ended up in the grass. And a 10-foot-long culvert shot out of the sky, found the bedroom and landed on Chick.

—  •  —

When the sirens went off, 16-year-old Linda Jones had been lounging on the couch, reading *Mad* magazine with her hair in curlers. She lived with her mother, brother, uncle, aunt and grandfather on Arter Street, not far from the airport. Her grandfather, John Goodall, was 80. He didn't trust the family's block house basement to hold up in a tornado, and he'd mentioned his fear once to the neighbors across the street, Carol Laird and his wife Edna Mae. The Lairds had a solid ranch house they'd built themselves in '54, and it had a big, poured concrete basement. Carol had told Goodall that his family was more than welcome to come over anytime the weather got bad.

So they did, and a lot of others did, too. There weren't many basements in the Garden Park neighborhood. Twenty-five people were in the Lairds' basement in all, family and friends, including Kitty Sims, the lady who lived in the next house to the north. Mrs. Sims had lost her husband to a heart attack the previous Friday and had buried him on Monday.

The group was listening to the radio and knew the tornado was moving their way. Linda's grandfather and Carol kept watch out the small basement window. Pretty quickly, they saw chunks of sheet metal and debris from Armco flying in the rolling blackness that was moving in from the southwest.

"Everybody get down! It's coming! God help us all!" Carol shouted. The large group squeezed together. Mrs. Sims, the woman who'd just lost her husband, started screaming. Then Linda heard the roof rafters crack and felt such a strong pull of suction that she was certain they all were about to be lifted into the air. When the tornado was on top of them, the world became deathly silent for a moment — like the eye of a hurricane — and Edna Mae Laird thought her eardrums were going to pop out of her head. Then the roar began again.

— • —

A friend of Linda Jones's brother, 19-year-old Bobby Coffman, was watching TV at his parents' house a block away with a buddy, Gary Fisher. When it became clear that the tornado was heading into Oakland, Bobby decided to make a run for the Joneses' house. He knew they had a basement. He urged his parents to come, but his father refused. So Bobby and his friend took off out the back door, dashing at a dead run through the wet grass, across a vacant lot to the now-empty house. As he ran, Bobby could see the black wall out of the corner of his eye, closing in from the southwest. They made it to the Joneses' back door, burst in and ran for the small basement, then huddled in a corner. The boys grabbed a trashcan lid to protect their heads.

Moments later, the entire house lifted off like a rocket ship above them and atomized in the thundering gale.

— • —

Fourteen-year-old Wanda Idlet had stopped trying to convince her mother that they needed to seek shelter and was instead thinking of fleeing on her own when she saw her dad, Charles Idlet, pull into the driveway. She hurried out to meet him.

"There's a tornado coming, and Mom doesn't want to go to the neighbors!" Wanda cried. "We've got to get out of here, Dad. Let's just get in the car. We can outrun it!"

Her father was tired and worn from a long day. He was a concessionaire, running a snack wagon downtown.

"Come on now, Wanda . . . We'll be all right."

They turned and looked to the southwest. Wanda could see sunshine. Her heart brightened. "Look! The sun's coming out," she said. "Maybe it's not going to hit."

But it was a ruse, because very quickly Wanda could see swirling darkness sliding in front of the sun and chunks of roofing and steel from Armco hurtling through the air. They could hear the rumble now.

"Get inside!" Charles yelled.

They dashed back into the little house. Wanda ran for the bedroom. She tried to get under a bed but the space was too narrow. So she and her mother climbed into the bedroom closet and pulled the flimsy, accordion door closed. She could hear the tornado grinding closer. Debris started pelting the house. Panicked, Wanda tried to stick her head under a small stepstool in the corner of the closet. The pressure against her ears became unbearable as the jet-engine roar reached its highest pitch. Debris was slamming the house like tank rounds.

Wanda closed her eyes. She prepared to die but first tried to work out a deal with God.

*If you let me live, I'll be a better person. I'll try to live for you. Please God. Let me live.*

—  •  —

David Briery's father was trying to reason with his 20-year-old son and convince him to leave the family's cinder-block house on Strait Avenue and come to a neighbor's basement.

"Come on, son. This isn't a joke or some kind of a science project. Don't be foolish. This could get you killed. We need to get out of here right now. Now let's go."

But Briery wouldn't budge. The University of Kansas student was home for the summer, working in the passenger accounting department at Santa Fe. He was studying biochemistry at KU. But he'd always been fascinated by tornadoes.

"No way, Dad. This is probably the only time in my life that I'll ever have a chance to see a tornado. I'm staying. I've got to see this."

"Suit yourself, but I think you're making a terrible mistake."

His parents departed, and Briery continued to listen as Bill Kurtis described the tornado's progress through the city. When Kurtis announced that the tornado was passing through downtown, three and a half miles away, Briery tipped a heavy couch over in the family room to make a shelter near the big picture window that looked out to the east. There was an alfalfa field across the street and beyond it, the low buildings of the Weather Bureau office and the airport.

Moments later, Kurtis reported that the funnel was approximately one mile southwest of the airport. Briery dashed to the back bedroom and looked out the window. He could see swirling clouds in the west and what appeared to be snow falling straight down from a windless sky. Except that it wasn't snow, it was paper. So he ran back to the front room. Now Kurtis was saying the tornado was crossing Strait Avenue.

*That's our street!*

The power immediately failed. From his makeshift bunker under the couch, Briery peered out the picture window. He could see the tornado a thousand feet to the south, moving diagonally across his field of vision. It was churning out of the Garden Park neighborhood and into the open ground around the airport — a towering, sprawling, rolling mass of mud and cloud, choked with debris. As the tornado approached the airport, its winds lifted several small aircraft high into the air. One of the planes burst into flames as it spiraled back to Earth.

⌒ • ⌒

Dave Perkins, the volunteer with the CB spotters group stationed at the Weather Bureau office, earlier had stepped outside with several others as the tornado tore through downtown. He could see debris swirling over the city. Then someone yelled, "Here it comes!"

The men dashed back into the Weather Bureau office. The building didn't have a basement, so people sought shelter wherever they could, in closets and under desks. Perkins got beneath a big military surplus table in the radar room. The whine and roar cranked up as the tornado drew near. Windows shattered, papers flew and doors slammed shut as though a deranged person were stalking the halls.

But the building held. When the winds began to subside, Perkins and several others ran outside in time to see the burning aircraft fall from the sky. The tornado, black and fulminating, was moving straight down the main runway like a jet on its takeoff roll. As the funnel slipped off the end of the runway pavement, it pinwheeled the huge trees that lined the banks of the distant Kansas River. And then, just as it reached the water, Perkins watched in astonishment as the entire funnel — from earth to sky — suddenly changed color from black to white. Instantly, like a shape-shifter.

And then it started to lift.

# CHAPTER FIFTEEN

# A World Transformed

Dominic Gutierrez, the eight-year-old who'd ridden his bike to the nearby market just before the tornado struck, was craning into the silence when he heard familiar voices outside. They belonged to his cousin, Phyllis Roacha, and her boyfriend, Phillip Hernandez. Phyllis lived next door. Dominic raced up to the trapdoor at the top of the basement stairs but the door was blocked. His mother shouted to Phyllis, and soon Dominic could hear Phil above him, moving heavy objects and then lifting the hatch. One by one, the Gutierrez family made their way up the narrow stairs to the parlor. The front of the house was gone. The roof was off, too, and a giant tree was leaning against a second-floor bedroom. Dominic walked out to the back porch and looked down the alley toward Guthrie's market. Homes were flattened, cars were smashed and once-tall trees were denuded and blasted and tall no more. The only things moving were the live wires snaking across the ground. The scene took Dominic's breath away. He thought he might cry but did not.

*Everything I've known is no more.*

— • —

Clarence Ginter and his co-worker at the Vickers station were plastered with mud, straw, sticks and blood but very much alive as they struggled up the slippery bank of the Shunganunga Creek. The gas station was scraped clean; only a bathroom wall and toilet stools remained. As the two men took in the devastation, a stranger appeared. He was medium-built and may have had dark hair. But it was hard to tell for all the blood on his head.

The man's name was Francis Bordner. He was a 38-year-old electrician at Santa Fe and a reservist with the police department. He'd been on his way to work at the police station and had just turned onto the 6th Street Bridge when he spotted the tornado coming on from the south. So he made a U-turn, swung into the station lot, and dashed inside the building seconds after Ginter and his co-worker ran for the creek. Bordner took cover in the women's bathroom. He wrapped himself around the toilet stool and hung on as the tornado ripped the building apart around him. The winds even sucked the water from the toilet. But the porcelain stool didn't shatter. And Bordner didn't let go. He was badly shaken and suffered several deep cuts to his scalp. But he was all right.

Ginter's co-worker, the kid from Gallatin, Missouri, was getting restless as the shock of events began to wear off. He looked to the northeast. The damage path was savage and unrelenting.

"My sister's house is over there, Clarence. I hope she's all right. I gotta go. I gotta go check on her."

"You sure you don't want to go to the hospital?" Ginter said. "You're cut up pretty good."

"Naw, I'm fine, really. I am. I'll see ya 'round."

And with that, the skinny kid from Missouri turned and jogged east into the apocalypse. Ginter watched him go and realized too late that the young man had a piece of wood sticking out of his shoulder.

He never saw the kid again.

*— • —*

Across the street at the pawn shop, Lanny Ellis could see sunlight filtering through the joints in the false ceiling. The roof was gone, but remarkably, the building and most of its contents were intact.

"I think we got lucky, Darrell," Ellis said. The half-brothers stepped out the back door and gazed in silence at the debris scattered the length of the Shunga. The open ground along the creek looked like a landfill as far as the eye could see. Wrecked houses were visible in the distance. Nearby, a broken hydrant sprayed a geyser high into the air. Ellis and Johnson returned to the front of the store. The plate glass windows were gone; the gas station and Dairy Queen across the street were destroyed. Apparently, a couple of kids who'd been working at the DQ had taken refuge in the walk-in cooler. The move undoubtedly saved their lives, as the metal box was the only man-made object still intact on the north side of the intersection.

The brothers went outside and helped free an elderly couple trapped in a basement a half block to the south. Then they returned to the pawnshop to find people gathering outside, milling aimlessly in front of the shattered windows. There was menace in the air.

"You all need to get out of here! We're not open."

Several regular customers appeared, desperate to pawn items for cash. Ellis and Johnson made them loans out of their pockets. But others were looking for different opportunities as the sun slipped lower in the west.

The men strapped on .38-caliber revolvers and awaited the night.

— • —

Norma Jackson, the young woman from Nicodemus, Kansas, and her sister-in-law, Tessa Hale, pushed away the mattress they'd sought shelter beneath and slowly climbed to their feet. Norma carefully placed her still-sleeping, 16-day-old son, Paul Frederick, on the bed. She took stock. She was itching from the many tiny pieces of fiberglass insulation that had lit on her body. But she wasn't hurt. Nor was the baby or Tessa. The house was gutted. As they looked around, the women heard a female voice outside.

"Tessa! Are you in there? Are you all right?"

Norma and Tessa went to the porch. A middle-aged white woman stood in front of the house. It was Jean from across the street. She was plastered from head to toe with mud and her clothes were ripped. Norma could see Jean's home in the background, reduced to a pile of kindling. Jean said she'd ridden out the storm in an overstuffed chair in her living room. As she spoke, Norma noticed something that made her gasp: The woman had a compound fracture of the lower leg. Jutting bone glistened through torn, bloody skin.

"Jean, your leg's broke!"

The woman slowly looked down. She had no idea. The color drained from her face. Norma and Tessa rushed to support her and then gently eased her down to the steps. Soon after, other neighbors arrived, brought a car and transported Jean to the hospital.

"We need to get out of here before dark," Norma said to Tessa. "I'm going to see what's left upstairs. Get some things together. We can go to my aunt's."

The 19-year-old ascended the stairs to catastrophe. The roof hadn't come off, but the kitchen wall was blown out and all the windows, too. Virtually every one of the young couple's possessions, modest though they were, was scattered and despoiled like trash. Norma did find some fresh diapers lying undisturbed on the dresser, and she pulled some bottles of formula from the darkened refrigerator. Then she threw some clothes in a sack and went back down the stairs.

Twilight was settling in as Norma and Tessa set off down Lime Street. Every house they passed was badly damaged or destroyed. People were milling and moving in the streets. Norma saw the body of a man, wearing overalls, lying in an odd, unnatural position on the floor of a destroyed house. A little further on, a huge, downed tree blocked the street, and Norma found herself struggling to get through the branches with Paul Frederick in her arms. She was nearly trapped by the brush when a set of hands appeared from the far side. She could see the face of a tall, slender black man through the limbs.

"I'll take your baby for you."

Norma smelled liquor on his breath.

"You better not drop him . . ."

"I won't. You can trust me."

So she did. Then she quickly fought her way through the branches, took her baby back, thanked the man and kept moving.

The scene became chaotic as the women approached 6th Street, the main drag through East Topeka. Looters were out in force and ravaging stores along the thoroughfare. A liquor store was hard hit and a drugstore, too. Cars screeched to a halt, and people jumped out and dashed into the buildings. A man ran past with a television. There were screams and shouts and curses and laughter. And all the while, the newly homeless, some bloodied and bandaged, streamed out of the damage path like an army in retreat, making for the bridge.

*This looks like a war zone . . .* , thought Norma.

Norma and Tessa crossed the 6th Street viaduct with many others, reached downtown and eventually spotted some friends in traffic and were able to get a roundabout ride to Norma's aunt's house in central Topeka. Her aunt's home, in fact, had been missed by the tornado but not by much. Lights were blazing like a beacon as they walked up the driveway. It had been two hours since the tornado hit. Norma handed the baby to her teary but relieved aunt, Lorene Powell, and then collapsed in a chair.

She didn't speak. She didn't cry. She just started shaking violently. Her teeth chattered and she couldn't hold a drink in her hand.

— • —

After the roar faded, Olen Robbins, the wheel shop foreman at the Santa Fe rail car shops, emerged from the small refinery building with his co-workers. The coal-black darkness that had engulfed the shops had lifted and the late-day sun still gave warmth. Devastation was everywhere. Cars were crushed, sheet metal torn and twisted; the roof of the sprawling car barn was entirely gone. A deafening silence settled in. But the quiet was soon broken by cries for help coming from nearby Ripley Park. Robbins and several others ran over. Tree limbs had come down on a '55 Buick and an elderly man was trapped inside. He had tiny cuts all over his face. Robbins and his companions struggled to remove the limbs but couldn't get the man out. An ambulance is coming, someone said. A couple of men waited with the trapped driver until help arrived.

Robbins could tell the tornado had moved into Oakland and he was worried about his family and home. He found his car, upside down, a half block from where he'd parked it. A co-worker, Gaylord Richardson, had parked farther from the shop, and although all the glass was out of the car, it was still serviceable. So Richardson offered Robbins a ride to his house. They battled down Seward and along side streets, frequently getting out to move limbs and debris.

When they finally reached his street, Robbins craned his neck to look ahead.

"Shit, Gaylord, it's gone . . ."

He jumped out and ran to the wreckage. Robbins's wife and children were nowhere to be found. He shouted their names.

"Bonnie! Randy! Connie! Where are you?"

Then he looked off to the west, toward the street behind the house where homes still stood. And against the setting sun, he spotted his wife and kids. They'd gone to a nearby relative's basement.

He ran to them, laughing and crying at the same time.

⁓ • ⁓

When Steph Esquivel saw the floor disintegrating overhead, she was certain death was seconds away. Now people were moving cautiously up the stairs in the silence of the Chavez home. The house was sheared away above the basement. Steph heard gasps as people filed into the yard. Every home in the immediate area was destroyed, including her own across the street. Women wailed and keened, clasping their hands to their faces as they looked around in shock and despair. Steph's mother was hysterical. Steph tried to comfort her as they walked through the wreckage of their home. The place was gutted. But in the living room, an 8x10 picture of Steph's older brother Greg — in his Navy uniform, just before he shipped out to Vietnam — still stood on a stereo speaker. Steph looked in the bathroom. A piece of wood the size of a ruler was driven through the porcelain tub, like a toothpick through cotton.

Steph's brother Ramon, the one who'd ridden out the tornado with his other sisters and father at the 10<sup>th</sup> Street underpass, arrived soon after. He'd been forced to abandon his motorcycle a block from his parents' home. He spotted Steph and his mother amid the wreckage. He let them know everyone else was okay. Then he checked the property. The family's Buick LeSabre was lying behind the house in a creek bed. Ramon also found one of his father's hunting dogs, a Brittany named Mister, laid open along the creek bank, dead. The other Brittany, Lady, was nowhere to be found.

Just before dark, Ramon Sr. walked up with daughters Marcia and Sylvia. He surveyed the destruction, pursed his lips and silently shook his head. He'd already lost all the equipment for his business. Now this. Then he spotted a tray of taco shells, five or six, lying in the rubble. The shells were unbroken, but each was packed solid with wood chips and bits of insulation.

"Hey, kids. Look at this! Here's our dinner!"

The children laughed.

The next day, a stranger pulled up as the Esquivels worked to salvage what they could. Much to their amazement, the man was carrying Lady, their second Brittany pup. He said he found her in his farm fields 15 miles northeast of Topeka. The wind evidently had carried her there. The little dog was unhurt, but for the rest of her life — whenever storms threatened — Lady would cower in her doghouse, quivering with fear.

— • —

Fern Taylor slowly regained consciousness in the middle of her bedroom floor. The concrete block house around her had been reduced in height to a single row of blocks. She could hear people coming to help. She could see Chick lying in the corner beneath the culvert. The man who owned the Miami Tavern on Seward arrived with several others and lifted the heavy pipe off Chick. Chick's eyes opened once and then closed. The man took Chick's pulse.

"He's dead, Fern. I think his eyes opening was just a reflex."

Fern didn't want to believe it, of course. The men put Chick's body on some bedsprings, and Fern stayed with him; eventually a car was found to carry him to the hospital. The coroner pronounced him dead later that night. His skull was fractured.

—  •  —

Carol Laird dashed up the stairs after the tornado passed, then reappeared just a few moments later. The neighbors and family waiting in the basement looked up as he came back down the stairs. Mrs. Sims, the neighbor lady who'd just lost her husband the week before, was still screaming. The children sobbed.

Laird looked directly at Linda Jones's 80-year-old grandfather, John Goodall.

"John, I hate to tell you this, but your house is gone. And I don't think we've got a whole lot left up there, either."

The group made their way up the stairs and found the home's first floor battered and torn; Sheetrock was cracked and marred with black marks from flying shingles, doors were blown off, windows broken, furniture smashed, all manner of trash scattered everywhere. The Joneses' house across the street was blown in chunks against Mrs. Sims's home one lot to the north. The two young men who'd sought shelter in the Joneses' cellar emerged, dazed but unhurt.

As Laird walked through the yard and took in the arc of destruction that had swept the neighborhood, he noticed something odd. Earlier that spring, he'd planted a sycamore tree in the front yard. The sapling was maybe 15 feet tall and six inches in diameter. The tree still stood, but all around it, in a perfect circle, a trench had been carved a foot-and-a-half deep. Evidently the tornado had bowed the tree over and then spun it around like a corkscrew with so much torque that the branches had opened the trench at the base. Yet the tree's trunk didn't snap.

There were other oddities. A pair of shorts and a pair of pants had been hanging on a chair in the Lairds' bedroom before the tornado hit. Afterward, the pants were twisted tightly around the legs of the chair, but the shorts somehow made it outside and had come to rest under the family car. A box of Kleenex facial tissues that had been on the headboard in the master bedroom was now empty and sitting on the living room divan. Later, when Laird climbed up to the attic to survey the damage to the roof (22 rafters were split lengthwise, but the roof held), he found facial tissues plastered all over the attic space. And all the family's framed pictures from the living room were coated with mud, like it was sprayed on. All except one: The picture of Jesus was virtually untouched.

Something else. The lady who'd lost her husband a few days before, Mrs. Sims? The Joneses' house had plowed into hers and completely wrecked the place. But the flowers from her husband's funeral the previous Monday still stood on a table.

⌐ • ¬

Much to Wanda Idlet's everlasting amazement, she and her mother survived the tornado in the narrow bedroom closet behind the accordion door. When the world finally grew silent, the two stepped gingerly out of the closet and peered out the bedroom window to the south. The house on the corner was gone.

*Where is Dad? Is Dad dead?*

Wanda pulled at the bedroom door, dreading what she might find on the other side. But the door was jammed. She was still fighting it when she heard a familiar voice. Her father popped the door free and the family embraced. No one was hurt.

Wanda's mother turned to her daughter. Her eyes were brimming. Her voice overflowed with regret.

"I'm so sorry we didn't go to the shelter, Wanda. You were right. You were right all along."

But Wanda was overjoyed.

*I've beaten the monster. I've beaten the thing I feared most. I'm alive!*

As for that bargain she made with God, Wanda kept her end of it as the years rolled on.

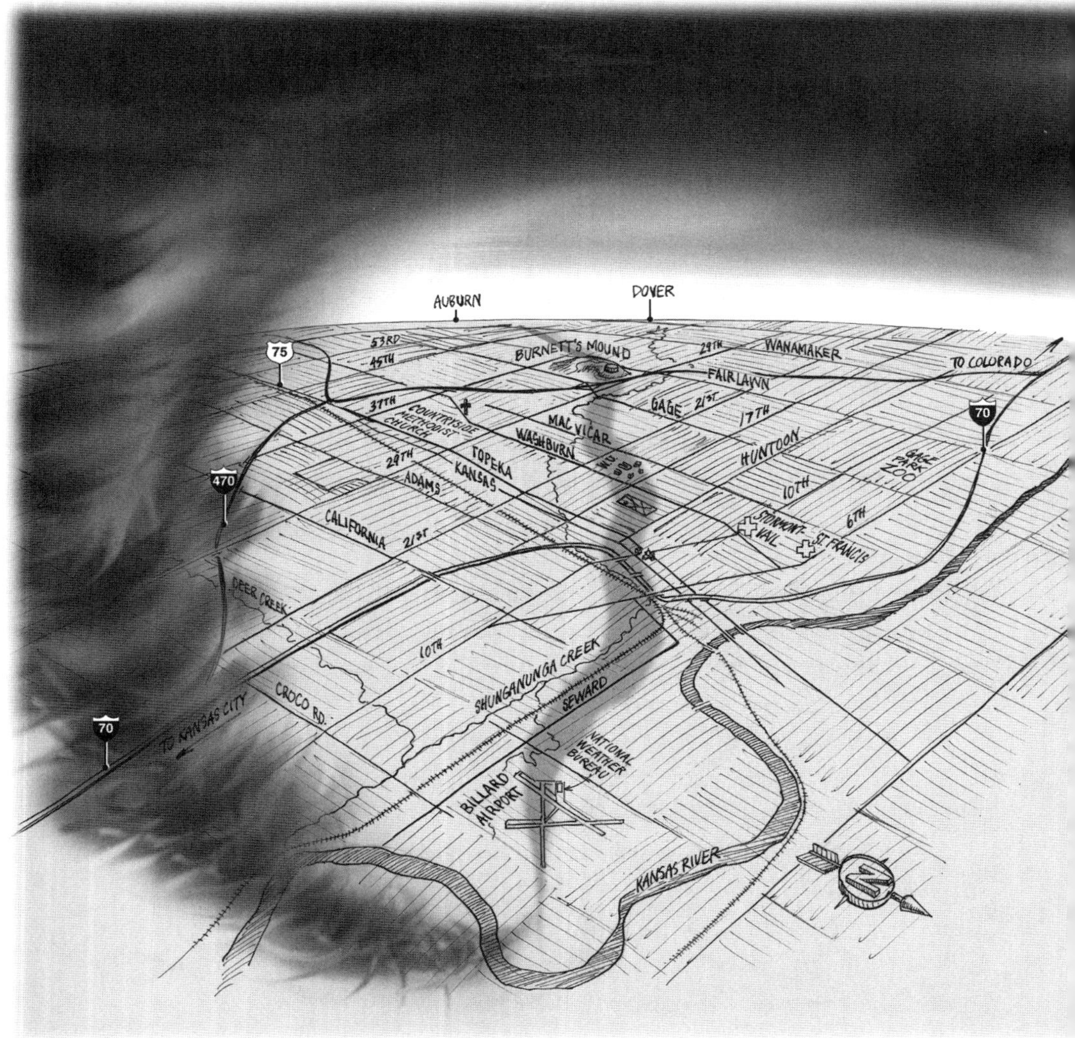


## The Tornado's Path

Total distance: 22 miles.

Distance through Topeka: Approximately 8 miles.

Touchdown occurred at about 6:50 p.m., four miles south and a half mile east of Dover, Kansas.

The tornado lifted just east of Billard Airport at 7:31 p.m.

# CHAPTER SIXTEEN

# Awaiting the Dawn

The still-white twister continued to lift as it cleared the Kansas River. The storm was committing suicide. The cascade of cooler air that helped create the funnel in the first place, the rear-flank downdraft, was swamping the tornado's base and choking off the supply of warm, moist air that fed the maelstrom. As the tornado strangled itself, it elongated and narrowed, or roped out, as if struggling to maintain contact with the earth. The winds of the parent thunderstorm then reasserted themselves and bent the weakened appendage into a fantastical serpentine shape that, ever so slowly, retracted into the sky. No longer the great, debris-choked wedge that had smashed through the city, the tornado in its dying moments became soft and ethereal, an attenuated, receding apparition that lingered in the eastern sky.

It was 7:31 p.m.

Almost 45 minutes had passed since the funnel touched down four miles south of Dover, Kansas. It had traveled 22 miles during that time — the last eight, through the city. If maximum destruction was the aim, the twister's route couldn't have been more effective. The storm followed the long axis across Topeka by slicing diagonally from southwest to northeast. Now a path of ruin one-eighth to one-half mile wide extended, block after block, from Burnett's Mound to the river.

The city was cut in half.

The sun wouldn't set until 7:47 p.m. and twilight would linger for 30 minutes after that. In the dead stillness and pale blue light of evening, thousands of stunned survivors emerged to confront a world remade. Then they tried to figure out what to do next.

Tom Noack, the electrician who lived near the base of Burnett's Mound (the one who'd started up the street, shutting off gas meters, immediately after the tornado passed), was still angry about the looters he'd seen come down from the nearby interstate. A police officer cruised slowly through the destroyed neighborhood sometime before dark, and Noack and a neighbor approached and told him what they'd seen.

"Do you have firearms?" the officer asked.

That was affirmative.

"Then get them out, load them and if anybody comes into the neighborhood that doesn't belong here and starts grabbing stuff, you holler 'Halt' twice, and then you shoot them, because that's what they deserve."

Noack and his neighbor glanced at each other and laughed nervously.

"No, that's what you do," the policeman reiterated. "Because that's what they deserve."

So they got their guns and loaded them.

Soon after, Noack spotted a familiar truck pulling to the shoulder of I-470. It was his boss, O. K. Johnson, owner of O. K. Electric. Johnson's shop man, John Powell, jogged down from the highway.

"Everybody all right, Tom?"

"Yeah, we're in good shape. We got lucky. But we could really use a generator."

Within 30 minutes, Johnson and Powell had returned with a 4,000-watt industrial generator. The men made quick work of tying it into the service of Noack's battered-but-still-intact house, and soon the generator puttered steadily against the gathering gloom. Lights blazed and appliances came back to life. Noack's wife, Connie, made coffee and sandwiches. Neighbors drifted in. Some brought stray dogs they'd rounded up, and the Noacks' garage was soon pressed into service as a temporary kennel.

At dusk, Noack walked down through the damage zone toward Gage Boulevard to let others know they were welcome to stop by for coffee and sandwiches. He found one elderly woman standing alone amid the wreckage of her home.

"Why don't you come up, ma'am? We've still got a house standing. We've got power."

The woman looked at him with angry, distant eyes.

"Well, aren't you a lucky son of a bitch . . ." she muttered.

Then she turned and walked away.

—  •  —

A chill settled in as night fell. The unseasonable weather seemed to accentuate the air of desolation that draped over the city. But wheels were turning. Kansas governor William Avery had immediately requested help from nearby Forbes Air Force Base, and by dark more than 400 airmen and Air Police, along with heavy equipment, searchlights and ambulances, were fanning out across the damaged areas. Avery also called out the National Guard and convoys of troop-laden trucks were rumbling into the city by 11:00 p.m. A total of more than 1,000 airmen and 600 guardsmen would be in Topeka within 24 hours. Law enforcement officers from across the state likewise converged.

Topeka mayor Chuck Wright was a broad-shouldered former marine, gruff and plainspoken. The morning paper on June 8 had carried a front-page story about Wright's ongoing battle to boost his salary and those of Topeka's four city commissioners. Wright had taken exception to an article that appeared the day before, about a survey suggesting that Topeka already had the highest-paid city officials in the state.

"I have not seen a copy of that report," Wright had thundered. "I hadn't seen anything until I saw the story this morning and blew my breakfast all over the wall." Wright claimed the article was part of a conspiracy to undermine the mayoral-commission form of government in favor of a city manager–style leadership.

But the controversy was ancient history by the end of this day. Wright arrived at the Shawnee County Civil Defense headquarters downtown not long after the tornado lifted and quickly took command. Reports of sporadic looting prompted Wright to issue a public warning through patched radio links to local TV and radio: Looters would be shot on sight. He made sure police received the order and underscored that this was to be no bluff.

With telephones down across the city, Wright also instructed Police Chief Dana Hummer to station patrol cars at each of the city's four hospitals to maintain communication, allocate health care volunteers and monitor casualty reports. Rescue teams would work though the night. Then volunteers would start walking the damage path at dawn to conduct a more systematic search for the living and the dead.

The prospect of hundreds, or even thousands, killed and injured did not seem far-fetched in the immediate aftermath of the tornado. About a dozen people already had been pronounced dead on arrival at the city's two public hospitals, Stormont-Vail and St. Francis, and given the breadth of the destruction, the likelihood that the number would grow exponentially seemed a given.

At Stormont-Vail, Henry Blake, one of the hospital's surgeons, was taking charge of the disaster response. He was well suited for the task. He had a forceful, commanding personality and had served as a battlefield surgeon during World War II. Fortuitously, the hospital had conducted an extensive disaster drill in the spring of '66 — a simulated airliner crash — and the experience proved invaluable when the real thing arrived. Still, conditions remained chaotic amid the crush of wounded. People were yelling for help, crying, speaking incoherently. The heat was oppressive. The light was dim. Yet the hospital coped, as did St. Francis Hospital, several blocks away. And help was coming. Topeka was home to one of the nation's top psychiatric hospitals and teaching facilities, the Menninger Foundation, and a number of the foundation's doctors showed up at both hospitals to lend a hand. Most hadn't done any clinical work since medical school, and their skills at stitching up wounds were rusty at best. But they nevertheless played an important role.

Among those receiving care at Stormont-Vail was Rick Douglass, the WREN disc jockey who'd raced down Burnett's Mound with the tornado on his tail, only to be caught in the twister at the base of the hill. Painstakingly, straight through the evening, nurses and physicians picked, plucked and washed mud, wood, glass and straw from his skin. They put him in a bathtub to soak and even used a household cleaner, Mr. Clean, to scrub off some of the wind-sprayed mud.

Officer David Hathaway, who had likewise been injured at the I-470 underpass, drifted in and out of consciousness as the night wore on. The extent of his head injury remained uncertain. The badly hurt boy Hathaway had pulled from the rubble near Burnett's Mound, Craig Beymer, was fighting for life. After physicians amputated what remained of his right leg and dressed his many other wounds, Craig was sedated and admitted to the pediatric intensive care unit. Nurse Nadine Gilbert sat with him all night long, like a guardian angel. His condition was grave.

Bill Hutton and his two teenaged sons, Craig and Chris — who'd been caught in the open on the Washburn campus — were treated and released. All had been badly mauled. Craig, hit in the back with a brick, ended up with more than 100 stitches for a variety of cuts and scrapes; Chris had 40 or 50 and Bill needed 20 stitches to close a long wound in his scalp. But they were going to be okay. The Washburn student who'd taken them to the hospital in his burgundy GTO waited patiently, and when the Huttons were released from the hospital, the young man offered to give them a ride home. But Bill instead asked for a lift back to the Washburn campus. He had to find out what had happened to his Corvair. He loved that little car.

It was late when they arrived at Washburn and police and National Guardsmen had cordoned off the area. The Huttons nonetheless were allowed to pass, and they eventually found the car 50 feet from where they'd left it. The Corvair was upside down; the glass was out and the roof smashed down.

"Were you guys in that?" one incredulous guardsman asked.

Hutton assured him they had not been. He studied the car for a moment and then turned to several of the soldiers standing nearby. "Any chance you guys could give us a hand righting this thing?" he asked.

Half a dozen men lifted and leaned, then flipped the car back on its tires and it landed with a bounce. Bill managed to pry open the driver's-side door, swept the glass from the seat, then squeezed himself in and turned the ignition. The motor fired.

He grinned. "Let's get the hell out of here, boys!" Chris and Craig climbed into the now-shrunken passenger compartment, and Bill swung out onto 17th Street, heading for North Topeka. It was a windy ride with the windshield gone and the men had to lean awkwardly to accommodate the partially crushed roof. When they arrived at the family home, Mrs. Hutton, the boys' significant others and friends poured into the driveway. Father and sons were still mud-caked and blood-soaked. At the hospital, the only areas the nurses had cleaned were immediately around where the men had been stitched. The result was a creepy kind of Frankenstein effect. Their hair still stood straight up from the mud and wind. They presented quite a sight as they slowly extracted themselves from the battered Corvair.

"We thought you were dead!" Mrs. Hutton exclaimed.

"Well, we damn near were," Bill replied.

It was some reunion.

There were a lot of those that night. Earlier in the evening, 16-year-old Carol Martin had driven downtown to attend the concert rehearsal with Job's Daughters, her singing group, in preparation for the trip to Hutchinson, Kansas, the next day. The choir had taken cover in the basement of the fortress-like Masonic Temple as the tornado approached. The twister passed very near the building. But the walls and floors were so thick that Carol barely heard it, and except for some broken windows, the damage was minimal. She and her companions emerged, of course, to find devastation all around. But Carol was relieved to see that her beloved, blue-and-white 1960 Dodge Dart had made it through largely unscathed. In fact, it was one of the few cars not totaled on the lot.

A friend, Patty Sellen, lived near Burnett's Mound, and reports were coming in of major damage in that part of town. So Carol offered to give Patty a ride home. They headed southwest but, like so many others, the friends quickly found their path blocked by debris. Eventually, they managed to make it to the Washburn campus. Carol was staggered by the destruction and immediately began to worry about her parents and her home just southwest of campus. She was able to drive a little farther but found the neighborhood cordoned off five blocks from her house.

So Carol got out and started down Randolph Street at a fast walk. The damage became steadily worse as she moved south with her friend. It was dusk now and power lines were down everywhere. A car somehow had slipped past the police line; the girls suddenly heard it roaring up behind them and barely had time to jump out of the way. A shaken Carol recognized the driver. It was a neighbor, no doubt frantic to see if his house still stood. Walking on, she spotted her friend, Patti McDiffett, standing on the corner with a group of others.

"Patti, how's your house?"

"What house?" Patti replied icily. "It's gone!"

Carol quickened her step and finally reached her block. Nothing was as before. She couldn't even tell which house had been hers. She had to count from the corner to get the right lot. The roof and the southern and eastern walls were gone. And all the grass in the yard had been uprooted, yanked clean away. Only mud remained.

Carol was starting up the driveway, calling for her parents, when she heard a familiar voice speak sharply from the gloom: "Don't come any closer!"

It was her mother, Hazel, standing in the shadows by the garage.

"Why not?" Carol asked.

"Power lines are down! We're not to move. You're not to come closer and I'm not to move!"

Carol didn't see her father.

"Where's Dad?" she asked.

"He was worried, so he went downtown to find you. He's on foot."

Carol's friend, Patty Sellen, was by now extremely concerned about her own family and she wanted to go. So the girls started back for the main drag where Carol had parked. Just as they reached 21st Street, a car pulled up and Carol saw a man get out. It was her father. He turned and saw her and they ran together and hugged for a long, long time. Forty years later, Carol still ranked the moment as the most dramatic of her life.

Cleve Martin evidently had made it down to the Masonic Temple on foot, jogging most of the three miles. After learning that his daughter was safe and had already left, he was able to catch a ride back to the neighborhood.

Carol and her father gave Patty a ride home. Thankfully, the girl's house still stood and her family was unhurt. On the drive back, Carol turned to her father and asked, in deadly earnest, "Dad, what are we going to do?"

Mr. Martin let out a deep sigh. "I don't know," he finally said. "I really don't know . . ."

Carol could always count on her father for answers. He was a practical, capable man and no stranger to hardship. He'd had an aircraft carrier sunk out from under him during the war. Now, with the family's house destroyed, their belongings scattered to the wind and a chilly night settling in, he didn't know what to do. This came as quite a shock to the 16-year-old. She worshipped her dad. In that moment, the enormity of all that had taken place hit home.

Father and daughter drove on and spoke no more.

—　•　—

Denny Benge survived the destruction of the barbershop on Kansas Avenue and legged it home after his '64 Chevy Super Sport was destroyed. He lived in southwest Topeka, not far from the mound. So he got out the family wagon, a '56 Nomad, and made numerous runs carrying wounded to the hospital with barber Terry Steele. In the course of the evening, the two were searching for survivors in a ruined apartment building near 29th Street when they came across two martinis sitting untouched on a coffee table. The cocktails still had olives in them and contained not a speck of dust or debris. It had been quite a day. The men knocked the drinks back.

—  •  —

John Fernstrom, the banker who'd survived the tornado in the basement of the Washburn law building after hearing the twister grinding closer as he took a test, grappled through the night with the sounds and images of the day. He was gloomy and restless. He tried to eat but could not, tried to sleep but got up and paced. He'd lie down, and then walk. He couldn't sit still. Over and over, Fernstrom kept replaying events in his mind. He ran through the images in super-slow motion, as if by reducing the speed, he could get his arms around what had occurred. Something extraordinary had unfolded. He'd been part of it. But his brain was playing catch-up, struggling to process the incomprehensible.

—  •  —

Elon Torrence was a veteran reporter who'd manned the local Associated Press bureau for 19 years. He was working late when the tornado passed very near his office in the *Daily Capital* newspaper building east of downtown, breaking windows and slicing power and phone lines. Torrence quickly sensed the scope of the disaster and guessed that if there was one place in town that would have working telephones, it would be the Southwestern Bell building. So he'd walked there and, sure enough, he was right. Company personnel provided him with an office and a working phone. The windows were blown out and the air grew chilly as night fell, but Torrence stayed at his station straight through until dawn and all the next day, gathering information and passing it along to the AP bureau in Kansas City, getting word of the calamity out to the nation and the world.

Maude Bishop Elementary School was just beyond the damage path, on the ridge northeast of Burnett's Mound. The school was pressed into service as a community shelter soon after the tornado passed. Just after dark, a couple of men who collectively constituted the entire public works department of tiny Bern, Kansas, a farming hamlet 80 miles north of Topeka, arrived and hooked up a big generator they'd hauled down from the country. The school's lights, warm and reassuring, blinked on.

In the gymnasium, a little blond girl, maybe five, sat alone on a mud-covered blanket. She was gripping a dirty doll. No one knew who she was or where she'd come from. Other refugees streamed in, mud-caked and dazed. A middle-aged couple sat in silence on an Army cot with a single suitcase beside them. Another woman was led in, sobbing over and over, "It's all gone, it's all gone."

A few blocks away, Ron Olson watched the stars come out. The junior high school teacher had lost his house as the tornado crested the ridge. Afterward, he'd sent his family to safety in Burlington, Kansas, 60 miles south. He was keeping an eye on the place through the night. Olson sat with his neighbors from across the street, the Michaelises. Their house was damaged but not destroyed and the little group made the best of it. They got out lawn chairs, fired up the grill and cooked steaks from the freezer before the meat could spoil.

Sleep was not an option for Olson; too much had transpired. So he watched the stars and watched the house and listened to the distant sirens as night drifted past. Around 2:00 or 3:00 a.m., Olson noticed flashlights moving amid the gaping, shattered rooms of his home across the street. He quickly woke his friend, Walt, and, gripping the pistol in his coat pocket, dashed over. Inside, two young men were standing in the darkness. Both carried gunnysacks.

"What do you think you're doing here?" Olson demanded.

"We're looking for survivors . . . ," one of the men replied.

"No, you're not. You're looting. I have a pistol in my pocket and if you don't leave immediately, I'll shoot you both dead. Believe me, I'm just out of my mind enough to do it."

The men didn't hesitate. They ran.

— • —

Eighteen-year-old Dan Woodward felt every bump on the hard bench in the back of a National Guard deuce and a half as he rolled north out of Ottawa, Kansas, in a five-truck convoy with 100 or so other guardsmen from the 169th Infantry. Woodward worked as a mechanic at the Ottawa Ford dealership. Until around 8:00 p.m., it had been just another Wednesday. But then the call came in to muster at the armory. Details were sketchy. Topeka was hit hard by a tornado; the unit would probably be gone five days.

The guardsmen reached the city around 11:00 p.m. and the men quickly deployed to patrol for looting in damaged neighborhoods near downtown. Woodward and another soldier found themselves walking alone amid darkened, ruined blocks. They had M-1 rifles with their bayonets fixed. A couple of hours into it, a man suddenly appeared in the darkness. The soldiers shouted for him to halt.

Woodward's flashlight caught the man's face. He was young, in his late 20s maybe. His clothes were disheveled. His skin was ashen and his eyes were fixed and strangely translucent, almost like you could see straight through him. Like his soul was gone.

"What's your business down here, mister?"

"I did live here," the man said. He gestured halfheartedly to one of the leveled houses nearby. His voice was a monotone.

"What are you doing out?" Woodward asked. "Don't you know there's a curfew?"

"I'm trying to find my family. I can't find them. I've been looking all over. I'm afraid they're all dead. I can't find them anywhere . . ." His words trailed off. Woodward didn't have a radio. No way to get help.

There wasn't much he or his companion could do. So they let the man pass. And as quick as he came, the stranger slipped back into the night.

The hours rolled on, the stars winked out and darkness gradually released its claim on the city. A stirring breeze seemed to kindle the embers of dawn, and in time the entire eastern sky was ablaze in a riot of orange and yellow. Then the red ball itself appeared, bloody and shimmering, lifting incandescently from the ground to the east.

Here was the new day. It would bring many changes.

# CHAPTER SEVENTEEN

# The Living and the Dead

Mayor Chuck Wright climbed aboard a National Guard helicopter at 6:00 a.m. Thursday and took off to survey the damage. From above, it appeared as if a giant lawnmower had made a ragged pass from one corner of Topeka to the other. The scope of the devastation was breathtaking, and before the chopper set down, the former marine was shedding tears of grief for his ravaged city.

But not for long. There was nothing for it except to get to work. So that's what people did. Relatives arrived from out of town or across the city to help families pick through the rubble and salvage what they could. Hundreds of volunteers poured in: Three hundred Mennonites from central Kansas, Boy Scouts, strangers unaffected by the storm, even people driving through the city on vacation stopped to lend a hand. Topeka bowed its neck and began the task of setting things right again.

Through it all, a strange mix of anguish and joy seemed to hang like a haze over the city. The death toll had reached 13 before bodies stopped arriving at the hospital morgues. More than 240 volunteers spread out at first light to look for additional casualties. But only one more body was found, an elderly woman in East Topeka.

Two more of the injured would die within 48 hours: Johnny Scheibe, the 19-year-old delivery driver who'd apparently been sleeping when the tornado struck his home, lingered in a coma until just before midnight on Thursday. The coroner listed the cause of death as extensive head trauma. The last to die was Craig Beymer, the five-year-old boy Officer David Hathaway had pulled from the rubble at the base of Burnett's Mound, the one whose leg had been amputated, the one nurse Nadine Gilbert had sat with through the night. He'd fought bravely. But he was just a little boy. His wounds were too much to overcome.

For the victims and their loved ones and friends, of course, these deaths were cataclysmic. Eternity had swallowed 16 souls whose lives had been full and real and flawed and blessed less than 24 hours before. Those left behind faced the silent void that arrived without warning and now would never leave. (A 17th victim, 65-year-old William Bachuss, died in rural Jefferson County about 20 miles northeast of Topeka on the night of June 8 after another tornado dropped from the same storm complex.)

As tragic as these losses were, the fact that the death toll wasn't far, far worse was legitimate grounds for wonder and celebration, given the ferocity of the storm and the path it had taken straight through the city. Approximately 820 homes or businesses were destroyed, and 3,000 more were damaged. An estimated 4,500 people had been left homeless. More than 10,000 vehicles were totaled. With the dollar losses pegged at $100 million ($662 million in today's dollars), overnight the Topeka storm became by far the most destructive tornado in U.S. history, nearly doubling the previous record of $52 million set by the Worcester, Massachusetts, tornado of June 1953. Topeka would remain the most costly tornado ever, until surpassed by the Lubbock, Texas, tornado of May 1970. Today, Topeka ranks fifth in terms of destructive tornadoes.[95]

The Fujita Scale for rating tornadoes wouldn't be invented for another five years. But a study of photos from Topeka conducted by severe weather experts in the 1970s confirmed that the storm was an F-5, the most powerful class of tornadoes, with wind speeds potentially exceeding 300 miles per hour. (In 2007, the F-Scale was modified to provide greater consistency in damage assessments, and today it is known as the Enhanced Fujita Scale, or EF-Scale.)

And while 550 people were injured, only 16 died. And two of the fatalities were due not to trauma, but to heart attacks that occurred during the tornado or immediately after it.

Why more hadn't lost their lives could be attributed to a fortunate convergence of factors that seemed to align perfectly to preserve life. First and foremost was the time of day the tornado struck. At 7:15 p.m. on a weekday, most individuals and families were home for the evening meal, watching TV or listening to the radio, and thus able to hear and heed the warnings. Had the tornado arrived two hours earlier, as thousands made their way home from work, the results no doubt would have been very different. And experts later speculated that if the tornado had come through in the dead of night — given the number of homes hit — the death toll conceivably could have reached 5,000.

There was, no doubt, an element of luck in the low number of fatalities. Commencement ceremonies for 500 seniors at Washburn University originally had been scheduled to take place in the school's football stadium on the evening of June 8. But the event had been moved back to the preceding Monday to better accommodate students and the travel plans of families and alumni. One shudders to think what the outcome might have been had the graduation gone on as planned, given that the tornado passed directly over stadium. As it was, the low casualty rate at Washburn was something of a miracle in its own right: An estimated 400 people were on campus when the tornado rolled through, but only 15 were seriously hurt.

One crucial factor in the high survival rate that had nothing to do with timing or luck was the early warnings provided by spotters stationed along the southwestern edge of the city. Reports of the tornado's approach from volunteer spotter John Meinholdt, Officer David Hathaway, WIBW cameraman Ed Rutherford, WREN disc jockey Rick Douglass and others bought precious time for citizens to seek cover. The fact that both Hathaway and Douglass had been injured in the execution of their duties only underscored the heroic nature of the task all spotters performed that day.

Similarly, the urgency of broadcaster Bill Kurtis's warning as the tornado slammed into the city — "For God's sake, take cover!" — undoubtedly saved many lives. In the years to come, the phrase and the man himself would for many become synonymous with the Topeka tornado. Kurtis would receive numerous accolades for the grace and command he displayed under pressure. But often overlooked was the cool play-by-play he subsequently provided as the funnel clawed deeper into Topeka. Field reports of the tornado's location and progress were coming into the television station, and Kurtis calmly relayed the information to the public in near real time via both TV and radio. Given the number of people who said they acted based on these reports, it could be argued that this service ultimately was Kurtis's most important contribution on June 8. Obviously, none of his warnings would have been possible without the individuals in law enforcement and among the general public who, at great personal risk, monitored the tornado's progress and quickly conveyed the information to the city's only television station. It's a fact Kurtis readily acknowledges.

The role played by meteorologist P. N. Eland and the staff of the Weather Bureau office likewise was crucial. They'd closely watched the building storms, activated the spotter networks, keyed the warning sirens nearly 15 minutes before the tornado hit the city, tracked it block by block and remained at their posts even as the funnel bore down directly on them.

That the Weather Bureau personnel performed so well underscored the importance of Richard Garrett's efforts. Indeed, if there was a single individual who deserved the bulk of credit for the amazingly low loss of life that day, it was the chief meteorologist of the Topeka Weather Bureau office. For almost 15 years, Garrett had labored to turn Topeka into a citadel of tornado preparedness. It was he who'd established the spotter network in the first place, who'd coordinated law enforcement and media communications, and who had pushed through bureaucratic roadblocks to harness the city's powerful airraid warning sirens. And it was Garrett who had worked tirelessly to raise awareness about tornado safety through the news media and public educational events. His efforts instilled in the community an acute sensibility to severe weather risks and a willingness to take action if danger was imminent.

Considering the range of techniques that Garrett employed in making Topeka safer and the years he'd invested in the effort, the fact that an EF-5 had barreled through the city without inflicting massive casualties represented a major personal and professional achievement. Here was a man whose life's work literally saved hundreds — if not thousands — of lives. How many people can say that? The lessons learned on June 8 were readily apparent to others in tornado-prone regions of the country, and in the years ahead, Topeka would become a model of tornado preparedness for communities nationwide.

Yet there would be no larger lessons learned, no great victories won for those who did not survive. The dead ranged in age from five to 91, although most were elderly. Perhaps many had struggled to reach shelter in time. The victims included 12 males and four females. They perished in all sections of the city. The aseptic, clinical language of the autopsy reports produced by Shawnee County coroner J. L. Lattimore, M.D., attested to the unimaginable fury that had accompanied many of the victims' final moments on earth:

- This lady shows a great many skin abrasions, a very severe cut on the right forehead with fracture of skull . . .

- This (man's) head is mutilated; the entire scalp is missing as well as the entire brain. There are very severe facial abrasions. Severe trauma to the left shoulder skin and upper left arm . . .

- This man shows a fracture of the occipital bone of the skull and extensive brain damage. There are very extensive lacerations to the forehead. Both elbows show very wide, open lacerations . . .

- This elderly, very frail female shows little trauma to the skin, shows a massive crushed skull with fractured ribs and sternum . . .

- This man was not identified for almost 24 hours after death. He was positively identified from his dental inlay work. (He) shows a tremendous number of lacerations about face and head, chest, abdomen, both arms and legs. The left leg shows a compound comminuted fracture, some 9 inches below the knee. There is a very large open wound, some 4 x 5 inches, on the right side, just below the umbilicus line. There are also two rather larger open wounds of the left chest, near the left nipple . . .

- This man has a completely crushed chest, massive hemothorax, a fracture of the right forearm, a very large number of abrasions to the face and right arm . . .

- This well-developed colored male shows a fractured skull on the left side, in the parietal region with brain damage. There is also a crushing type wound to the occipital portion of the skull. There is larger laceration to the forearm. There is a severe open laceration over each knee . . .

The first to die were Calvin and Clarice Wolf, the couple who lived one house north of carpenter Glenn Nicely and his wife, Inge, on Auburn Road in rural southwest Shawnee County. As the tornado approached, Hazel Nicely, Glenn's mother, had picked up the phone and heard Mrs. Wolf talking on the party line. Hazel warned her neighbor of the approaching danger but the Wolfs did not act. Inge later spoke with Mrs. Wolf's sister (the person on the other end of the call that evening) and learned that Mrs. Wolf had dismissed the warning, telling her sister something to the effect that "Calvin says it's just a little wind, that's all." A few minutes later, the house blew apart. The couple was found more than 100 yards away, near their car. Authorities consequently assumed, erroneously, that the Wolfs had been trying to outrun the tornado when they were killed.

Calvin Wolf was 64 years old. He was a big man who operated the road grader along the gravel roads west of Auburn for the Mission Township road maintenance department. Clarice was 60. She was from St. Mary's, Kansas.

In addition to the Wolfs; Sterling "Chick" Taylor, the man killed in his home by the flying culvert; Lisle Grauer, the proprietor of the bowling alley; Johnny Scheibe; and the little boy, Craig Beymer, the other fatalities were, as follows:

- George Sklenicka, 61, died in the open near the gas station at the base of Burnett's Mound. He was a certified public accountant and worked part-time for the firm of Brelsford, Hardesty and Battz.

- William R. Crouch, 44, was a World War II vet. He was a foreman for the maintenance department of the State Highway Commission. He died of a heart attack as the tornado pressed within a half mile of his home in southwest Topeka. He'd previously been under a doctor's care for a heart condition.

- Bertha M. Whitney, 83, lived with her husband, Von, near Washburn University. Neighbor Neil Bartley had dashed over as the tornado approached in an effort to warn the couple and bring them to safety. According to Mrs. Whitney's grandson, Bertha went to the basement but was coming back up the stairs to get her husband when the tornado hit. The roof came off and the house folded up. She was buried in debris and died that night in the hospital.

- Mary I. Beasley, 90, died on Byron Street, not far from the Whitneys and a few houses up from the home of 11-year-old Tony Stein. Mrs. Beasley was born in Leavenworth and was a member of the Central Congregational Church. Tony said the story in the neighborhood was that she was a semi-invalid and had been killed after an aide had been unable to get her to the basement.

- Edward J. Lyons, 71, died in his apartment near 11th Street and Kansas Avenue. He may have been the older man Denny Benge had urged to come to the basement barbershop just before the tornado swept through the car lots along Kansas Avenue. Lyons was born August 25, 1894, in Burlingame and lived in Eskridge before moving to Topeka in 1928. He was a retired housepainter.

- John T. Wells, 59, was born May 20, 1907, in Tyler, Texas. Wells was a big man of Indian and French-Canadian descent. He had jet-black hair and bronze skin. Folks called him "Chief." He had been a brakeman for many years on the Missouri Pacific but was working construction in 1966, running a jackhammer. He lived in a big rooming house downtown near 10th and Monroe. He'd lost his wife to sudden illness in '39. According to his daughter, Wells was sick in bed on June 8. He had been ill for a couple of days. So when the woman who ran the boardinghouse told him he needed to get to the basement with the rest of the tenants, Wells had said no. He wasn't up to it. They eventually found him, still in his bed, crushed.

- Oliver Jacob Milton, 68, died in the same boardinghouse as Wells on Monroe Street. He was born in 1897 in Pulaski, Iowa.

- Gareford Lee, 63, died in his house on East 8th Street. He was born in Tulsa, Oklahoma, and had lived in Topeka for 31 years.

- John D. Culver, 59, was a native of Iowa and a graduate of the University of Nebraska. He was manager and secretary-treasurer of Midwest Wholesale Lumber Company. He died of a heart attack as he drove down East 4th Street to the rail yards to check on damage to the lumberyard immediately after the storm passed. He left a wife, Vivian, and a grown daughter, Joan.

- Hattie L. Anderson, 91, was found by search crews on Thursday morning. She was born October 12, 1874, in Council Grove, Kansas, at a time when a few wagons still rumbled past on the Santa Fe Trail. She and her husband ran a store in Halstead, Kansas, for many years. She raised five boys with a gentle hand and an iron will, according to her grandson, R. R. Her husband passed in 1958. Mrs. Anderson was only five feet tall and weighed barely 100 pounds. One of her sons, Herb, looked after her in her later years and lived in the home on a corner lot along the west side of Ripley Park in East Topeka. But Herb was fishing on the evening of June 8. Grandson R. R., a 29-year-old Korean War vet, was there Thursday morning when a dozer lifted a large section of more-or-less intact debris from the backyard and Mrs. Anderson's body was discovered beneath it. She was still lying in her feather bed but crushed nearly flat. The bed was pressed deep into the ground. Mrs. Anderson had come to rest under her favorite tree, or what was left of it. She'd spent many hours sitting beneath that tree in the cool of summer evenings. When he spotted the body, the dozer operator told R. R. to get Mrs. Anderson's sons out of the area. He was worried they might have heart attacks if they saw their mother. Mrs. Anderson might have lived had she made it to the basement. But R. R. didn't think so. The cellar had immediately filled with water from broken pipes and hot wires were in contact with the water. R. R. believed his grandmother would have been electrocuted. He told Herb that it was a lucky thing he'd gone fishing, for he probably would have died, too, even if they had reached the basement. But Herb didn't buy it. He blamed himself for his mother's death until the end of his days.

Among the more than 60 people who remained hospitalized citywide the day after the storm was Lois "Dorothy" Decker, the 46-year-old woman who'd been so badly mauled as she was pulled up Kansas Avenue by the tornado. Fortunately, Dorothy was rapidly improving, and her condition was upgraded from poor to satisfactory by Friday morning. She would make it, although she remained in intensive care and had stitches in nearly every portion of her body. Her daughter, Barbara Rainey, flew in from Indiana to be with her. When Barbara arrived at the hospital, she didn't recognize Dorothy at first, so severe and numerous were the wounds. And then, when the two started talking, the trauma of seeing her mother so badly cut up became too much and Barbara fainted. Dorothy desperately wanted to see her grandchildren during that first week. But children weren't allowed up onto the hospital floor. So when she was strong enough, Dorothy got in a wheelchair and went down to the lobby to meet them. It didn't go well. The kids were badly shaken by the encounter. They started crying when they saw her. And the youngest, Joyce, who was five, was terrified of weather after that. If it would just start sprinkling, she'd begin to scream. Her mother would ask, "What in the world is wrong with you?" and Joyce would say a tornado was coming.

It took a long time for those fears to go away.

— • —

In the community as a whole, serious concerns existed about a potential tuberculosis outbreak, of all things, in the tornado's aftermath. The Kansas State Health Laboratories were housed in the National Reserve Life building. That was the 10-story structure that Gary Fleenor had seen the funnel coiled around like a snake. A large incubator on the seventh floor containing deadly cultures had been knocked over, and no one knew whether the bacteria had escaped or not. Fortunately, authorities eventually determined that the cultures were contained, and a 20-ton crane was brought in to gently lift the heavy incubator out of the building. This was accomplished with great care and the hazard was taken to a landfill and burned.

— • —

Evidence of the tornado's fiendish powers was everywhere as people continued to dig out.

Glenn Nicely found all of his father's guns — rifles, shotguns and a pistol — neatly placed by the tornado inside a driveway culvert 100 feet from his parents' destroyed house. The guns were undamaged. Electrician Tom Noack noticed that in one house with the walls and roof ripped away, a large aquarium stood untouched along a center wall. Fish were still swimming in it. Schoolteacher Ron Olson found pieces of asphalt shingle driven like darts through a wooden privacy fence in his backyard. Teri Huffman, the 10-year-old who was nearly carried away when the tornado wrecked her house near Burnett's Mound, discovered two dozen unbroken eggs inside the family's refrigerator lying in the backyard. Dan Hudkins returned to the destroyed service station where he worked and marveled at cases of soda pop with the caps still on and the bottles intact, but the liquid sucked out — somehow pulled through the microscopic gap between bottle and cap. A towel was driven into a door at the Embassy Apartments with such force that a man was unable to pull it out.

Janifer Wallace lived in a second-floor apartment at the Embassy apartment complex. She never heard the sirens because she was under one of those large, old-style hair dryers at the time. A friend who wasn't supposed to arrive until 8:00 p.m. showed up early and warned Wallace of the approaching tornado, and together they fled to the basement. After the tornado passed, Wallace emerged to find the roof of her apartment building gone and a Chevy Corvair parked in her second-floor living room, exactly where the hair dryer had been. At first, she told a reporter, she was mad to see a car in her living room. But then she realized how lucky she'd been and started to shake.

At Francis Clay's home on 33$^{rd}$ Street, ripe tomatoes blew out of Clay's garden and were strained through a window screen, coating the pale green bathroom walls in bright red. A stack of 12 dish towels was carried from an open drawer in the kitchen down a hallway to the bedroom. The towels landed on the bed, still neatly stacked.

J. B. Hart lost the roof of his home on 17$^{th}$ Street, although lamps and glassware in the attic were untouched. A pickup truck near Washburn University was wrapped around a tree so tightly that tailgate and front bumper overlapped.

Heavy crane operator Ted Mize (the man who'd carefully hoisted the potentially deadly bacteria incubator from the seventh floor of the wrecked National Reserve Life building) was also called in to recover a 20-foot steel I beam that had been ripped from a gas station in the College Hill area. The 1,000-pound beam had come to rest two blocks away. Somehow, it had dropped down in the narrow gap between adjacent, two-story houses and then turned horizontally to shoot through a second-floor bedroom window. The beam had swept across a bed, gathered up the linens, and rammed them through the plaster and into the studs of an interior wall. Half the beam stuck out the window; half was in the house. Even stranger, an eight-foot fluorescent light fixture was still attached to the beam, and the bulbs were unbroken.

While working late at Pelletier's Department Store downtown, employees thought their building was on fire when the tornado rolled through. They reported the store filled with a "white wind" that looked like smoke.

The tornado's black magic was particularly evident at Joe Smith's car lot on Kansas Avenue. Salesman Jerry Estes returned to the lot the next morning. There was a '65 Covair with the rear hood completely crushed down, concaved against the motor, with both rear tires flattened and both rear springs broken. Something huge had struck the car with enormous force, but whatever it was, was long gone. Nearby, a brickbat — a brick-sized piece of soft masonry — had shot through the passenger-side window of a 1962 Pontiac Catalina and struck the interior door panel just below the driver's-side armrest. The missile then continued through the panel and punched out through the steel exterior like a cannon shot. And it was there still, sticking partly out of the torn door. But when Estes pulled it out and dropped it on the ground, the brickbat shattered. Why the soft material didn't disintegrate when it was slammed against the interior door, who could say? Two cars over, a '63 Galaxy had a two-by-four driven straight through the grill and radiator like an arrow. The thing was that the two-by-four had come from the west, while the brickbat that hit the Covair two cars down had come from the northeast.

As Estes and Smith worked to salvage what they could that morning, a truckload of Mennonites pulled up. The men, dressed in their plain garb, suspenders and straw hats, piled off the truck and offered to help clean up the lot. Old Joe was grateful and told them by all means. He happened to notice that one of the men was the fellow who'd come in the day before trying to buy the blue '64 Impala. Estes and the man had been unable to agree on price and there'd been no sale. Now the car was flattened, crushed by a fallen brick wall.

Smith called Estes aside.

"Hey, Jerry," he whispered. "Go tell that guy we'll take his offer for the Impala."

Estes approached the man and informed him that, after careful consideration, Mr. Smith had elected to accept his price for the Chevy after all. Everyone laughed, the Mennonite hardest of all.

—  •  —

In the late afternoon of June 9, after a fitful day at work, banker John Fernstrom walked from his home back over to the Washburn campus. He managed to avoid the National Guard patrols and found himself standing outside the ruins of Carnegie Hall, the building where he'd been taking the banking test when the tornado struck. With no one around, Fernstrom climbed through a window and made his way up the rubble-covered stairs. He wanted to retrieve the raincoat he'd left in the classroom the night before. Now the room was open to the sky and chairs and desks were scattered in heaps. Eerily, the teacher's written instructions for the test still stood unmarred on the blackboard.

*My God, we were here. We would have all been killed if we had stayed. We would have been carried off toward downtown. I still can't believe this happened . . .*

Fernstrom looked at the chair he'd been sitting in. A two-by-six was driven through the seat like a dagger. Then he spotted his raincoat wrapped tightly around the legs of a nearby desk. He untangled it, took one last look around and departed. When he got home, Fernstrom realized that the coat was riddled with glass and splinters. So he tossed it in the corner of his garage and never wore it again.

# CHAPTER EIGHTEEN

# To the Stars Through Difficulties

On Saturday, June 11, U.S. armed forces in Vietnam awoke to news of the Topeka tornado plastered above the fold on page one of *Stars and Stripes,* the official military newspaper. The United Press International story didn't quite get the facts right: The headline and opening paragraph claimed that a barrage of 15 twisters had struck Topeka, killing 13. Evidently, the reporter or editor had been confused by the fact that while 15 tornadoes hit the state as a whole on June 8, only one had gone through Topeka.

But the story otherwise was accurate, and included on the inside page was a small map of the tornado's damage path. Among those who studied the map with growing alarm was 35-year-old Captain Edward (Ted) Marvin. The tall, soft-spoken Virginian was a C-130 pilot assigned to the 29th Squadron of the 463rd Troop Carrier Wing, based at Clark Air Base in the Philippines. The unit had deployed from Forbes Air Force Base the previous January. The squadron's mission was to fly men and materiels up and down the length of Vietnam for two-week rotations, return to Clark for a few days, then head back to Vietnam. And that's where Marvin was — at Tan Son Nhut Air Base in Saigon — when he picked up the newspaper. He was worried because it looked from the map as if the tornado had passed very close to, if not right over, his home near Washburn University. Marvin feared for his wife and two daughters.

*Are they alive? Are they dead? Injured? Did we lose our house?*

There were no cell phones or satellite phones in 1966, of course, nor was there an Internet. Radio telephones did exist, but they were hard to come by in Vietnam. In any case, most phone service in Topeka was down. So Marvin and others in his 15-plane squadron had no way of knowing the fate of loved ones at home. The hours turned to days, and the worry metastasized into a hard, ever-present knot of dread.

Still, Marvin had a job to do. So he pushed aside the uncertainty and stayed on task, continuing to fly missions to forward combat bases along the DMZ. Aircraft cargo could include anything from 105-mm howitzer shells to 30,000 pounds of Velveeta cheese. Most of the landing strips in country were cut from the jungle and were sometimes no more than 3,000 feet long. It took guts and skill to stick a fully loaded, 130,000-pound C-130 down on a short, dirt or steel-planked runway. The grunts called the C-130s "mortar magnets" due to the plane's propensity to attract incoming rounds once on the ground.

For most of that week Marvin and his crew flew at 5,000 to 10,000 feet above the vast, green canopy of South Vietnam. After four or five days of grinding worry, word finally came through the chain of command that all the squadron's families in Topeka had been physically located and all were okay. None had suffered property damage. Marvin was overjoyed. But the anxiety he experienced no doubt was replicated hundreds of times over in the tornado's aftermath among servicemen and women in Vietnam with family or friends in Topeka.

⚊ • ⚊

Back in the city, recovery efforts received a major leg up on June 10, thanks to nearby Kansas City, Missouri. Topeka mayor Chuck Wright had appealed to area communities for assistance the day after the storm, and at around 5:30 p.m. on Friday afternoon, a mile-long convoy of heavy equipment rolled in from the east like a mechanized army. The machinery was manned by 160 employees of the Kansas City Parks and Recreation, Water, and Public Works departments. The convoy included 40-plus dump trucks, two Cat D-7 dozers, low-boy trailers, front-end loaders, cherry pickers, chippers, winch trucks, street sweepers, pickup trucks and dozens of chain saws. The fleet represented just about every construction and maintenance asset K.C. had.

For the next five days, the Kansas City crews worked in shifts around the clock to clear the streets from Washburn University to downtown. Rubble and tree limbs were loaded into dump trucks or dozed into burn piles around the city. Smoke from the fires lifted into the blue summer sky as the bulldozers clanked and dump trucks rumbled in. George Eib was the K.C. Parks and Recreation Department superintendent in charge of the operation. He recalled that flat tires were a huge problem that week, due to the enormous amount of glass, metal and nails littering the streets. To meet the challenge, tire trucks and repair crews raced back to the shops in Kansas City every night to repair flats and bring up additional spares. It was all they could do just to keep up.

Supporting the Kansas City workers themselves was no small feat, either: Lunches were carried to the field; breakfast and dinner were served from a mobile kitchen at the Shawnee County garage near the fairgrounds. Much of the food was donated by Topeka restaurants, families and individuals after appeals were made on radio and TV. The men slept at the city's municipal auditorium and at Topeka High School.

Although the Kansas City workers were on the clock in Topeka, it was clear the effort became more than just a job for many. One hi-loader operator worked 24 hours straight and wouldn't stop until a supervisor finally showed up and basically ordered him off the machine. According to the newspaper, the man became "extremely emotional" about his desire to continue working. All told, the assistance provided to Topeka for those five days cost Kansas City $37,000 (about $245,000 in today's dollars). It was a selfless act. But it wasn't isolated.

Thousands of men from municipalities and utilities across the Midwest descended on the city and worked 16-hour days until the streets were cleared and basic services restored. Many of the cleanup crews were volunteers. On the utility side, Southwestern Bell had more than 800 men in the city, replacing cables that served 18,000, or about 25 percent, of Topeka's 73,700 telephones. The job required 20 miles of cable and 1,100 poles. Kansas Power and Light likewise deployed more than 500 men from towns across Kansas to restore power along the damage path. Within four days, 80 percent of the homes and businesses capable of receiving power were back up and running.

The level of federal involvement in the aftermath of the Topeka tornado was relatively modest, unlike many future American disasters. The morning after the tornado, Mayor Wright received a telephone call from President Lyndon B. Johnson. According to Wright, the conversation went something like this:

> "Mayor Wright, this is President Lyndon Johnson in Washington. I just want to tell you how sorry we are to hear what happened to your wonderful city, and we're here to do everything we can to help."
>
> I said, "Mr. President, I certainly appreciate that. I know our people do. We're Republicans out here." And the president said, "Well, this is a catastrophe, and it doesn't make any difference whether it's Democrat or Republican." I said, "As soon as I know what we need, I'll get back to you."

Wright and other city officials quickly concluded that temporary housing was Topeka's most pressing requirement. And sure enough, by the end of June, the first of more than 500 mobile trailers provided by the General Services Administration began arriving in the city. Temporary communities were laid out in parks, at the airport and on the grounds of the veterans hospital. The trailers were hot, smelly and cramped. But they provided essential shelter — in some cases for a year or more — for those fighting to get back on their feet.

Donations of clothes and other materials poured in from around the country. Central Airlines set up an airlift to bring the donations in from several eastern cities. Truckloads of clothing, bedding and other supplies arrived from surrounding states. Everyone gave what they could. Even the inmates at the Kansas State Penitentiary in Lansing set up a relief fund.

Throughout the city, a powerful spirit of sacrifice, cooperation and hard work was pervasive in those first days after the storm. It was a unique period, to say the least. As a result, three psychologists on staff at the Menninger Foundation seized on the opportunity to conduct an in-depth psychological study of how a community reacts to disaster. The three — James B. Taylor, Louis A. Zurcher and William H. Key — all had volunteered in the cleanup operations, and as the work wound down, they fanned out to interview more than 100 victims, volunteers, city officials and others. The effort resulted in a book titled *Tornado: A Community Responds to Disaster,* which was published in 1970.[96]

Because the book was written by, and largely for, mental health clinicians, the content reflected the heavily academic, often densely analytical mind-set associated with the profession. But the effort was sincere, the research comprehensive and the writing clear. In detail, the book described the psychological journey that many individuals and the community as a whole experienced, from the shock and trauma of the event through adaptation and recovery. According to the authors, a "post-disaster utopia" fleetingly reigned in the wake of the tornado:

> For a period after the disaster, ordinary cares and concerns seemed laid aside. The city was caught up in a collective excitement and a profound sense of shared destiny, wherein the fate of one's neighbor was as important as one's own. The result, for a brief moment, was a kind of community coherence seldom encountered outside of war or the transcendental states of mass religious excitement. For a while the city became a different organism and functioned by different rules.[97]

The book included many keen observations and anecdotes. One tornado victim described the cognitive dissonance he experienced when confronted with the eerie normalcy that existed just beyond the tornado's path:

> I have a truck drop me off at the edge of Westboro, where I am to have dinner with friends. And as I walk into Westboro I have as great a sense of disorientation, of unreality, as anything I've experienced all day. Here the lawns are carefully manicured, birds are singing in the confident stately trees, children are laughing, discreetly it seems, and I envy them. A woman is talking with her gardener about begonias, in a quiet voice, but it is so peaceful here that I can hear every word of the conversation as I walk by the house. It would appear that all was not well with the begonias. I am dead tired, the contrasts of the day have been so great that I feel I've gone from one side of the moon to the other — but where is the Earth?[98]

Another report described a humorous collision of cultures that occurred during the storm cleanup:

> He had to laugh about some of the things that happened. The helpers were so anxious to help, and yet they made for difficulties. The men who were trying to salvage the things came from a farm background and had different values than his. They would pull out some half-destroyed article, and tell him, "If you take a hammer to that, you can fix it up okay" — and then they would put it on the truck. The informant didn't want to discourage them, because they were being so helpful, but he was quite sure he would never fix up the article. So, surreptitiously, after the helpers had put it on the truck, he would sneak up behind them and throw it away again. They caught him at this late in the afternoon, and he had a difficult time explaining what he was up to. When they did

finish loading up the truck at the end of the day and moved everything to his new house, he had to phone the Salvation Army so that he could give away the useless junk.[99]

Yet another individual interviewed by the psychologists was an elderly Mexican man who'd fought under the Mexican rebel leader Pancho Villa as a youth. The old man had refused to seek cover when the tornado approached. Shelters, he explained, were for women and children.

Instead, he'd gone outside to see "the face of God."[100]

— • —

Despite the spirit of selflessness that dominated the city in the tornado's aftermath, not everyone subscribed. Sightseers had been a major problem from virtually the minute the tornado lifted. For days, streets around the damage path were choked with motorists trolling slowly through to take in the epic destruction. The problem got so bad that one fed-up individual whose home near Washburn had been jacked open like a dollhouse erected a large sign in his yard that read: GAWK, YOU BASTARDS! YOU'RE A LOT OF HELP.

— • —

Volunteers from both the Red Cross and the Salvation Army were ubiquitous. They operated mobile canteens, fanning out to provide food and clothing. Shelters were established, kitchens were stocked and for weeks, both organizations continued to play a vital role in pulling the city back from the abyss. Yet very different perceptions emerged about the value of the respective charities among some storm survivors. Tom Noack, the electrician who lived near Burnett's Mound, remembers Red Cross canteens demanding monetary donations before they would provide food or drink. In contrast, he said, the Salvation Army handed out food, drink and even hand tools, free of charge and no questions asked.

"I still have tools in my garage that were given to me by the Salvation Army," Noack said 40 years later. "I have no use for the Red Cross."

Noack's sentiments were echoed by Lanny Ellis, the pawnshop owner in East Topeka. "The Salvation Army was giving out sandwiches and coffee and shelter and asking for nothing back. They were fabulous. But the Red Cross was down here charging for food. It left me with a real sour feeling. To this day, I do not give to the Red Cross. I give directly to the Topeka Salvation Army."

Inge Nicely, the wife of carpenter Glenn Nicely and among the first victims of the tornado, was taken by her sister-in-law to a Red Cross shelter several days after the storm. She went there to gather clothes and other necessities. Still reeling from the loss of her home, possessions and nearly her life, Inge found herself sitting across a desk from a Red Cross woman. According to Inge, the woman looked up and asked, in a condescending, almost accusatory tone, "And just what is it that you want?"

Inge stammered and stood up.

"You can stuff it!" she replied and turned and walked away.

No doubt, many storm victims benefited from the efforts of the Red Cross and its volunteers. But the charity apparently made a bad situation worse for others.

— • —

On June 16, a radio-television marathon fund-raiser featuring stars of the Grand Ole Opry was held at WIBW's studios. The program was picked up by stations across Kansas and included 24 country-and-western singers. Ferlin Husky headlined the show. Husky had topped the charts in 1960 with the hit "Wings of a Dove." Radio reception must have been exceptional that night; donations came in from as far away as Maryland and California. The telethon raised $54,000. Estimated in today's dollars, the amount would equal about $358,000.

— • —

The mighty, 90-foot-tall cottonwood tree on the statehouse grounds, which supposedly had sprouted from a construction stake when work started on the building back in 1866, lost half its branches in the tornado. But the battered old sentinel hung on and survived for years to come.

— • —

And so the days rolled past, the cleanup continued and the impossibility that recovery posed in the tornado's immediate aftermath began to recede like a mountain washing slowly to the sea. Washburn University epitomized the transformation under way. The university had been effectively destroyed in what was perhaps the single most devastating disaster ever to befall an American institution of higher learning. Losses totaled $8 million (an estimated $53 million in today's dollars); 11 of 13 major buildings had been badly damaged or destroyed. When the school's vice president for academic affairs, Arthur F. Engelbert, asserted the day after the tornado that the school would open in the fall and emerge stronger than ever, the words sounded like the desperate boasts of a delusional man. But progress was relentless. Soon after the storm, giant tarps were brought in to cover exposed buildings and protect undamaged books and other materials. Work crews from Washburn and the University of Kansas in nearby Lawrence, along with private contractors and student volunteers, salvaged much, and before long, heavy equipment operators were bulldozing the stately old ruins into the ground. The single exception was Carnegie Hall, the law building, which was restored.

Plans for replacement structures soon emerged. Fortuitously, the university's board of trustees had rewritten the university's property insurance in early 1966 and switched from standard, depreciated coverage to a replacement cost policy. The change was made at the recommendation of the university's treasurer, Richard Vogel, and would have profound implications for Washburn's future. Instead of receiving a payout based on the aging structures' assessed value or depreciated construction costs, Washburn could look forward to receiving enough money to build a brand-new, state-of-the-art campus.

In the meantime, summer classes quickly were reconstituted at Topeka West High School and began the week after the storm. As summer wore on, 41 portable trailer-classrooms provided by the General Services Administration arrived and were anchored with concrete piers in open ground and parking lots. And just as Engelbert had predicted, the school opened its doors for classes on September 12. Washburn had a new nickname after that: Tornado Tech.

— • —

In a roundabout way, the destruction at Washburn would produce one of the most significant public safety advancements to emerge from the Topeka tornado. Few stories were more publicized in the wake of June 8 than the harrowing tale of the near-tragedy at the MacVicar Chapel music recital. After the sirens sounded, 40 or so recital attendees had — as tornado safety doctrine directed — sought shelter in the southwestern corner of the basement. But because the piano in that room had been out of tune, Robert Snyder, the Washburn music professor, moved the group to a practice room at the other end of the building. This decision saved many lives, since the original, southwest corner room ended up buried beneath tons of stone and heavy timbers. Aside from triggering imponderable questions about the role of luck, fate or divine intervention in tornado survival, the event begged a more practical issue: Was it really true that the southwestern corner of the basement was the best place to ride out a tornado?

One of those intrigued by this problem was a young assistant professor of meteorology at the University of Kansas. Joe Eagleman was 29 and a native of southern Missouri. He'd always been interested in tornadoes. So when he read about the MacVicar Chapel incident, it occurred to him that the destruction in Topeka might offer a unique opportunity to statistically assess whether the southwestern corner was in fact the best place to be during a tornado. The logic behind this long-standing convention was that debris from a tornado (which typically approached from the southwest) would blow up and away and therefore would be less likely to fall in on someone seeking shelter just behind and beneath the point of impact.

Two weeks after the storm, Eagleman and two graduate students began a field assessment of homes across the city. The professor designed a worksheet that could be used to document the location of damage and debris within each house, regardless of design or construction. All told, 135 structures were surveyed and documented over three days.

Eagleman returned to KU and began crunching the data. Immediately, he was struck by what the numbers revealed. According to the survey, the southwestern corner was definitely *not* the best place to be during a tornado. In fact, it actually was among the most dangerous locations in which to seek shelter. Only the southeastern corner was more vulnerable to falling debris. In contrast, the northeastern corner of the building, farthest from the tornado's impact, statistically offered the highest level of safety.

These conclusions flew in the face of long-standing Weather Bureau public safety recommendations. Consequently, when an article about the study appeared in the *Topeka Daily Capital* in early August, the reaction was fast and furious. Richard Garrett, meteorologist-in-charge of the Topeka Weather Bureau office, stormed into Eagleman's office at the University of Kansas the very next morning to confront the young heretic.

"He was very angry," Eagleman later recalled. "He basically told me he'd been studying tornadoes all his life and that I didn't know what I was talking about. But I had seen the data, and I've always been a stubborn person, and I believe in myself. So I listened, thanked him for stopping by and basically brushed him off."

Eagleman's survey results were published in a scholarly journal, *Monthly Weather Review*, in March 1967. That same year, the National Weather Bureau's tornado safety rules changed: The southwestern corner recommendation was abandoned and replaced instead with the general suggestion that individuals go to the basement and "seek shelter under a sturdy workbench or heavy table if possible." Over time, the accepted guidance became that individuals go to the lowest, most interior portion of the home.

Despite the fact that the agency clearly had taken Eagleman's work to heart, his paper later drew a lengthy rebuttal from a meteorologist in the Kansas City Weather Bureau office, who attacked Eagleman's data, methodology and conclusions. But Eagleman was able to duplicate the findings through five subsequent studies involving hundreds of homes damaged by tornadoes in Texas, Florida, Kansas and Mississippi through the late '60s and early '70s.

Years later, Eagleman lamented the fact that the Weather Bureau never credited or acknowledged, formally or otherwise, the significance of his work. Nor did Garrett apologize for his hotheaded reaction. In fact, Eagleman never heard from him again.

"It would have been nice to have been recognized by the National Weather Service," said Eagleman. "It was disappointing." In the years after the Topeka study, Eagleman would continue to make pioneering contributions to tornado science. He developed one of the first realistic simulations of a tornado in a laboratory setting and came up with early, breakthrough, ultimately accurate theories regarding the role of double-vortex circulation in tornado formation. Interestingly, Eagleman later played a role in destroying yet another tenet of 1960s-era tornado safety dogma: Wind tunnel experiments showed that opening the windows of a home as a tornado approached had no effect whatsoever in equalizing the pressure and keeping a house from exploding. Just the opposite, in fact: Open windows made it easier for high winds to get inside a house and tear the structure apart.

Eagleman's findings about the risks associated with seeking shelter in the southwestern corner did raise one final, intriguing question: If that was indeed the most dangerous place to be, then how come more people in Topeka didn't die, given that the location was where most of those with a basement would likely have gone? Eagleman acknowledged that this had always remained a mystery to him, although he theorized that given the sudden pressure drop inside the tornado, many walls tended to fall outward rather than inward.

The remarkably low loss of life in the Topeka tornado would remain the subject of considerable scrutiny and approbation in the years ahead. For vulnerable communities in Kansas and elsewhere, the lesson was clear. The *Coffeyville Journal* in southeast Kansas noted that 15 years of preparedness work in Topeka had preceded the devastating tornado: "Cities such as Coffeyville, which have not stressed tornado safety in recent years and have no adequate warning systems, therefore should pay heed. We should start at once putting our house in order. Let us not find ourselves saying after a disaster hits, 'If we had only . . . '"

Echoed the *Parsons Sun*, "The city of Parsons well might investigate the possibility of a genuine storm warning system. Air raid sirens may be available through the federal civil defense program. Their installation and maintenance would not be costly, and certainly can constitute prudent insurance against grievous disaster."

A year after the storm, the Disaster Research Center at Ohio State University in Columbus published a lengthy research report examining the nature and impact of warning systems in place in Topeka on June 8. Author Robert Stallings described Topeka's comprehensive tornado defenses and the extensive coordination that existed between public agencies, the media, civilian volunteers and the community at large:

It is clear that an elaborate tornado disaster subculture has emerged in response to [high tornado risk]. A complex organization and technology, along with corresponding attitudes and values, is present among the residents and organizations of the city. There is not only an elaborate pattern for sensitizing the community to a particular kind of danger but equally as important, there is widespread knowledge about the appropriate course of action to follow when certain cues are presented.[101]

Stallings went on to note that while many other communities in the country were subjected to the same level of tornado risk as Topeka, the response in the city had been of "a different order." The high survival rate, he said, had much to do with the advanced warnings. But just as important, if not more so, was the fact that "Topeka is psychologically and socially prepared for tornadoes whereas other localities are not."

The pivotal role played by the U.S. Weather Bureau's Richard Garrett in fostering that mind-set was formally recognized in 1967 when Garrett received the Bureau's Exceptional Service Award. The citation noted his "unusual awareness of and sensitivity to the public needs in the severe weather warning realm, as well as his imaginative leadership and response to these, which led to his developing, implementing and maintaining such an effective tornado warning system that resulted in the saving of many lives when an extremely destructive tornado struck Topeka."

Mary Patricia Fleenor, Garrett's daughter, said her father seldom talked about the tornado or his work in the years after June 8, 1966. But she was certain he was proud of all that had been accomplished and was particularly proud of the resolute performance turned in by Weather Bureau staff on that fateful day. Garrett retired in 1971 and died at age 97 in 2003. His wife of 65 years, Margaret, passed away three years later.

# CHAPTER NINETEEN

# Beneath the Shadow of June 8th

The pervasive sense of shock and unreality that dominated the tornado's aftermath gradually abated in the first frenetic, then grinding pace of cleanup, recovery and reconstruction. In fits and starts, for individuals and the city as a whole, a new reality emerged. It was much like the old one, only different.

Carpenter Glenn Nicely and his family moved in with Glenn's sister in Scranton, Kansas, 25 miles south of Topeka. Despite his many cuts, bruises and puncture wounds (not to mention burns from the ruptured hot water heater), Glenn was back at work the following week. The horses that were lifted across Auburn Road in the tornado were rounded up and all were unhurt. Mitzi, the Nicelys' Chihuahua–toy terrier mix, surfaced a few days after the storm. She'd been in the family's trailer with Tommy the cat when the tornado hit. The trailer vanished; only its chassis remained afterward. Yet somehow Mitzi survived with a broken leg and a chunk missing from her tongue. A couple of days after the dog reappeared, a friend of the Nicelys said she thought she'd spotted a cat near the ruins of the family home. So Inge drove over, got out and called Tommy's name. And, sure enough, the big Siamese bolted at a dead run across the grass and launched himself into Inge's arms. He was unhurt.

Two years after the storm, Glenn had a strange encounter concerning the tornado. He was building a gas station in Valley Falls, a small town 45 miles northeast of Topeka. As it happened, he and a co-worker stopped in for a beer at a local tavern one day after work. But when the sky turned dark and menacing, Glenn figured they'd better go.

"I'm not going to get caught in another tornado up here," he said.

A local man asked Glenn if he'd been in the Topeka tornado. Glenn replied that he had, and the stranger asked him his name. When Glenn told him, the man said, "Well, I think I have something that belongs to you. I don't know what it is, but it's got your name on it." Turns out the guy had found Glenn and Inge's German marriage certificate in the middle of a field, impaled on a weed stalk, the day after the tornado.

What are the odds of that?

Glenn and Inge eventually built a nice ranch home on Glenn's parents' property, and after making do in a small trailer for two and a half years, they moved into it in January 1970. Glenn built the home on a poured, reinforced concrete basement, and the Nicelys set up a bedroom below ground for nights when severe weather threatened. And to this day, Inge said, Glenn will sit up and watch the Doppler radar on TV, all night if necessary, until he's sure the danger has passed.

He was never going to let a tornado take him by surprise again.

⌒ • ⌒

Disc jockey Rick Douglass remained in the hospital for about a week after June 8. He became something of a celebrity due to the warning he'd broadcast as he raced down the mound. A picture of him — grinning and lying in his hospital bed, smoking a cigarette — made the front page of the *Kansas City Star*. At one point, Douglass was being interviewed by a TV reporter when he felt a sharp pain in the back of his head. A nurse came in and probed around in his bushy, wiry hair. Then she said, "You're not going to believe this," and pulled out the jagged base section of a soda pop bottle that had lodged above his right ear.

The WREN-mobile, the storm-chasing Chevy II wagon that had vanished in the storm and consequently had caused Douglass so much angst, turned up a week after the tornado in the ruins of the nearby Huntington Apartments. The car was mauled and every window shattered. But the keys were still in the ignition and Douglass hung onto them as a reminder of that day. His wallet was found, too.

The photograph taken of a mud-and-straw-caked Douglass being helped into Stormont-Vail Hospital became one of the more memorable images to emerge from the Topeka tornado. It ran in *Life* magazine and elsewhere nationwide. For a long time after, wise guys would approach Douglass in White Lakes Mall or elsewhere in town, and their line was always the same: "Boy, you sure look better than the last time I saw you!" A lot of people wanted his autograph.

Douglass said he never saw himself as a hero; he was just doing his job. Psychiatrists evaluated him later that summer and suggested to WREN management that Douglass should do no more storm spotting from the field. Evidently they were concerned that, given all he'd been through, he might flip out and drive straight into the next tornado he encountered.

Douglass stayed at WREN until 1971 and then took a job in Kansas City before moving to the Phoenix area in 1979. He got out of radio in the mid-1980s and today is an account manager with an advertising firm in Phoenix.

Along with the flying '59 Pontiac Bonneville he saw as he lay on the I-470 entrance ramp, one of Douglass's most potent memories of the tornado was the smell that literally permeated his skin for many months after the storm.

"It's a unique, very strong, pungent smell," he said. "Very earthly, like mud after a rain, but there was this other top note to it — it could have been the blood from the dead ponies at the pony farm — that just made you draw back and burned your stomach. We drove past Washburn a few weeks after the storm and it was the same smell. I got sick to my stomach."

Douglass never dwelt on his experience. But for more than 20 years, he received regular and painful reminders of that day: Tiny pieces of straw, wood and glass periodically would work their way out of his skin.

— • —

One footnote about WREN: About 18 months after the tornado, station manager Bob Fromme received a stern letter from the Federal Communications Commission, informing him that the station would soon be the subject of an investigation. Officials in Washington, D.C., were concerned that the station's trademark severe weather watch alert — a series of four beeps that went out every two minutes over whatever else was being broadcast — was in fact some kind of nefarious signal, perhaps to enemies of the state.

Fromme and the station's chief engineer immediately drafted a letter explaining the purpose of the beeps. They noted that Topeka was in the heart of Tornado Alley and had in fact experienced a devastating tornado less than two years before. The beeps were a public service, they said, nothing more. The agency eventually backed down but still sought repeated reassurances that everything was on the up-and-up as far as the beeps were concerned.

— • —

WIBW anchorman Bill Kurtis caught his big break with the tornado. He would later say that "just like Dorothy in *The Wizard of Oz*, I rode out of Kansas on a tornado." The day after the storm, Kurtis was asked to do a live broadcast for the *CBS Morning News*. He seized the opportunity. And although he'd made the decision a few months earlier to join a law firm in Wichita, Kurtis quickly realized that everything had changed for him with the tornado. So he sent his tapes out and was hired in July by WBBM-TV's *Channel 2 News* in Chicago. From there, Kurtis went on to CBS, first as a correspondent and then as anchor for the *CBS Morning News*. Not only did he get to work with his hero, Walter Cronkite, but the two became close friends. In the early 1990s, Kurtis formed his own production company and subsequently created a series of popular news documentary shows for the A&E Network, including *Investigative Reports*, *American Justice* and *Cold Case Files*. Kurtis also purchased a ranch near Sedan, Kansas, that once was the home of author Laura Ingalls Wilder. In Sedan, he formed Tallgrass Beef Company to promote the health and environmental benefits of non-feedlot-fattened, grass-fed beef.

It was to his wife, Helen, that Kurtis's famous warning, "For God's sake, take cover," had been in part directed. Fortunately, she'd already sought shelter in the science building at Washburn, and neither Helen nor the couple's six-month-old daughter, Mary Kristin, was hurt. They had another child, Scott, in 1970. But Helen tragically died of cancer just seven years later.

Kurtis said he's proud of his performance on June 8.

"I do look back at it; I refer to it as 'The Test,'" he said. "Because had I not done it, it would have haunted me for the rest of my life. Some people may look at it and say, well, 'For God's sake, take cover,' that was not such a big thing. But at the time, in the context, at that moment, at the crucial point when people needed to know what was happening, it was the right thing at the right time."

A few years ago, Kurtis was asked to give a speech at the dedication of a statue in Council Grove, Kansas, honoring pioneer women. It was a sweltering Kansas summer afternoon and Kurtis figured only a few hard-core history buffs would show up. But much to his surprise, the bleachers were full when he got there. He visited with a number of people from the audience afterward and learned that many had driven down from Topeka for the event.

"I told them that it was nice that they'd come out on such a hot afternoon," he recalled. "And they said, 'Well, we were there that day. You saved our lives. And we wanted to thank you.' I can tell you, I come to tears every time I think about it."

—  •  —

Officer David Hathaway recovered from his injuries and was back on duty within a couple of weeks. But in 1970, he decided it was time for a change. So he resigned from the Topeka P.D. and moved to Mobile, Alabama, where he went to work in the boat business. Hathaway was on track to earn his captain's papers and run charter fishing boats out of Mobile Bay when Mother Nature again reached out to him, this time with more serious results. Hurricane Fredric struck southern Alabama on the night of September 12, 1979, with 125-mile-an-hour winds. In the aftermath, Hathaway was helping with the cleanup. He was on a roof cutting tree limbs when he slipped and fell. His neck was broken. The doctors told him he'd spend the rest of his life in a wheelchair. But Hathaway said he couldn't live like that. So he battled and fought and years later, he was able to walk again with the aid of a cane.

— • —

Along with Hathaway, volunteer spotter John Meinholdt received a plaque of commendation from Topeka mayor Chuck Wright in recognition of the men's service in providing the earliest warnings of the approaching tornado. Meinholdt later worked with the Weather Bureau to help set up volunteer storm-spotting groups in other communities across Kansas. But he never went on weather watch again.

— • —

Electrician Tom Noack's wife, Connie, was sitting in her kitchen with the morning paper one day not long after the tornado when she let out a gasp: "Oh my God!" She was reading about Craig Beymer, the five-year-old who was severely injured just a few blocks from the Noacks' home and who later died from his wounds. It was only then that Connie realized who he was: Craig's mother had been a close friend to her while growing up in Leavenworth, Kansas. Connie had heard before the storm that the Beymers had moved to Topeka. But she had no idea they'd been living just down the street. The thought of what might have been haunted Connie for a long time after that. If only she'd known, she thought, she could have reached out when the sirens sounded, and Mrs. Beymer and Craig could have come to safety in the Noacks' basement.

⟶ • ⟵

Teri Huffman (now Teri Colpitts), the little girl who lived nearby — the one whose house was swept away and who was herself nearly sucked into the winds but for her father's strong grip — fought the tornado's legacy for years. The blow to the back of her head and the psychological trauma of the day did lasting damage. After the tornado, Teri's personality changed; she found it hard to concentrate and learn. She would become angry and agitated easily. She acted up; as an adolescent, she started smoking and often skipped school. She ran away from home. The behavioral problems persisted as an adult. She had a hard time holding a job. It wasn't until 1990 that neurologists and psychologists were able to link her problems to the injury and trauma she experienced on June 8. And in time, with the help of her second husband, she was able to get to a better place. But she really battled with the anger.

*Why did this happen to us? Why did it hurt my family? Why did it hurt me? This just shouldn't have happened.*

"The anger would just kind of sit there and build up until after a while, you couldn't handle it," she said.

Teri said she still dreads the spring.

"If the sirens go off, I start shaking," she said. "It scares me to death. I go to the basement. I'm just waiting to hear that sound again, that sound I heard when the tornado was coming."

The Huffmans struggled with money and insurance and everything else after the tornado. But the family eventually regrouped and rebuilt. One thing, though: They never talked about the tornado itself, about those terrible seconds when the funnel was blotting out the sun and nearly on them and then ripping their house away. In fact, Teri didn't even know her father had reached up to save her until after he died. Her mother finally told her. When it came to June 8, Mrs. Huffman said, the family just didn't go there.

The memories were simply too terrifying.

—  •  —

Assistant U.S. Attorney Jim Ward, who shot footage of the tornado as it crested Burnett's Mound, made it back home to find his own house severely damaged, twisted on its foundation and dangerously askew. Within a couple of days, he and his family had taken up residence at a local hotel. He also managed to get his film developed. The footage is dark and grainy and lasts only a minute or so. But the images are unmistakable; the black funnel is silhouetted against the lighter sky to the west as it draws closer to Burnett's Mound and then crests the ridge. In the last frames, the funnel fills nearly the entire view. Ward shot additional footage of storm damage, and within a couple of weeks, he put an advertisement in the Topeka newspaper pitching his movie. He sold more than 200 copies of the film at $12.95 apiece.

—  •  —

Like so many others, Paul and Peg Marmet — the couple who watched the tornado bear down on them and who were sure the sound alone would kill them — clawed their way back. They linked up with a capable contractor and, remarkably, moved into an entirely rebuilt home on the same lot just 85 days after June 8. Their biggest headache came later, courtesy of the Internal Revenue Service. One of the few items they'd managed to recover after the tornado was a drawer containing receipts for all the new furnishings they'd purchased for their house in the days, weeks and months before the tornado took it all away. A lot of the stuff was brand-new, many wedding gifts were still in boxes and none of the furnishings were more than a year old. But when Paul tried to deduct the expenses as losses, the IRS came back and said the Marmets could only get fair market value for the possessions. This amounted to about 20 percent of the costs. The upshot: The IRS claimed they owed $1,300. The couple lawyered up, went back and forth with the agency, and eventually was able to reduce the liability. But the IRS still hit them for $750 in back taxes, plus a 10 percent penalty — a pretty decent sum in those days, particularly when you've just lost everything.

"We decided afterward that dealing with the IRS might have been worse than the tornado itself," Paul said.

—  •  —

Schoolteacher Ron Olson — the friend of the Marmets who'd confronted the looters on the night of June 8 — came across some still-intact bottles of homemade apple wine a few days after the storm in the basement of his wrecked home. He put the wine in his pickup with some other salvaged items and was leaving the neighborhood when he came to a checkpoint manned by a single National Guardsman. As a thank-you, Olson pulled out one of the bottles and told the guardsman, "Now, take this home tonight, but be careful drinking it. It's pretty potent."

Much to his embarrassment and regret, Olson spotted the guardsman passed out on the sidewalk with two MPs attending to him when he returned to the neighborhood an hour later.

Olson worked like a dog for days, wheelbarrowing debris out of his house. A couple of weeks into it — after he'd moved his family to one of the temporary trailers set up on the grounds of the VA hospital, after much of his help had lost interest and moved on — Olson was working alone cleaning out the last of the wreckage. The day was very hot and he began to suffer from heat exhaustion. So he found a shady spot and sat down. And it was only then, in that moment, that the harsh reality sank in: He'd really, truly lost his house and nearly everything he owned.

He just sat there alone and sobbed.

Kert Scheibe lost his older brother, Johnny, in the tornado. The family didn't know that night which hospital he'd been taken to, so they raced first to Stormont-Vail and then to St. Francis. A nun finally got on a two-way radio and determined that Johnny was at the veterans administration hospital, not far from his home. It was kind of ironic, because Johnny was well known at the sprawling VA and well liked. When he was younger, he'd had an early-morning paper route there, delivering the *Kansas City Star* to patients. He also worked in the hospital's bowling alley for a time. But no one could have imagined he would return like this.

Kert recounted a strange incident surrounding the tornado and its aftermath. He and his brother shared a bedroom and a closet. When the tornado leveled the house, it carried all of Kert's clothes away. Every stitch. But all of Johnny's stuff — including the suit he would be buried in — was left unsoiled and undamaged in a heap on the floor.

Kert said his mom and dad struggled with depression for years after Johnny died. They never did get over the loss.

Sue Breuninger (now Sue Coleman-Muñoz) was the woman who experienced the strange and comforting phantom touch to her shoulder after she began to pray as the tornado drew near. She didn't speak of the incident to anyone for nearly 40 years.

"I didn't want people to think I was some kind of religious nut," she said. "But I don't know why, I just started talking about it a few years ago. I guess I've reached the age in life where, if you want to think of me as a nut, go ahead. That's your problem, not mine."

She remains mystified by the experience.

"Some people believe in guardian angels, and I'm not sure I do, but I don't know how else to explain this presence. I know it was there. I know that it protected me. I know there is something beyond us that watches over us. I feel certain about that much."

— • —

For John Fernstrom, the banker who'd heard that strange, growling sound as he took a test at Washburn, the tornado was life-changing.

"After 1966, I had a totally different idea about possessions, things, furniture, art, all that stuff," Fernstrom said. "None of it meant nearly as much as it did before, because it could be gone in an instant. And life meant quite a bit more. It's a very fragile thing. We're just like little ants. We can be stepped on."

Fernstrom had nightmares for a time. He'd dream about the tornado coming and he would hear that sound again. In some of the dreams, the events were even worse than the reality he'd experienced: Dozens of people were dead or dying amid the chaos of the Carnegie Hall basement.

— • —

Mary Hatke lost her big, beautiful house across from Central Park. She lost her Thunderbird and her Plymouth wagon, too. Never saw either car again. Mary was no shrinking violet. She'd been among the first class ever of female marines in 1942. She'd worked in the paymaster's office in Washington, D.C., for the rest of the war. She was a fearless, independent woman in a man's world and ahead of her time that way. But this tornado was a hard thing. Mary and her husband had put most of their money into their art store downtown. They hadn't had it for long. So their home and car insurance weren't what they should have been. And, yes, they rebuilt. But life was a steep, uphill climb after June 8.

"We never really recovered financially," Mary said. "I was very bitter for a while. I said to my husband once, 'Why me?' And he smiled and said, 'Well, why not you, Mary?'"

What hurt even more than the material losses, though, was the destruction of the tight-knit Central Park community and the once-beautiful park across the street. Mary assumed that her neighbors would rebuild and life eventually would return to normal. But in truth, nearly all of her neighbors did not rebuild and they never returned. And the park became a 15-acre rubble dump and burn pile after the tornado. Debris was bulldozed into the center lagoon. Eventually, the park was restored but only as a shadow of its former self.

"It was very sad," she said. "It broke my heart."

Mary said she stopped feeling sorry for herself after her husband was diagnosed with Parkinson's disease not too long after the tornado.

"He had Parkinson's for 41 years. It was very difficult. And I thought, well, the tornado wasn't so bad after all."

—  •  —

The sudden loss of community was something a lot of people grappled with, particularly the kids. Groups of close friends literally were scattered by the winds overnight. Tony Stein, the carpenter's son who grew up not far from Mary Hatke, said he never saw some of his friends again after the tornado. Same thing with Dominic Gutierrez, the eight-year-old boy who bravely rode his bike to the store to pick up some flashlight batteries just before the sirens sounded.

"I felt like I lost a part of my childhood," Gutierrez said. "The memories I had from before the tornado are a lot different than the ones I had after. Things were never as good again. Before, everything in my neighborhood was so beautiful — big trees, flowers, grass, and the houses looked real nice. But afterward, it was turmoil. The tornado came through and it just devastated everything. It took people and friends away, and I never saw them again. It's just like a whole chunk of that time is gone."

—  •  —

At 19, Pete Maxon rode out the June 8 tornado huddled alongside his girlfriend's house, hanging onto the edge of the siding for dear life. Twenty-two years later, Maxon was working at a bank in west Topeka when another tornado came at him. This time, the funnel was rain-wrapped and impossible to see. Maxon and a couple others were watching a thunderstorm approach when debris started hitting the bank. They sprinted for the vault just as the windows shattered and objects began flying across the lobby. The tornado (unusual for November) was far less powerful than the '66 storm. But it still injured 22 people and did $3.9 million in damage as it skipped across the western side of the city.

— • —

Like Maxon, Guy and Jean Shuck experienced a tornado's wrath more than once. The couple's home near 13th and Harrison was badly damaged on June 8, although the Shucks and their three small children fortunately escaped unhurt. Then, more than 40 years later — on May 4, 2007, to be exact — the now-retired couple was living in Greensburg, Kansas, when that town was wiped out by a massive, nearly two-mile-wide EF-5. The Greensburg tornado wrecked the Shucks' house and trashed most of their belongings. But once again neither Guy nor Jean was injured.

What's it like going through two EF-5s?

"Well, after Greensburg, we tried not to tell anybody where we were going to move to, because nobody wanted us around," Guy joked. "We have some friends up in Newton, and I was just teasing and I told them, 'We're thinking of moving up there near you,' and they said, 'Oh, please don't!'"

As for losing their home, two cars and most of their worldly possessions in the Greensburg tornado, Guy Shuck said, "We were just in shock for quite a while afterward. But I think maybe it was God's way of telling us that we had too much stuff."

— • —

If the '66 tornado hadn't killed Lisle Grauer, the proprietor of the Pla-Land bowling alley, the loss of his beloved bowling alley would have. That's what his son, Ron, always believed.

"I had to go down there and take all the bowling balls home because a lot of them belonged to other people," Ron said. "They weren't all house balls. And, God, what a horrible mess it was. He would have collapsed just looking at the place."

Ron said his father was "a hell of a good dad." He recalled how Lisle had chartered a plane to fly him to Kansas City on the day Ron was scheduled to report to the Navy, and how his father was standing there at the gate on the day he was discharged; how his dad lent him money for a down payment on his first house and then sent him a note when Ron's first child was born that read: "Paid in full!"

"He was a rough, tough, sentimental guy," Ron said. "He was a real character."

⁓ • ⁓

Denny Benge was the former marine and concrete finisher who watched the tornado devour the bus barn from the back door of the barbershop before diving for cover as the building came down around him. Afterward, he couldn't find his car and jogged most of the way home.

A few months after the storm, Benge was finishing a concrete patio at a physician's home when the sirens went off. He was covered with cement but didn't think twice. He bolted straight through the wet concrete and went in the patio door, across the man's white carpet and down to the basement.

"I guess it still had me a little spooked," he said. "This man and his wife knew. They didn't say anything. I apologized and tried to clean it up. But when you go through something like that, you pay attention to the sirens."

⁓ • ⁓

Southwestern Bell was harshly criticized after the tornado for failing to warn company telephone operators about the approaching danger or allowing them to seek shelter. Pressure from the union helped force a policy change, and operator Laura Dalrymple was among those who took cover in the telephone building when the sirens next sounded in early August of '66.

— • —

Tim Lyle watched the tornado churn across the city and then straight for him from the 10th floor of the Santa Fe office building. More than forty years later, the funnel still lived in his dreams.

"I wouldn't call them nightmares as such," he said. "But I have dreams of tornadoes, and I get a real apprehensive feeling and I wake up abruptly. I just feel fortunate that we came through it unscathed. It gave me an acute awareness of my mortality as far as nature is concerned. And when I hear the sirens go off today, I go to the basement. I don't go out and look."

— • —

Carol Martin (now Carol Yoho) was the girl in the Masonic singing group who returned home to find her house destroyed and who finally reunited with her father on the street at the end of that epic day. She had nightmares for a time after June 8. And even today, the tornado reaches out across the years.

"Whenever I really think about it, my heart races and I start breathing heavily," she said. "It was traumatic, dramatic, dangerous, exciting, memorable. It was amazing and it was hard. But most of us survived it. If it taught me anything, it is that you don't mess with Mother Nature!"

— • —

The woman pulled down Kansas Avenue by the tornado, Dorothy Decker, was hospitalized for a month after June 8. The doctors stitched her up and put her ankle in a cast. But they didn't get all the shards out of her body. In the late 1960s, Dorothy began to develop sores on her legs and rear end. She'd go in for X-rays, but nothing would show up. In time, though, glass and splinters slowly began to work their way out of her skin. Some of the pieces of plate glass were huge: a quarter-inch thick, an inch wide, and two or three inches long, according to her son, Don Berry. Dorothy ended up with a mason jar full of shrapnel before the stuff stopped coming out. Her physician, Lester Saylor, evidently believed humor played a part in healing: He called Dorothy "Glass Ass" and "Peg Leg."

Not surprisingly, she was terrified of tornadoes after June 8. The sirens went off later that summer, and Dorothy still couldn't walk yet because of her broken ankle. So she bounced — no doubt, painfully — down the stairs on her rear end. Her daughter, Barbara, said Dorothy didn't complain in the years that followed, despite the constant physical reminders of that day. She just kept going. But in 1976, Dorothy died unexpectedly in her sleep while visiting Barbara in Muncie, Indiana. She was just 56 years old.

—  •  —

Nine-year-old Jill Nauman (now Jill Poole) was the girl from Washington State whose summer driving vacation had ended abruptly under the 10th Street Bridge. She spent about a week in the nearby Santa Fe Hospital, receiving treatment for the nasty scalp wound she'd received as the tornado came over. The Santa Fe Hospital was set up for railroad employees and retirees, so it didn't really have a pediatric department. But the staff improvised pajamas for Jill, and she made friends with the nurses and followed them on their rounds. She met a lot of the older patients and, all in all, it turned out to be a pretty neat experience for her.

Except for one night: On Sunday evening, four days after the tornado, heavy thunderstorms once again rolled through Topeka. The thunder crashed and vivid lightning ripped the sky most of the night. Jill was petrified. She wasn't used to storms like this. It rained a lot in Washington State, but seldom with such ferocity. Plus, Jill was still badly shaken by her experience in the tornado. And her parents were not there. So one of the hospital employees, a man named Mario, came and sat with her and held her hand nearly the whole night through, until the storms moved on.

The Esquivel family also sought shelter under the 10th Street overpass. They'd fled there from the nearby dental building they'd been cleaning. The family made it home to find their house destroyed but Mrs. Esquivel and Steph unharmed. Fortunately, Ramon Esquivel Sr. had recently taken out additional homeowners insurance. The decision had been a real sore spot with his wife, Phyllis, in the weeks leading up to the tornado, according to son Ramon Jr. Phyllis didn't think the family could afford it. They were "insurance poor," she argued. But she didn't complain afterward. The family rebuilt a bigger and better home and moved in just before Christmas.

A number of people — the Esquivels, Jill Nauman, Rick Douglass, Dave Hathaway and others — sought shelter beneath interstate highway overpasses on June 8. It seemed like the place to go at the time, and evidently it was, given the lack of available alternatives and the fact that none of them died.

But subsequent events have shown that those who survived under bridges on June 8 were extremely lucky. In fact, highway overpasses can be death traps in tornadoes. The National Weather Service conducted an in-depth study of overpass safety, or the lack thereof, after a particularly fierce tornado outbreak hit Oklahoma and southern Kansas on May 3, 1999. At least three people were killed by tornadoes after they'd sought shelter beneath interstate bridges. Others suffered horrific injuries, including compound fractures and shattered bones, missing fingers, missing ears, missing noses and impalement by debris.

The problems with seeking shelter beneath overpasses are three-fold, according to the Weather Service study: 1) The flow of the already-fierce wind is constricted by the bridge and accelerated, thus increasing the likelihood that people will be sucked out, blown away or seriously injured by debris; 2) Seeking shelter at the top of the abutment puts individuals above ground level and at greater risk of being struck by flying debris; and 3) The underside of most highway bridges lack exposed I beams that can afford some degree of protection from the circular, swirling winds that attack first from one side and then from the other.

Today, the National Weather Service strongly advises against seeking cover under bridges and is working hard to dispel the widespread public notion that doing so is a good idea. The best option if caught on the highway, according to the National Weather Service, is to attempt to determine which way the tornado is moving and, if time and distance permit, drive out of its path. Failing that, individuals should get out of their vehicles and seek shelter in the lowest spot possible.[102]

—⋅—

Francis Bordner was the Santa Fe electrician who survived the tornado by clinging to a toilet at the Vickers gas station in East Topeka. He recovered from the cuts and wounds he received during the tornado. But his sister, Catherine Schmidt, said he wasn't the same afterward. Bordner's hearing bothered him for a long time, evidently from the roar of the tornado or the pressure drop. And at the slightest risk of severe weather, the lifelong bachelor would immediately leave work and retreat to his basement. He set up a bedroom there, and he would stay in his lair until any threat, real or imagined, had passed.

"He didn't talk about it much, but I think the experience really took a lot out of him emotionally," his sister said.

Bordner died of cancer in 1980.

—⋅—

Olen Robbins, the wheel shop foreman who took cover in the old refinery building at the Santa Fe shops, lost his house and all his possessions in the tornado. Fortunately, he had good insurance and was able to rebuild. As was the case with his first house, Robbins built the new one himself. He came out whole in the end. But the tornado changed him. "One lesson I learned was how fast you can lose everything you've got, everything you've accumulated over a period of years. It's gone like it was never there." What made it worse, he said, was that even after everything had been ruined or destroyed, he still had a mess to clean up.

"I would have been better off if there was nothing left."

Robbins said he still thinks about the tornado every month or so.

—— • ——

Norma Jackson, the woman who rode out the tornado on the floor under a mattress with her sleeping baby in her arms, said her son, Paul Frederick, never showed any ill effects from the experience. But events haunted Norma.

"You looked at life differently after that," she said. "You were thankful to be alive. You heard about people who didn't make it. You put your life back together. But there was still something missing — I mean, in the way it used to be versus what it had turned into. You just kept pushing. You had to continue. And I guess being young and growing up like I did on a farm, whatever was wrong, you just worked to get it fixed."

—— • ——

The changes came fast and hard for "Chick" Taylor's wife, Fern, and her mentally handicapped brother and sister, Everett and Stella, after Chick was killed in his home on B Street by a flying culvert. The timing of Chick's death couldn't have been worse, as if there can ever be such a thing as a good time to lose a spouse. On June 8, Chick was just two months shy of retirement. He'd been looking forward to collecting a full pension from Hill's Packing Company in September. But the payout was not to be. Nor was there any life insurance. Consequently, Fern couldn't afford to rebuild. So she moved in with her daughter, Katherine, and son-in-law, Wayne Boline Sr.

Stella, Fern's sister, was shipped off to a home for the developmentally disabled in Silver Lake. Stella had suffered from a large goiter for most of her life, and on June 8, she'd been struck in the neck by debris. The injury complicated her condition and the doctors said the goiter would need to come out. They operated, but it was not a good outcome. Stella died just six months after the tornado.

Her brother, Everett — also developmentally disabled — likewise was injured in the tornado: hit hard, twice, in the forehead. The doctors said the blows would have killed any other man. But Everett was strong. He had a temper, too, and was hard to handle. So he was sent away. But he didn't last long anywhere due to his violent ways. For the next quarter century, Everett was bounced from institution to institution across Kansas, before finally coming to rest in Goodland, out near the Colorado line. He died in the early 1990s.

— • —

Wanda Idlet (now Wanda Bulmer) was the girl whose mother refused her daughter's plea to seek shelter as the tornado approached. Mrs. Idlet was certain Burnett's Mound would protect the city. The family was not hurt, but their home was badly damaged and Mr. Idlet had let his homeowners insurance lapse. So they struggled coming back. One thing Wanda remembered was how the animals suffered from the tornado. Cats and dogs were lost, injured and killed. Baby birds were blown from their nests.

It was a hard time for all God's creatures.

— • —

After June 8, Topekans were forced to acknowledge that the legend of Burnett's Mound had been just that. The hill could not protect the city from tornadoes after all. Not by a long shot. Some pointed to the water tank erected on the side of the mound five years before. The reservoir had disturbed the sacred Potawatomi burial grounds, it was said. A terrible curse had been unleashed.

Whether you believed that or not, a person couldn't help but wonder about why the tornado did what it did. It was just human nature. Was the destruction really about the reservoir and the Indians buried on the mound? Or was the water tank merely a symbol and the tornado actually payback for a much larger injustice, for the way Indians were treated generally in Kansas — dispossessed, dispersed, humiliated and ultimately, as a people, destroyed? Did the state's collective karma come back on the capital city a hundred-plus years on? It was spooky how the tornado made for the mound from miles away, just like it was drawing a bead on the hill. And then, amazingly, the funnel had gone straight over the top of the water tank. But the reservoir was strong — built to hold back 20,000-plus tons of water — and it had been undamaged.

Even then, though, the tornado seemed to act with malice aforethought and vengeance in its heart. Chief Burnett's creek, the Shunganunga, pointed like an ancient, crooked finger toward the heart of the city, and the tornado more or less followed the creek's path. It shattered Washburn, the crown jewel of Topeka, and then took aim at the state capitol, the ultimate symbol of the white man's power. It even hurled a small building at the capitol dome, as if to underscore its fury. Finally, the tornado made its grand exit, rolling down the airport runway and changing in color from black to white before starting to lift. And then, when it roped out, the funnel was over Tecumseh, a town named for the Shawnee leader who'd united the Potawatomis and the other Woodland tribes against the whites so many years before.

But if that was all just coincidence, if the tornado wasn't an agent of Chief Burnett or the Great Spirit, then was it God who informed its actions? Did an angry God unleash the destruction to punish the city? Or was it a merciful God who protected so many from the pitiless wrath of Satan? Then again, maybe it was just physics: a tiny wisp of an updraft on a sultry afternoon — the precise mixture of vapor, heat and motion, a permutation and chain reaction that quickly mushroomed into a killer.

The answers, of course, could never be known. Not in this lifetime, anyway. And even if they were, it wouldn't change anything. The tornado was what it was. It had come and it had gone. And all you could do, all Topeka could do, was pick up the pieces and move on.

Still, the terror of that day hung around. On Wednesday evening, June 7, 1967 — exactly 364 days and four minutes after the sirens sounded on Wednesday, June 8 — they went off again when a tornado once more was spotted growling in from the southwest. Pandemonium ensued. People scrambled for shelter. One woman was injured when she ran straight into a barbed-wire fence in a headlong dash for cover. Cars careened on the streets. Some people, irrationally, climbed on roofs to watch the tornado approach. Fortunately, the twister lifted before it reached the city and the danger passed.

But the whole thing was still pretty strange.

And so the days gathered in pools like water and collected into months and years. Time ran on. People coped. They rebuilt. They adjusted. They learned to forget. And the city recovered. Trees grew on Burnett's Mound and eventually all but obscured the water tank. Development pressed in on its flanks. Washburn University came back stronger than ever. A damaged, 30-foot section of the capitol dome was re-clad in new copper, and the patch stood out for years like a great bandage against the green, oxidized dome. A construction boom lasted for a while. Devastated portions of the city were rebuilt. Some homes, though, never did come back, especially in older, poorer parts of town. Even today, if you follow the damage path, a curious pattern of oddly vacant lots, newer ranch homes, incongruously placed apartments and much older frame houses can be discerned.

And the trees: It was amazing how many survived. For decades, you could always spot a tornado tree: They were twisted and deformed like something from a hideous dream, clawing and stabbing at the sky with shriveled, truncated or unnaturally crooked limbs. But living and growing just the same.

As for the people, it's hard to say what the tornado did to the psyche of Topeka. But the collective trauma of the event, along with the hard work of recovery, probably colored beliefs and attitudes in the city for a generation, and not necessarily in a bad way. There were scars, of course. But the knowledge that, at any given time and for no apparent reason, nature can take you out — along with everything you own — has a galvanizing effect. It strips away that which is superficial and extraneous. It crushes pretention. It forces you into the here and now. And it instills a certain indifference to adversity and a gritty determination to overcome any obstacle, no matter what the days may hold.

# Notes


1 Thomas P. Grazulis, *The Tornado: Nature's Ultimate Windstorm* (Norman, OK: University of Oklahoma Press, 2001), 119.

2 Tim Marshall, "A Tribute to Dr. Ted Fujita," Stormtrack.org library, http://www.stormtrack.org/library/people/fujita.htm (accessed February 17, 2006).

3 Severe Weather Database Files (1950–2007), Storm Prediction Center, National Oceanic and Atmospheric Administration, Norman, OK, http://www.spc.noaa.gov/wcm/#data; Storm Events Database, National Climate Data Center, http://www4.ncdc.noaa.gov/cgi-win/wwcgi. dll?wwEvent~Storms.

4 Ibid.

5 Ibid.

6 Ibid.

7 Grazulis, *The Tornado: Nature's Ultimate Windstorm*, 138.

8 Ibid., 220–221.

9 Ibid., xiv.

10 Thomas P. Grazulis, *Significant Tornadoes, 1880–1989, Volume 1: Discussion and Analysis* (St. Johnsbury, VT: Environmental Films, 1991), 18.

11 Severe Weather Database Files (1950–2007), Storm Prediction Center, National Oceanic and Atmospheric Administration; Storm Events Database, National Climate Data Center.

12 Ibid.

13 Thomas P. Grazulis, *Significant Tornadoes, 1880–1989, Volume 1: Discussion and Analysis* (St. Johnsbury, VT: Environmental Films, 1991), 22; also "F5 & EF5 Tornadoes of the United States, 1950–Present," Storm Prediction Center http://www.spc.noaa.gov/faq/tornado/f5torns. html (accessed June 5, 2009).

14 Joseph G. Galway, "John Finley: The First Severe Storms Forecaster," excerpts from the NOAA Tech Memorandum ERL-NSSL-97; *Stormtrack.org*, Vol. 23, No. 6, September–October 2000, http://www.stormtrack.org/library/archives/stsep00.htm (accessed February 17, 2007).

15 Tim Marshall, "John Finley's First Tornado Damage Survey," *Stormtrack.org*, Vol. 23, No. 6, September–October 2000, http://www.stormtrack.org/library/archives/stsep00.htm (accessed February 17, 2007).

16 Ibid.

17 Marlene Bradford, *Scanning the Skies: A History of Tornado Forecasting* (Norman, OK: University of Oklahoma Press, 2001), 36.

18 Ibid.

19 Galway, "John Finley: The First Severe Storms Forecaster."

20 Grazulis, *The Tornado: Nature's Ultimate Windstorm*, 82.

21 Bradford, *Scanning the Skies*, 45–46.

22 Ibid., 43–44.

23 Ibid., 44–45.

24 Ibid., 49–50.

25 Ibid., 40–42.

26 Ibid., 43–55.

27 *Wikipedia.org*, "1899 New Richmond Tornado," http://en.wikipedia.org/wiki/New_Richmond_Tornado (accessed February 18, 2007).

28 Grazulis, *The Tornado: Nature's Ultimate Windstorm*, 230–231.

29 Peter S. Felknor, *The Tri-State Tornado: The Story of America's Greatest Tornado Disaster* (New York: iUniverse Inc., 2004), 4.

30 Bradford, *Scanning the Skies*, 54.

31 *Wikipedia.org*, "Tri-State Tornado," http://en.wikipedia.org/wiki/Tri-State_Tornado (accessed February 18, 2007).

32 Grazulis, *The Tornado: Nature's Ultimate Windstorm*, 232.

33 Bradford, *Scanning the Skies*, 59–62.

34 Ibid., 61–64.

35 James L. Crowder, "Tinker's 1948 Twin Twisters, Birth of Tornado Forecasting," *Air Weather Association*, released April 1, 1998, http://www.airweaassn.org/Library/aws/Tinker.htm (accessed February 18, 2007).

36 Ibid.

37 Robert C. Miller, "The Unfriendly Sky," transcribed by Charlie A. Crisp from an unpublished manuscript written in the 1970s, National Oceanic and Atmospheric Administration, http://www.nssl.noaa.gov/GoldenAnniversary/Historic.html (accessed February 18, 2007).

38 Crowder, "Tinker's 1948 Twin Twisters."

39 Miller, "The Unfriendly Sky."

40 Ibid.

41 Bradford, *Scanning the Skies*, 66–67.

42 Miller, "The Unfriendly Sky."

43 Crowder, "Tinker's 1948 Twin Twisters."

44 Bradford, *Scanning the Skies*, 73–75.

45 Ibid., 71–77.

46 Ibid., 78–85.

47 William E. Unrau, *Indians of Kansas: The Euro-American Invasion and Conquest of Indian Kansas* (Topeka, KS: Kansas State Historical Society, 1991), 16–25.

48 Ibid., 33.

49 Ibid., 31, 37.

50 R. David Edmunds, *The Potawatomis: Keepers of the Fire* (Norman, OK: University of Oklahoma Press, 1978), 234.

51 Ibid., 15–23.

52 Ibid., 198.

53 Ibid., 220.

54 Unrau, *Indians of Kansas*, 55.

55 Ibid., 56.

56 Tom Hamilton, "Potawatomi 'Trail of Death' March and Death of Father Petit," Potawatomi Web, A Kansas Heritage Group Site, http://www.kansasheritage.org/PBP/people/trail_map.html (accessed February 18, 2007).

57 Gary Wis-Ki-Ge-Amatyuk Jr., "Chief Abram B. Burnett Family," http://wiskigeamatyuk.com (accessed February 18, 2007).

58 "Father Benjamin Petit and the Potawatomi 'Trail of Death,'" Fulton County Historical Society, http://www.icss.net/~fchs/petit.htm (accessed February 18, 2007).

59 Edmunds, *The Potawatomis*, 267-268.

60 "Father Benjamin Petit and the Potawatomi 'Trail of Death,'" Fulton County Historical Society.

61 R.C. Obrecht, "Burnett's Mound," *Bulletin of The Shawnee County Historical Society,* No. 18, March 1953, 16.

62 Ibid., 14–16.

63 Ibid., 16.

64 "Man of Muscle," *The Topeka Journal*, Oct. 19, 1929.

65 Obrecht, "Burnett's Mound," 17.

66 Douglass W. Wallace, *"Before Kansas Bled: Pre-Territorial Shawnee County"* (Topeka, KS: Shawnee County Historical Society, Bulletin No. 82, September 2007), 26–31.

67 Obrecht, "Burnett's Mound," 17.

68 Steve Fry, "How the West Was Won," *The Topeka Capital-Journal,* February 2, 2003, via cjonline.com, http://cjonline.com/stories/020203/our_westwaswon.shtml (accessed February 20, 2007).

69 Barbara Brackman, "Kansas Troubles: This Week in Territorial History, December 5–11, 1854," www.kshs.org/sesquicentennial/series.htm.

70 F. W. Giles, *Thirty Years in Topeka: A Historical Sketch* (Topeka, KS: George W. Crane & Co. Publishers, 1886), 77–78.

71 Giles, *Thirty Years in Topeka,* 57–59.

72 Giles, *Thirty Years in Topeka,* 134–135.

73 Giles, *Thirty Years in Topeka,* 105.

74 Douglass W. Wallace and Roy D. Bird, *Witness of the Times: A History of Shawnee County* (Topeka, KS: Shawnee County Historical Society and Shawnee County American Revolution Bicentennial Commission, 1976), 252–253.

75 Fry, "How the West Was Won."

76 Ann Marie Bush, "Larger than Life: Chief Abram Burnett Remembered as Colorful Topeka Character," *The Topeka Capital-Journal,* November 23, 2000, via cjonline.com, http://cjonline.com/stories/112300/swn_chief.shtml (accessed June 7, 2009).

77 W.C. Campbell, "Heap Big Injun," *Topeka Mail and Breeze,* May 22, 1896, unknown.

78 Edmunds, *The Potawatomis,* 221.

79 Campbell, "Heap Big Injun."

80 Aileen Mallory, "Burnett's Mound," *The Territorial: Where the West Was Won,* Vol. 6, No. 6, November–December 1986.

81 Wis-Ki-Ge-Amatyuk Jr., "Chief Abram B. Burnett Family," http://wiskigeamatyuk.com (accessed February 20, 2007).

82 Milton Tabor, "They Still Hunt for Burnett's Gold," *The Topeka Capital,* March 11, 1928.

83 "The Original Kansans," *Kaw Mission State Historical Site,* http://www.kshs.org/places/kawmission/mainmenu.htm (accessed February 20, 2007).

84 Unrau, *Indians of Kansas,* 80–91.

85 "The Original Kansans," *Kaw Mission State Historical Site.*

86 Fry, "How the West Was Won."

87  Spencer L. Duncan, *Historic Shawnee County: The Story of Topeka and Shawnee County* (San Antonio, TX: Historical Publishing Network, 2005), 39.

88  Gene Smith, "Cleared for Take-off," *The Topeka Capital-Journal,* May 30, 1999, 2-B.

89  Ibid.

90  "Forbes 2nd Largest Base in SAC," *The Topeka Sunday Capital-Journal,* December 10, 1961.

91  *Strategic-Air-Command.com,* "SAC Bases: Forbes Air Force Base," http://www.strategic-air-command.com/bases/Forbes_AFB.htm (accessed February 3, 2007).

92  Ralph Marsh, "Tornado Watch No. 201," *Midway* magazine, *The Topeka Sunday Capital-Journal,* June 4, 1967, M5.

93  Ibid.

94  Ibid., M6, M9.

95  Harold E. Brooks and Charles A. Doswell III, "Normalized Damage from Major Tornadoes in the United States: 1890–1999," *Journal of Weather and Forecasting,* Vol. 16, No. 1, February 2001, 168–176.

96  James B. Taylor, Louis A. Zurcher, and William H. Key, *Tornado: A Community Responds to Disaster* (Seattle: University of Washington Press, 1970).

97  Ibid., 17.

98  Ibid., 30.

99  Ibid., 41.

100  Ibid., 9.

101  Robert Stallings, "Research Report #20: A Description and Analysis of the Warning Systems in Topeka, Kansas, Tornado of June 8, 1966," Disaster Research Center, Ohio State University, June 8, 1967.

102  Daniel Miller et al., "Highway Overpasses as Tornado Shelters: Fallout from the 3 May 1999 Oklahoma/Kansas Violent Tornado Outbreak," 1999 National Weather Association Annual Meeting Presentation, Biloxi, Mississippi, http://www.srh.noaa.gov/oun/?n=safety-overpass-slide01 (accessed May 1, 2009).

# Index